SO-CKJ-535

3 2528 06384 6788

WORKING TOGETHER IN TROUBLED TIMES

Community-Based Therapies

Jane Piazza

University Press of America, Inc.
Lanham • New York • Oxford

Copyright © 1997 by
University Press of America,® Inc.
4720 Boston Way
Lanham, Maryland 20706

12 Hid's Copse Rd.
Cummor Hill, Oxford OX2 9JJ

All rights reserved
Printed in the United States of America
British Library Cataloguing in Publication Information Available

Library of Congress Cataloging-in-Publication Data

Piazza, Jane
Working together in troubled times : community-based therapies / Jane
Piazza (editor).
p. cm.
Includes bibliographical references and index.
1. Psychiatric social work--United States. 2. Family psychotherapy--
United States. 3. Social work with inorities-United Sttes. 4.
Community mental health services--United States. 5. Community
organization--United States. I. Title.
HV690.U6P53 1997 362.2'0425--dc21 97-1465 CIP

ISBN 0-7618-0694-6 (cloth alk. ppr.)
ISBN 0-7618-0695-4 (pbk: alk. ppr.)

♾™ The paper used in this publication meets the minimum
requirements of American National Standard for information
Sciences—Permanence of Paper for Printed Library Materials,
ANSI Z39.48—1984

This book honors the memory and the work of
three distinguished mentors of community-based therapy:

Barbara Carr-Eubanks

Carmen M. delValle

Velma Thomas

CONTENTS

PREFACE

This book grew out of the desire to share with therapists a whole body of community work which I have been exposed to and learned a great deal from over the years, but which is often not available for therapists to read about. The specific inception and goals of this five-year project are spelled out more in the body of the work in Chapter Two. Here, I want to express gratitude.

Readers need to remember that this was a *group* project, with the author having transcribed conversations with about *seventy* people in nine different groups. Most of these people are named in the chapters which report on their work. Only a handful could not be named, since they had changed jobs, moved, or could not be enlisted by the time they were contacted 2-4 years later to sign formal permissions for publication. These group conversations form the core of this project, which guided all other additions.

While I knew some of the chapter contributors very well, many did not know me well at all, but took time from very busy lives in the hope that some of what they wanted to say would reach those current and future therapists intending to work in their own or similar communities. Some of these people need special mention as experts in community-based therapy: Carmen M. DelValle; Margo Villagomez; Nancy Padilla; Anne Marie Smith; Elsie Maldonado; Myrtle Parnell and Jo Vanderkloot; Velma Thomas; Barbara Carr-Eubanks; Leta Cooper; Mel King; Agnes Williams; and E.H. Auerswald. They need to be named, but I hesitated, knowing that there are so many more here who I do not know as well. I am grateful for their sharing of themselves with such wisdom, patience,and generosity; and for the many who stand behind them, who passed on the community traditions which I have only had time to touch on here. Writing this book was a wonderful learning experience for me.

I never would have actually approached any of those who contributed here without the encouragement of Virginia Goldner, who took me seriously about this project when I was only joking about the urge to write. I am fortunate to have had the support and advice of my sons Stephen and Joseph and my daughter-in-law Sarah; and to have had the consistent moral support of Virginia Solomon and Margo Villagomez.

Help was given to me time and again by Cecilia Gaston, who readily offered consultation and lent me her apartment for meetings, as a "home away from home", even when she was extremely pressed for time. Original manuscripts were improved many times by the comments of chapter participants, es-pecially Nancy Padilla, who took considerable time and effort to advise me and correct inaccuracies; and by those not grounded in community-based work, but who still took time to offer good advice, such as Anne Lockwood at Children's Hospital of Buffalo; and by some editors who could not publish the book, but took the time to guide me with helpful comments, anyway. It has been important to incorporate the perspectives both of those very familiar with community work and those not familiar with it.

I am especially grateful to the Editorial Board of University Press of America, Inc. for taking a chance on work by an author who had never written material more complex than articles, and not part of the university system; and to Dorothy and Don Taylor, Betsy Webber, and Bill Talmadge for their tremendous technical assistance which enabled me to get the work from manuscript form into a book format.

I hope that this book can give some back to the fields of social work and family therapy which informed it; and to the "City of No Illusions", Buffalo, New York, and its Lower West Side community, which educated me well. Special thanks to Fleeta Hill, the Hispanic Women's League, and Maria delValle and the whole delValle family, who provided invaluable models of personal wisdom, sharing, and giving.

In the past ten years, I have felt quite a lot of personal guidance from the Great Creator, and I have become more aware of the tremendous influence in my life of my mother Janice Brollier Gray, who has provided me with a model of persistence during adversity, and who helped me to seek truth and assistance beyond my own immediate family and culture.

JANE PIAZZA

CHAPTER ONE:
POWER, COMMUNITY, AND THERAPY

"What will happen when we can cure symptoms without even considering their causes?"

Seymour Halleck
The Politics of Therapy

******

As the world gets smaller and power intensifies globally, the benefits of that power do not seem to be trickling down to local communities in the United States or elsewhere. The increased distance between the life/work experience of wealthy international corporate business classes and those unemployed and unable to support their families in urban and rural areas does not encourage charity and non-profit investment by those with resources. Economist Robert Reich warns about the increasing lack of responsibility for local communities among multinational corporations, and the rapidly growing detachment of this class, much more elite and powerful than ever in our history (Reich 1991). American companies have increasingly relocated to Caribbean or Asian locations where workers can be underpaid, and companies need not feel any loyalty to the communities of their workers. Nike, for example, closed its New Hampshire and Maine factories and increasingly subcontracted work to factories it did not own in Korea and Taiwan, where workers were poorly paid and denied basic rights. When unions spread there, it shifted its suppliers to Indonesia, China, and Thailand, where governments suppressed union activity. In 1992, Nike paid Michael Jordan more than the combined yearly income of 30,000 young women piecing together sneakers in Indonesia (Cavanagh and Broad 1996).

To paraphrase a quote by Frederick Douglass, power concedes nothing without a demand; it never has and never will. When multinational power is concentrated we need to organize *across* national boundaries in order to make a powerful enough demand to be listened to. But, as we organize, we need to *think locally* and ecologically (reversing the slogan "Think global, act local" to "Think local, act global"), according to the needs of our own areas and populations, so that the demands we make at international levels protect *diverse local* needs. International labor, health, peace, and ecology movements depend on healthy local communities. Our own form of government provides an example of national organization intended to protect the integrity and diversity of individual communities. While the size and scope of our government have mushroomed from the days of its inception, we are still a very young country able to learn from our original intentions and practices.

Community Roots: the North American Idea of Democracy

Those who came to what is now the United States from northern Europe had left behind them years of struggling for basic political rights, and were determined to guarantee individual freedoms here in a vast land which promised unlimited resources without the constraints of Europe. They came from a nation ruled by monarchs who claimed that God conferred their right to rule and had, then, no real model for democracy. Initially, they set up many different colonial administrations, each with its own policies.

According to Jack Weatherford, the Iroquois chief Canassatego, in 1744, complained that the Indians, who had lived peacefully in this land before the Europeans came, found it difficult to deal with so many different colonial administrations. He suggested unification of the thirteen colonies which would be like the League of the Iroquois, which had been founded by Hiawatha and Deganawidah sometime between A.D. 1000 and 1450 under a constitution called the Great Law of Peace. When the Europeans arrived in America, the League constituted the most important and extensive political unit north of the Aztec civilization (Weatherford 1988).

Weatherford cited writings of the settlers which showed that they were intrigued by this model, but Benjamin Franklin was the first to apply it to their new government, having been the Indian commissioner in Pennsylvania in the 1760's. He advocated a council composed of elected delegates from each territory, like the League's sachems from each nation. The sachems represented each nation, but also represented the whole league, so that all decisions were law for the totality. New "states" were to be treated as future partners, rather than being given the status of colonies ruled by the original thirteen, as would have been the European practice (*Ibid.*). This prevented the establishment of a military ruling class, as has happened in Latin American democracies. Iroquois sachems did not own land or receive any financial compensation for their work; and so our founding fathers worked to prevent property qualifications for holding office, and to limit the salaries paid to officeholders(*Ibid.*). Europeans who wanted to escape from the evils of hierarchial monarchial systems had only had experience in those very systems. They needed to rely on the practice of democracy which had existed before they settled here in order to achieve their goals.

Indeed, in the formative years of the American nation, the use of Iroquois ideas and phrases was common, when settlers found that European ideas were not always adaptable to the new environment. Native American thinking has been reflected in the ideas of the Tammany Society and in the editorial practices of the American Museum (Grinde 1992). John Locke and Jean Jacques Rousseau derived their ideas about democracy from travelers' accounts of Native American governmental structures (*Ibid.*). Locke believed that absolute monarchy could not be the basis for civil society because the dictates of the majority and the consent of those governed *defined* civil society. This was like the Great Law of the Iroquois, except that Locke held to the concept of private property, while the Iroquois did not (*Ibid.*).

Contradictions, Class Structure, and Idealism

While our political traditions have not been the product of any single heritage, but a unique amalgam of many, we have lacked awareness of our Native American roots. Lyons noted that the colonists were quick to embrace egalitarian and community-spirited Indian traditions, but then attributed the love of liberty and equality to their Greek and Roman roots (Lyons 1992). Colonists enjoying newfound equality here nevertheless expected Native people to adapt to colonization by the Europeans just as Europeans had adapted to that by the Romans: by giving over to the conquerers (Venables 1992). The European perspective was then assumed to be *central* here, just as the Roman perspective had been in Europe; and the interest in world cultures experienced during the Enlightenment was only a peripheral embellishment to the European "mainstream" (*Ibid.*). Our conquering meant the forced migration and slaughter of whole nations of Native people, in the interest of establishing a government of privileged property-owning classes who, after taking native lands, would thereafter continue to tax the people living on them--thereby maintaining their wealth just as the British oligarchy they had revolted against (Mohawk 1992).

Out of their European history of class stratification, the settlers biased their protection of individual and community diversity in favor of *landowning individuals*. Our violence to Native Americans also did violence to the *common good* ethos we had adopted which balanced the evils of a class system. European immigrants who had escaped Old World control then established a New World capitalist "democracy" system in which the government would stay out of voluntary transactions between buyer and seller (the free market), and thereby protect the individual freedoms of those who could bargain best. Lekachman and VanLoon characterize capitalism in the United States as grounded in the belief that individuals can escape

communal and governmental control and that, being left alone to pursue their own self-interest and desires to better themselves, they can be controlled only by market prices (Lekachman 1981). In this system we expect the market to automatically produce order and limit greed.

Lack of governmental "interference" encouraged the making of vast fortunes from a world system of trade, without any accountability as to how the fortunes were made. Companies of exploration kidnapped Africans to the United States in chains, and used their labor on huge cotton-producing plantations, as well as Indian labor in gold and silver mines,"Coolie" Asian labor on railroads, and Chicano labor in migrant farming camps. Oppressive practices allowed for low operating costs and huge profits (Weatherford 1988). Unregulated trading policies have allowed wealthy Western nations to dominate and annex smaller less wealthy nations. Since we are a nation founded from egalitarian principles, we euphemistically refer to our own piracy as "economic development"of "underdeveloped areas". Immigrants from countries directly or indirectly colonized by the United States have escaped dictatorships and dire poverty to come to a "Land of Milk and Honey", using sixty percent of the world's resources.

Native American identification of individual with community rights has been reduced to rhetoric which has served a purpose in our history, creating an image of a free society, with profits the just reward for unleashed capitalist ingenuity and hard work. Children in our schools learn a myth about Europeans who escaped oppression and, by hard work and pioneer sacrifice, survived and prospered in a new (founded by Christopher Columbus) land. The fact in the myth is that, of course, our European ancestors *were* often very hard-working and creative, but their importance has been exaggerated, and credit has not been given at all to the material and cultural influence of those subjugated.

Predominant in the contributions of, not only indigenous, but later African, Hispanic, and Asian people to the United States is *experience in building and sustaining community* (participatory democracy). Our history texts have not recalled and appropriately credited these contributions. But now, when multi-national corporations threaten to extend the class system so as to exclude from the mainstream the vast majority of North Americans, it is important to unearth those traditions which can provide some balance. Before annexation by the United States, New Mexico and Texas were Mexico, and people had organized a wilderness into many towns according to the indigenous *pueblo* principle of shared communal lands, as well as the Spanish hierarchial hacienda system (Meier and Ribera 1995). The sophisticated organization of the Black Church helped African Americans survive slavery and post-slavery injustices by more than prayer and preaching. Martin Luther King and other Civil Rights leaders, working in the context of the powerful community-building Black Church, accomplished large-scale social change by organizing *local communities*.

To avoid the unemployment and class/caste excesses of capitalist technology, we must unearth what we have learned from those we have silenced, that balance of community values and small-to-mid-range economic and political development.

Small-Scale Technology

Large-scale universal "solutions" often deliver far less than they promise. A startling book, *The Coming Plague: Newly Emerging Diseases in a World Out of Balance*, documents the serious effects of unbalanced large-scale development in the fields of medicine and agriculture. It is problematic, for example, when we develop a particularly hardy genetic strain of corn which can grow anywhere and produce more corn than previous strains. We come to think of the previous diverse strains and farming methods as outmoded. The new crop and large-scale method become the wave of the future, passed on primarily by youthful newcomers who replace the idea of development-as-continuity with develop-ment-as-discontinuity. We imagine a future which breaks with the past. We limit ourselves to whatever will develop the biggest market, fit for the largest population, and we standardize many possible solutions into a few or one (Garrett 1994). Prior to the development of large-scale corporate agriculture, mass production was rare. Different farmers used slightly different methods. Planting was done according to the ecology of certain areas, without plans for larger markets. Now many small communities are protecting and growing these old minor genetic strains of seeds, to protect the planet from loss of options and famine when disease or natural disaster strikes. Agricultural researchers estimate that, if we can encourage this reversal within the next ten years, we will have time to prevent increased famine (*Ibid.*).

The field of medicine in the West is another example of this standardizing process in which we equate better health with increased technology to combat disease. We have radically reduced funding for public health/epidemiology, believing that immunization has erased the scourge of earlier diseases, and that our research and sophisticated techniques of surgery are rapidly conquering heart disease and other killers, so that we think Americans enjoy much longer happier lives than in most parts of the world. While it is true that we are a wealthy country, and that that wealth enables many Americans to live in a style not enjoyed by most of the world, it is also true that we rank 19th in the world in infant mortality, 29th in low-birthweight babies, and 49th in the world for child immunization for our non-white children (*Ibid.*).

Many diseases thought to be wiped out have survived in poor countries in which sanitation and diet are poor, and export crop systems were developed in the 1960's and 1970's in pursuit of foreign exchange. The latter meant a decline in domestic food production and higher local prices for grains, vegetables, dairy products, and meat. Food scarcity became a function of global food distribution systems monopolized by very few multinational corporations, which could effectively manipulate prices and supply. Malnutrition in these areas, and in poor areas in the United States, strongly affects the immune system,in which cells are most dependent on a steady supply of nutrients (*Ibid.*).

The prevailing view in the world's leading capitalist agencies has been that nations had to modernize first and develop industrial capacities and consumer classes, and that the benefits of economic modernization would eventually trickle down and result in overall improvements in education, transportation, and health (free market capitalism). Intellectuals such as Theotonio dos Santos, Fernando Enrique Cardoso, and Enzo Faletto from South America and Africa argued that loans and aid from multinational corporations would produce greater dependency and debt, as has proven to be the case. But they did not spell out alternatives, in the way that Ghandi had set out a system of small technology development. Political unrest accompanies economic oppression, and war and political tyranny in poor countries also strongly increase disease epidemics (e.g., Idi Amin in Uganda, deposed in 1979; epidemics of malaria, TB, leprosy, cholera, and others between 1975 and 1980, diseases thought to be conquered) (*Ibid.*).

As people travel more, previously rural diseases concentrate in urban areas and spread easier there. Diseases such as AIDS do not stay only in poor areas of the world. However, it is extremely difficult to organize global strategies for disease control, due to political and economic divisions and differences; for example, in 1992, the World Health Organization was forced to admit that there was no global strategy for malaria control, but every individual ecology in each endemic nation needed to develop its own environmentally and socially tailored plan of action.

Furthermore, the use and overuse of antibiotics by those who believed that they would permanently kill bacteria has tended to produce an antibiotic-resistant strain of bacteria. As we develop more and more new types of antibiotics to replace those no longer working, we keep applying the same kinds of solutions in terms of developing pharmaceutical technology. More money goes into drug research and developing medical expertise with drugs than goes into public health and training physicians in prevention techniques in wellness medicine, helping people to strengthen their natural immune systems. And so old illnesses come back, and infect those populations in which immune systems have been severely compromised--the old, the indigent, the homeless, those living in big cities in which budgets for city garbage pickup or sanitation have been cut. But diseases do not stay with the poor...and so in recent years in the U.S. we are coping with lethal HIV/AIDS, tuberculosis, Legionnaires Disease, and other forms of viruses originating in Third World countries.

While coping with these diseases has rapidly driven up the cost of our health care, we are not coping with them as public health epidemics with mass prevention campaigns. In 1992, the Center for Disease Control and the New York City Department of Health adopted what amounted to a Third World tuberculosis control strategy, training nonprofessionals to work as officers monitoring patient compliance with medication. This came on the heels of an 80% success rate or better in disease control in the world's poorest nations, while the U.S. performed poorest of all in terms of identifying TB cases, treating them, and keeping track of outcome and possible contacts. Our health care industry is organized to provide drugs and specialized health care to individuals *after* they become sick, rather than to educate general populations how not to become sick *before* they are sick. We have put a bit too much faith in the effectiveness of new technologies to cure, once people are sick (*Ibid.*).

Meanwhile, automated technologies in industry have been reducing the need for human labor in every manufacturing category. The number of factory workers in the U.S. has declined from 33% of the work force to under 17% in the past thirty years; and, by the year 2020, less than 2% of the entire global work force will still be engaged in factory work. But these workers won't find jobs in the service sector, as it too automates its banking, insurance, wholesale and retail, and layers of management corporate infrastructure (Rifkin 1996). Productivity is increased with a decrease in the work force (and this harkens back to the functions of slavery and colonialism in U.S. capitalist history, referred to earlier in this chapter). But our government could offer tax incentives to companies which reduce their work-weeks, and offer shareholder dividends so that employees can share in productivity. Civic organizations need to come together to restore work and civic life in their communities. Rebirth of civil society is needed, with this becoming the third vector in the old polarity of government versus the market. Social capital in the next millenium will need to be equal in importance to market and public capital. This will change the political discourse, and open possibilities of re-envisioning the economy and the nature of work and society (*Ibid.*) Drawing on our town hall, pueblo, Civil Rights, feminist, and labor movement traditions will help us to break out of paralyzed thinking which polarizes government and the market. In expanding our thinking, we encourage diversity and discourage dependence on only one race, one class, or one gender.

Since social service provision is institutionalized according to the norms and values of this society, it is no surprise that the problems and solutions in social service agencies parallel those in the larger society . With increased productivity demands and loss of staff, social workers no longer work in the collaborative environment which has been essential in social work practice. Is less teamwork and case consultation, less mediation, brokering and advocacy services a loss of essential professional social work treatment, or increased efficiency? The 1980's saw an increase in the centralization of departments and the size of catchment areas served; and case management, day treatment, and residential services were substituted for more costly clinical services such as prevention and outreach, consultation and evaluation, and direct service. A qualitative study done on the perspectives of social workers and clients about their experience of these changes indicated that they felt the changes were a reduction in service to the point that service could no longer be called professional social work (A.K. Motenko, E.A.Allen, P. Angelos, L. Block, J. deVito, A. Duffy, L. Holton, K. Lambert, C. Parker, J. Ryan, D. Schraft, and J. Swindell 1996). It seemed that social workers were caught between market and government, and so (a la Rifkin above) might need to heed the suggestion to use community as a third vector to empower their work.

Bringing together diverse viewpoints is very important in order to get new ideas and creative solutions in our work; and, to escape "stuckness" in a group, says Auerswald (1995). We have to change collectively   the vantage point from which we approach the topic at hand, the context. We need to identify restrictive thinking, such as 1) "either-or" solutions rather than those more inclusive, and 2) ego independence, in which I am unique and don't have to consider what others think. The best way to get creative solutions is when we-ness, not I-ness prevails, shared synthesis and energy, group creative thinking. It is hard to get energy and creativity at the poles of either isolation or bureaucratic organization.

Economist E.F. Schumacher (1973) advises that our technology and organization must be on a scale understandable to the common man, and that, when they get out of hand, they will not be able to sustain large-scale profits and will result in large-scale depression. Schumacher holds that *Small Is Beautiful* because economic stability depends on building a system in which people matter, and can come together, at the community level.

Definitions of Community

The contradictions in our history play out in our current confusion about what community means and how it relates to our individual identities, as exemplified in this quote from *The New Yorker*:

> The deeper problem with the communitarian view is that it asks us treplace one abstraction, the autonomous individual, with an   even   greater abstraction, the group. What determines the group to which we belong? Nationality, religion, race, gender, economic class, generation, physique, profession, sexual kink, hair color? Each "group" we nominally,belong to has interests that conflict with those of other groups we belong to; and we often identify with the interests of groups that we don't belong to at all (Menand 1994, 85).

The author concludes that the politics of these warring group identities is largely responsible for the violence in our society:

> It's not primarily a lack of respect for the community that accounts for the abusive and violent behavior we feel assailed by today. It's lack of respect for individuals. Victims aren't communities, and neither victimizers (Ibid.).

In this essay, Menand polarizes the abstractions of the autonomous individual versus sociological categories to which we can assign individuals. He seems to then equate these categories with community and, in a repeat of the old nature-nurture controversy, sides, in the Western tradition of individualism, with the individual:

> Morality is an attribute only of persons. Individuals can benefit by identifying consciously with a group, but no one is a better person simply by virtue of belonging to a group. Groups are essentially imaginary. Souls are real, and they can be saved, or lost, only one at a time (Ibid.)

The Menand essay speaks to a sizeable part of the American experience in which the individual feels raised in a vacuum, cut off emotionally and physically, in a geographically and upwardly mobile world, from formative connections and accountability. A person's morality is not learned in the company of beloved others. Attachments are not the foundation of the individual's morality, but are only illusion. This alienation, and its accompanying fear and anger, provide justification for violence. Individuals who cannot raise themselves without some support, and who also cannot be raised by mental health systems, experience psychic overload. Mental health clinicians have been trained to provide treatment for many forms of psychic overload one individual, or one nuclear family, at a time. Therapy is a European invention, often sharing the same biases as the Menand essay,such that the only reality is the individual and that one cannot treat both the individual and the supportive context.

Spiritual and religious leaders generally understand that alienation breeds violence, and so they preach community involvement, often as a way to prove one's unselfishness in this life in order to gain a place in the next. As with Menand, this view of community tends to polarize either the individual or the community. Sociological analyses of community, as exemplified bv Lasch's *The Culture of Narcissism* (1979) and Bellah, Madsen, Sullivan, Swidler, and Tipton's *Habits of the Heart* (1985), often focus on the historical development of community. They see it decreasing over time, so that modern individuals have become increasingly narcissistic and isolated. When community is thus plotted on a time continuum, solutions for its demise would seem to be a nostalgic return to the past.

Coontz (*The Way We Never Were*) warns us not to seek solutions in the past. She extends the period of community analysis beyond this half of the century, and arrives at slightly different conclusions:

> Twenty per cent of American children live in poverty today. At the turn of the century, the same proportion lived in orphanages, not because they actually lacked both parents, but because one or both parents simply could not afford their keep. As late as 1950, after ten years of low divorce rates, one in three children lived in poverty. Modern statistics on child support evasion

are appalling, but prior to the 1920's a divorced father did not even have a legal child support obligation to evade. Until that time, children were considered assets of the family head, and his duty to support them ended if he was not in the home to receive the wages they could earn. As for child abuse, it has far too long a history to be blamed on recent family innovations....While overpermissiveness may create problems among some modern youth, overwork was responsible for the prevalence of delinquency and runaways in the late nineteenth century. Today's high school dropout rates are shocking, but as late as the 1940's less than half the youths entering high school managed to finish, a figure much smaller than today's. Violence is reaching new high in America, but before the Civil War, New York City was already considered the most dangerous place to live in the world; the United States has had the highest homicide rates in the industrial world for almost 150 years...There have been many transformations in family life and social relations in American history, but they have been neither as linear nor as unitary as many accounts claim...No one family form has ever protected people from poverty or social disruption...and no traditional arrangement provides a workable model for (organizing)family relations in the modern world (Coontz 1992, 4-5).

Coontz goes on to emphasize that a focus on personal responsibility for strengthening family values encourages a way of thinking which leads to moralizing rather than mobilizing for concrete reforms:

The problem is to build the institutions and social support networks that allow people to act on their best values rather than on their worst ones (*Ibid.*).

The Black Church in America has focused *both* on moralizing *and* mobilizing for concrete reforms. The National Baptist Convention in Washington in 1991 spoke to 40,000 delegates from 33,000 churches and 100,000 pastors in this, the largest black organization in the nation (Billingsley 1992). The National Baptist Convention of America, the second largest denomination, represents some 11,000 churches and 2.4 million members; and the African Methodist Episcopal (AME) denomination represents 6,200 churches and 2.2 million members. The rapidly growing Church of God in Christ is third to Baptists and Methodists, with memberships representing 16% of the total, and 2 million black Catholics in 1989 accounted for about 8% of the total (*Ibid.*). This means not only a "church on every corner", but community centers and recreational centers encouraging education, business development, and democratic fellowship. C. Eric Lincoln has called attention to its multiplicity of functions, necessarily very different from white churches:

> Beyond its purely religious function, as critical as that function has been, the black church in its historical role as lyceum, conservatory, forum, social service center, political academy, and financial institution, has been and is for black America the mother of our culture, the champion of our freedom, the hallmark of our civilization (Lincoln 1986, as quoted in Billingsley 1992, 354)

Black churches are owned and controlled by members, who have financed organizations over a span of 140-150 years stable and substantial enough to involve, as does the Concord baptist Church in Bedford-Stuyvesant, Brooklyn, a whole city block of institutions: an academic school through the twelfth grade, a scouting program, nursing home, homes for the elderly, a housing rehabilitation program, a credit union, and a foundation to support a wide range of political, social, and economic activities in the community (*Ibid.*) Most black churches, even those not so well endowed, offer a wide range of social and economic services in addition to worship. When we understand the depth and breadth of the church's involvement in the lives of black Americans, we can better understand how it mounted and sustained enough organization for national Civil Rights activities in the 1950's and 1960's, and certainly in times prior to that and since. It is a model of organization *both* broad *and* deep, both social/political/economic and personal. Black churches combine messages of Christian salvation as a reward for diligent hard work and community responsibility in this life with extremely supportive and nurturing structures and rituals which preserve the black culture and soul.

The Native American *spatial* religious focus contrasts sharply with the European *temporal* lens which casts community sharing as a way to move up and away from original sin in the present to rewards in the afterlife. Deloria (1994) explains the spatial orientation:

> Changing the conception of religious reality from a temporal to a spatial framework involves surrendering the place of teaching and preaching as elements of religion. Rearrangement of *individual* behavioral patterns is incidental to the *communal* involvement in ceremonies and the continual renewal of community relationships with the holy places of revelation. *Ethics flow from the ongoing life of the community and are virtually indistinguishable from the tribal or communal customs. There is little dependence on the concept of progress either on an individual basis or as a means of evaluating the impact of the religious practices. Value judgments involve present community realities and not a reliance on the part of future golden ages toward which the community is moving or from which the community has veered* (Deloria 1994, 68; emphases mine).

Western views of community seem to approach it from the perspective of the individual, as to the its importance in forming and sustaining *individual identity*. Our indigenous traditions make the place of the individual take a back seat to the maintenance of *communal relations* amongst humans and all of nature through renewing ceremonies and rituals. The Black Church exemplifies another way of understanding community, in its role of organizing and reorganizing for *institutional reforms*. The community in small geographically and ethnically identifiable areas offers social and leadership structures as mediator and power broker between usually poor and working-class individuals and larger societal structures which would not be so responsive to the needs of poor persons without organized brokerage.

All of these understandings of community are part of our heritage, and are useful and important. They are paralleled particularly by different social work fields: casework, group work, and community organization. These specialty areas were developed in social work historically in work with the poor *in* their communities.

The Relationship of Therapy to Community

"Therapy" is a class- and culture-bound word. It is accepted as a solution for a wide variety of problems among middle- and upper-class persons and those of European heritage. According to the primary   value of individualism in these cultures, personal problems are seldom seen to be political and social problems, at the same time. One seldom relates one's individual depression to any of the power imbalances in society mentioned previously in this chapter. Moreover, it is primarily the woman in the family who is thought to have the problem, or to be the one who should seek help for it in therapy. Most men do not request therapy and do not imagine themselves to be the ones it should involve, since it is a service for the "weak" female who needs and fosters interpersonal connections. The focus on feelings and on talking solutions has been left to "minorities", while white middle-class males have been assumed to be responsible for making the "more powerful" economic and political connections. These assumptions separate interpersonal and emotional bases of power from economic and political ones, denying the importance of the former; and therapy becomes a sort of consolation prize for the underdogs, a process which would help the underdogs *self-correct*, rather than one which helps them build on their already-existing power.

The popular conception of therapy is of a very private practice in which one person has a problem and bares his/her soul to another person who can bring a new perspective to that problem, based on training rather than friendship with the client. The therapist is expected to be detached and objective, and is not expected to advocate for the client or press for group or institutional change relative to the client's problem. To do so would be to get into the economic and political sphere, again not seen to be the domain of therapy. When the split between economic/political power and personal/ relationship power is maintained in therapy, therapy is not expected to acknowledge or participate in larger political spheres. Training for therapists focuses on the understanding of their own personalities and family histories vis-a-vis their ability to be objective and subjective in intimate relationships with clients. When the assumptions underlying professional training are of a split between political and personal realities, training does not often help therapists understand their own culture, class, and gender biases in work with clients who have backgrounds more or less similar to, but also radically different from, their own. While some researchers specify the racial, cultural, class, and gender compositions of their sample populations, those who teach and write journal articles and books read by other professionals seldom specify the populations they themselves come from and have worked with. Traditions of the therapist as "tabula rasa" (a "blank slate", detached, objective) and racial and class guilt combine to protect the therapist from examining his/her political biases and how they affect the therapy process.

Those in the public sector often get information from "experts" who have never worked with poor populations or people of color. Most trainers, whether in private institutes, universities, or agency settings, have developed their clinical practice with middle- to upper-class populations in private practice. They also tend to live in middle- to upper-class areas predominantly white; and the similarity of their life and work experience carries a power which tends to make this experience *seem* universal to them. Unconsciously, this sets a standard against which they measure training and work experience in the public sector, especially since work in the public sector carries less salary and status and so may not be expected to have its own store of wisdom and knowledge. Workshops attended for continuing education credits are commonly focused on a particular school of therapy, model of work, or presenting problem seen in practice, *as if these could be abstracted from the backgrounds of the person doing the therapy or the setting in which it occurs.*

We have come, then, to gravitate toward educational expertise in one *abstract* area of work or another, further and further away from actual *particular lived experience*. We are encouraged to deny differences amongst ourselves and to keep hidden those aspects of our history which are "unsettling": classism, racism, and sexism. University, medical and insurance institutions,which would need to undergo changes in structure if they acknowledged the ability only to serve white middle- and upper-class clients, are protected by this umbrella of universal assumptions. Indeed, the practice of therapy has been institutionalized along the same lines as the rest of society, so that we repeat society's unresolved class, race, and gender biases in our practice of therapy. Such is the meaning of institutionalization. It is not that we discriminate intentionally, or that therapists want to serve only those who pay well or are similar in background to themselves. But our history together in the United States provides encouragement to "helping professions" to help in some ways more than others.

In our history, in times of social unrest or depression, the country pulls together enough to consider the needs of the poor and the disenfranchised. In the 1960s, the biases of training institutions were confronted, and many departments recruited minorities to help in restructuring to meet needs they had not taken into account. Some of these changes were institutionalized, but most were not. Since the time, particularly of President Reagan's withdrawal of federal support for such efforts, "therapy" definitions have swung back to more individualistic medical interpretations for human behavioral, interactional, and political impasses. However, paradoxically, as therapists bump into managed care and experience some of the same political/economic barriers as those faced by the poor and the working poor, many can see more clearly the effects of these external factors on the therapeutic relationship.

Clinical social workers, due to their history of work primarily in the public sector and their recruitment more from diverse ethnic groups than other clinical professions, often have incorporated advocacy and institutional coordination functions into their roles as therapists.They have generally been given less status and salary than other therapy specialty fields, and have often been seen more as environmental manipulators than therapists (again, the split between the two). Clinical social workers have been trained to incorporate both the private and the interpersonal, institutional aspects of therapy, and so have felt more constrained than psychologist and psychiatrist counterparts, the author believes, when the therapist's role has been reduced to only the private sphere. However, this strain in the clinical social worker's role can certainly foster some of the creativity needed now.

Suppose, for a minute, that the therapist sits in the client's chair seeking help for job burnout. He/she is reeling from the constant focus on paperwork and statistical service quotas, in the face of peers losing jobs and clients increasingly cut off frorn the institutions which previously served them. With both client and therapist in overwhelmed states, their is little progress in the work of the therapy. When behaviors seem unable to be controlled within one's family, and unable to be modified by therapy, institution-alization and medication are increasingly likely solutions, just as prisons seem more likely solutions for criminal behavior when employment and job training in the community are drastically reduced This hopeless scenario repeats itself often when families under extreme financial and social pressures work with therapists whose frameworks include only individuals and dyads.

With sharp reductions in funding to social services over the past fifteen years, and with sharp increases in disease, poverty, and unemployment affecting family life it is hard to maintain optimism and faith in our own and our clients' strengths. However, when significant support becomes available to us in times of crisis, that crisis can become an opportunity. It will no longer work for us to solve our economic and ecological problems by dividing along class, race, and gender lines, and then using only those solutions offered by the dominant groups. Constructionist/postmodern therapists and theorists (e.g., Anderson and Goolishian 1988; Hoffman 1991, 1993; White 1991; and Foucault 1980) have tried to expose the particular historical foundations of so-called universal approaches, in an effort to help other particular, but less used, approaches define the dialogue between therapist and client. This is for the purpose of unearthing "new" information in order to give us better options as we design practiee to meet the needs of an increasingly polarized, violent, diseased, and spiritually barren population .

Agencies are places where clinical social workers, who can systemically address concrete resource and power issues within the treatment context, can work with generalist BA-level social workers trained broadly in the needs of the field and its clients, but without clinical practice and supervision; and with a variety of less-trained"aides" or "case managers", whose roles have become diverse and ill-defined in the past fifteen years when we have sought to maintain comparable levels of service with less pay and reduced personnel in agencies . However, this diversity can enable clinicians to be influenced and taught by their co-workers with backgrounds closer to those of their clients, and can then enable the resulting agency services to better relate to community realities as well as the more abstract academic realities which are not enough by themselves, given the class and racial polarization in our society.

Family therapists also comprise an increasing wedge of the pie of service providers over the past thirty years, since the proliferation of many family therapy training centers 1960-1980; a system of credentialing family therapists which developed through the American Association for Marriage and Family Therapy (AAMFT); and the licensing of marriage and family therapists in many states. However, since the field is young and standards have been recently set, it is hard to tell what training a particular family therapist has actually received. Most clinicians have taken some institute or agency training in family systems approaches to therapy, but few to the degree of AAMFT credentialing. Since most organizations' job descriptions for clinicians still only include certified or licensed social worker, psychologist, and psychiatrist categories, most family therapists who have had to have prior clinical degrees in these fields, get to be recognized not as family therapists, but as social workers, psychologists, and psychiatrists.

Since family therapy is a postgraduate discipline requiring work 2-5 years beyond the clinical degree, and since this added education is expensive, most well-trained family therapists do not come from or return to the public sector. Yet many in agencies have received some training from family therapists, being drawn to its systems applicability for work with the poor and its practical interactional strategies. Family therapists in early years of the Philadelphia Child Guidance Family Therapist Training Program made attempts to recruit and train minority therapists, and to train in a mutual way which respected and built upon the community experience of trainees. Out of this came a focus on *power* in family therapy: power primarily in internal family dynamics, and with respect to social services systems(e.g., Minuchin and Fishman 1981; Haley 1976; Montalvo 1976; Aponte 1976; and later, Imber-Black 1986, 1988; and Schwartzman 1985). Feminist family therapists extended this work by helping us to understand that power interactions between family members are never solely determined by those persons, as if the family existed in a vacuum. Rather, the family tends to act out power scripts designed by the larger society's models of male-female relationships (e.g.. Goldner 1985; and Goodrich, Rampage. Ellman, and Hallstead 1988). Feminist therapists and theorists have often included class and race in these analyses of the effects of power imbalances on women and families(e.g., Collins 1991; and Jones 1993).

When we understand that family dynamics parallel power relationships in society, we should be reminded that therapy can only be part of the solution, and that therapeutic solutions in isolation from more powerful contextual reforms can only be band-aids. Social workers and then family therapists have learned to go out to homes, not as investigators or anthropologists, but to get a feel for the reality of peoples' lives and to encourage clients to educate us as to their connections. How far away is the corner store, and how expensive? How dangerous is the community, apart from media stereotyping, and do children go out to play, or spend all day in small apartments glued to their overwhelmed mothers or TV sets? Are there any recreational opportunities for families and children? Do family members live close to one another, to support each other at a moment's notice? Which church does the family attend, and what programs exist there, and in other local churches? How far away are drug dealers? How much do family members know about housing, welfare, food stamps, health, education, and job training resources and services they are eligible for? How much do they know about social service policies and appeal procedures?

Accumulating information in these areas with the client helps the therapist to learn about the client in the context of his/her community. Knowledge of the community enables the therapist to make referrals within it, of course, but also to find clinical approaches which would strengthen symptomatic families' own internal and community supports, and increase the power of the therapy. All of us need networks of social support in the normal course of our lives, but those who do not have class or racial or gender advantage have tended to value community connections more than those who would have a financial or status cushion in hard times. We are only now beginning to discover that these advantages are not enough, and that the community strengths of the poor and people of color and women need to be more valued and developed for all of us.

Community organizers have helped families to link to others in block clubs and other advocacy organizations, and have helped to link youth to opportunities other than drugs and crime. Therapists have often worked in close liaison with such organizers, or with natural spiritual and political leaders in the community, beyond only social service agencies. Family therapists such as Attneave (1969, 1976, 1990), Speck and Rueveni (1969) and many network therapists since then have taught therapists how to convene large networks as a tool in their work. Landau-Stanton has taught "link therapy" as a way for therapists to work with large systems with severe internal feuding, and a model of supervision to be used with a group in work with such systems (Landau 1981; Landau and Stanton 1983). Agency administrators have often recognized that having a branch office in a community did not, in and of itself, make the agency a part of the community; so they have often worked to establish structural links between natural leadership and organizations in the community and their own leadership, making it easier then for line staff to follow their example in work with clients. Community-based clinical work in agencies has been published (e.g., Auerswald 1982, 1983; and Brown and Parnell 1990), as well as efforts to base clinical training in the community experience of trainers and trainees (e.g., Piazza and delValle 1992).

However, such work in agencies and in communities, which builds a bridge between the personal and the economic/political facets of solutions offered by therapy, needs clearer conceptualization, with examples which remind us that it is possible, do-able, and successful, even with managed care and budget restrictions in the public sector. This volume is an attempt to contribute to the growth of knowledge of clinical *and* community-based approaches across practice fields. These approaches can offer more power to social service delivery systems in crisis now, and more hope to families of all classes, races, and cultural groups.

Culture and Community

Racial/cultural divisions and the primarily individual/dyadic verbal practice of therapy are factors which have separated it from community solutions for individual problems. Those with therapy expertise seldom link with those with community expertise, and vice-versa. While therapists often have not even thought of community approaches as solutions, political and economic conditions now obviously directly affect their work with individual clients. Therapists are beginning to re-envision community and enlist its help in intervening between the larger society and the individual.

A recent example of this clinical use of community work is in work with domestic violence in a program directed by family therapist Rhea Almeida at the Institute for Family Services in Somerset, New Jersey. In this program, the claustrophobic privacy of the abusive couple is treated by assigning "cultural consultants" as sponsors to family members at the beginning when a court order for treatment is made. This network of volunteers, generally former clients, operates like a natural community in which private behaviors in the family are accountable to the larger network supporting it. They participate with family members in, first, separate men's and women's groups,and then family groups, getting a sense as to how violence happens in families, and addressing the assumptions undergirding it. Domestic violence is not treated as a private problem within one family in a therapist's office, but as a societal problem needing community intervention in order to help individual families change (Wylie 1996).

The use of "cultural consultants" in this work is a good example of the importance of culture in communities, and of the distinction between the two. Volunteers are sought who will mirror the cultural experiences of the family member, realizing that it is important for vulnerable people attempting to change serious symptoms to be involved with others who can "walk the walk and talk the talk" (similart to the philosophy of Alcoholics Anonymous) and be *close*, having a personal sense of one's own experiences. The process of linking with someone who has "been there" (using culture in its broad sense, including, but not restricted to, ethnic or class or gender membership) is different from linking to the *distant* expertise of therapy. The value of therapy is intensified when it can offer community identification and authority. Community offers many kinds of such identification and connections, many kinds of cultures which interact at different points or in different projects such as this one (*Ibid.*).

Often we talk of culture as if it were structure. Therapists without experience working with certain populations seek information about "African- American" cultures, for example, in courses which teach cultural profiles. These focus on cultural values and histories which explain differences from the "mainstream", since this is the knowledge sought initially, when students have not had exposure. Unfortunately, when knowledge of culture stops at the level of these profiles, the net effect of the education tends to be to produce only more abstraction and polarization (Montalvo 1976). When this education happens in the community context, in which concepts are related to the actual coming together of different groups to get solutions for problems they experience, students can see culture as *process*. The process is determined by a multiplicity of factors beyond only the cultural characteristics of the constituent groups, so that students will not so easily come up with facile abstract solutions which will apply in many different communities. Placing culture in the structure of community makes our understanding of culture more complex. In this book we will be exemplifying clinical approaches based in specific Hispanic, African-American, and Asian- American communities. This work flows from time-honored ethnic traditions, and these traditions are explained at some length. However, the work happens now in this country, according to local needs and resources which are partly, but not totally, the dominant cultural traditions in the community. Defining our work as "community-based" enables us to see the importance of culture as a living reality in our lives and usable in our work (Chapters Three and Four perhaps being the clearest example of the difference between culture and community here, when they contrast work with the same culture in three different cities).

Clinical work is about application, about use, about what to *do* to help the client. What we do always occurs in relationship: to ourselves, the therapists doing the therapy; to the setting in which the therapy occurs; and to the natural community support systems of the client and the therapist. Adequate training for this work involves moving away from "first step" cultural profiles toward the greater complexity *between* cultures in all of our lives. The community offers us dynamic ways to process and support change and diversity at these junctures, overcoming the isolation of clients and therapists alike.

CHAPTER TWO:
FOUNDATIONS, GOALS, AND
KEYNOTE DISCUSSION

"A powerful approach to the empowerment of all marginalized groups is to work together to develop critical consciousness, to develop together the tools to critique frames of reference, ideas, information, and patterns of privilege."
--Nobles and Goddard, in *The Black Family: an Afrocentric Perspective*

******

Personal Influences

The author grew up in Dayton, Ohio in the 1940s to the 1960s, an only child in a very small Anglo-American family. We were working-class, but aspiring always to the middle-class, with our "success" being the purchase of a small suburban home when I was a sophomore in high school. What extended family I did know were out of town, and most were far out of town. In one generation, both sides of my family had gone from farm or small-town to city folk, and my mother was determined to work, during World War II, much more than her mother had ever thought to work outside the home. Still, although my parents were both working a lot and we were rather isolated in the mid-size city of Dayton, we knew our neighbors and developed strong friendships. My friends were from larger families in which adults, generally mothers, were always home. I grew up with the sense that the world was a friendly place, although racially segregated and strongly disapproving of dependence on others outside the nuclear family. Graduate school at University of Wisconsin-Milwaukee School of Social Welfare in the 1960's challenged my culture's value of individualism. Seeking to major in "casework", I had to meet the requirement of the department to take a number of courses in "community organization". This simple requirement made a statement to those social workers wanting to do "therapy". It said that therapists had to put their work in the context of the community, first and foremost. Of course, this fit the times then, in which communities were demanding control of programs. And so this work owes a lot to the University of Wisconsin-Milwaukee School of Social Welfare, 1965-1967. Milwaukee also marked the beginning of my indebtedness to Puerto Rican culture and communities.As an undergraduate, I did some volunteer work with pre-teens which was organized by an order of nuns based in Puerto Rico. Surprisingly, the nuns offered me a scholarship to a summer institute in language and culture to be held at the Catholic University of Puerto Rico in Ponce, P.R. in 1964. It was an intense three months. Thereafter, fate often landed me in Puerto Rican communities which showed me ways to build community while doing therapy, especially the Lower West Side of Buffalo, New York, from 1976 to the present. In this community, I began to learn how the extended family, rather than the individual, could be the basic unit with which to work; and pursued family therapy training to increase my skills in family work.

Increasing my skills as a family therapist and a family therapy trainer/supervisor introduced new contradictions. The culture of family therapy often seemed to reinforce Anglo and middle and upper class biases. I began to seek out other clinicians who could bridge the gaps for me between my professional training and my work in the community. Again, the common denominator in these collegial relationships was our service to the same community of people. During this twenty- year period, my work was affected very much by two partners, Carmen M. delValle and Margo Villagomez, who co-founded and co-directed with me a community-based family therapy training institute (see Chapter Nine); and by numerous individuals and organizations on the Lower West Side of Buffalo. It also was affected by raising my two sons Steve and Joe as a divorced parent, with the support of years of soccer teams and school parent organizations and friends, as well as their father; and by having participated in the Civil Rights and women's rights movements. All of these experiences contributed to the fabric of community for me. Later I moved briefly to New York City and to Dover, Delaware, where I met many of the other authors in these chapters.

The Organization of This Book

This is a modest book, coming from my own attempts to educate myself and integrate those professional and life experiences which have taught me the most. My experiences are not unique, certainly, just as the various examples given in this book could be multiplied a hundred-fold. But now, when various therapy fields are losing financial and institutional support, I want to share with others a source of support which it is often difficult for therapists to tap into and use adequately in their work: their own and their clients' communities. My goal in this book is to expand the clinical vision of the reader, as others have expanded mine. I hope that readers can use some of these examples of community-based clinical work to explore the connections between their own and their clients' community memberships and their clinical approaches. Such exploration offers a third source of power to therapists during these troubled times, in addition to their own professional training and the corporate or government financial and administrative support in their treatment setting.

This book represents conversations with nine groups of therapists, some seventy people in all, who have worked together to develop creative community-based approaches to therapy. These therapists do not always call themselves "therapists", but answer to titles such as social worker, community organizer, community healer or spiritual leader, community political leader, administrator, mental health aide, case manager, alcoholism counselor, educator, family therapist, psychiatrist, psychologist, nurse, and nurse practitioner. Thus, we use the word "therapist" in a generic healing sense here. These were groups of people I met in the states of New York and Delaware who were doing community-based work in different kinds of agencies or in community-based organizations (CBO's), and with different cultures and different kinds of problems presented. In interviewing them, I organized their accounts into book form, so that this is a co-authored product of group thinking and definitely not the ideas only of the primary author.

Readers will note that, in chapters reproducing a group's dialogue, the voice shifts from third to first person. I hope that this is not too confusing, but it is intended to remind readers of the communal thinking involved. The keynote discussion in this chapter is the only one in the book in which the people interviewed have not worked together previously in the same agency or on the same project; and so I identified the content by individual participants here, unlike in the rest of the group discussions. These chapters do not provide examples of community-based work which are representative of the whole country. The examples come from my own contacts along the way, and are used to provide food for thought as to *the connection between clinical work and the community membership of the therapist and the client.*

Most of those therapists in our examples use ethnic community traditions in their work as much or more than formal clinical training; so I have reported on those traditions, insofar as I could research them for the scope of this book. The reader is urged to consult the bibliography at the end for further knowledge of these traditions, in order to better inform his/her own practice.

It is not my purpose to collapse these richly different examples into one overarching model called "community-based therapy". Such has been done before, and while models are reassuring to the beginning practitioner and easily marketable, they do not do justice to the advanced levels of expertise of most who will be reading this book. Some readers may be more advanced at community levels, and some more advanced at clinical levels. We try here to honor the complexity of both worlds by extracting common themes from our examples, along with the unique diversity of particular traditions and histories in each community. In interweaving the particular and the general, readers are then invited to put themselves into the work and build their own models in their own comrnunities. Therapy can then be grounded in the specific ecology of each community, and each community creates its own "model".

The Keynote Group Discussion

With Edgar H. Auerswald, Miriam Azaunce, Dionisio Cruz, Brenda David, Cecilia Gaston, Virginia Goldner, Ena Johnson, Mel King, Eliana Korin, Bolaji Oladapo, Barry White, and Agnes Williams*

Our group has come together from many different work settings, occupations, and communities. We are experienced as social workers, family therapists, educators, administrators, community organizers and spiritual healers. Our experiences might match the diversity of those who read this book, and the themes developed in the following chapters. We hope that our questions and concerns about our work and ourselves has some connection to your own questions and concerns; so that our conversation here serves to orient you to the following chapters.

The Power of Relationship

Certainly most of us here seem to have had some connection to doing therapy or work in agencies or communities. We might ask whether you

* See List of Contributors, Chapter Two in the end notes after the Index, for a more complete identification of participants and listing of their work.

Have to be of the same culture as your client in order to help him or her or be from the same community. There are opinions at both extremes, but many say that you work as part of a team with defined roles in an agency, and that part of your professional knowledge base is an understanding of cultural diversity. Thus, you can, on that team, help a client from whatever culture with whatever problem he or she experiences.

Gaston: But that kind of language is too intellectual, as if education conquers all. That belief in this society is a problem in relating to people. What about the "skills" of the uneducated person?

David: Of course, one extreme denies that clinical skills are real: ghettoization. And then, the other extreme does not recognize the importance of education beyond that provided in a university. Being an African-American therapist does not mean that I can only work with African Americans. In fact, in my agency, I am often an outsider with my own people due to my age or education, it being assumed that, since I got that piece of paper, I must be from wealth. What I do is start by being very honest with the client about who I am and how I got here, and I try to demonstrate my concern and compassion for that person in an active, caring way. There is more to me than this degree.

Azaunce: In your agency, you must remember that you represent the system! When I work with immigrants, I know they can't disclose to me. I know that I can't really work with the true person because they have to lie so much.

Cruz: Language, dialect, and slang are short-cuts to making us co-participants in the therapy process, and helping us trust one another. When I speak Spanish to a Spanish-speaking client, I get a different set of problems and a different affect than when I speak English. The use of English tells the client that s/he is on the therapists's turf, whether the therapist is Anglo or Hispanic. The client then will have to conform to institutional expectations, and will have to do more of the adapting than the therapist will have to do.

When I work in the community in which I live, I have a certain respect there, especially when my work setting is one which the community feels it has molded and shaped. Not only do I have a track record which clients hear by word of mouth, but the work setting in general has one. Then, therapists have power by virtue of the community's belief in them. When residents determine that program changes have been made which are not helpful to them, they stay home and seek what they need elsewhere.

Auerswald: We need to make a distinction between power and skills. Power has to come from the people who live in the community, although skills can certainly be brought in from outside.

King: We need to be careful not to throw one blanket over everything. We're talking about a lot of different situations and people and about "do you trust me, do I trust you?"--a lot of different issues here. We can't overgeneralize about community. Whether or not therapy occurs in a community-based setting, it is a European invention. It has some of the information needed for change, but not enough information, by itself.

I do not think In terms of a "poor" client or a "poor" community, but of what information that person brings with him or her to get the job done, to get from here to there. Perhaps the client's child is out of control and she is upset or depressed about it: What resources or skills are needed to get the child to behave better? Who can we get to help? Who are the effective ones and experts in the family, and how has the mother gotten good results with the child herself? What is the culture of the family, and how does that culture say the child should be controlled? What would the mother be doing to change the behavior if she were in Antigua or Santo Domingo?

Oladapo: I am African, from Nigeria, and I do counseling to prevent the hospitalization of kids with drug problems, emotional problems, behavior and family problems. There is a lot of death and AIDS in these families, and the kids just can't cope. These are mostly Hispanic children aged 4-18 years, in Broadway-Flushing and Bedford-Stuyvesant sections in Brooklyn. My program is supposed to be for four to six weeks, but clients stay six to nine months due to lack of places to refer them to in their neighborhoods or catchment areas. Most families just find it difficult to follow up when they have to travel far away, and so they just keep cycling back to us. I do family therapy and involve the grandparents on home visits, trying then to introduce families to facilities in their own neighborhoods.

According to my culture, when children behave, then they are the father's children. But when they don't behave, then they belong to the mother. It seems like that here, too, when it is hard to get fathers to come in with the kids. But I really have no problem getting them in. When a child acts out. I believe that the whole family is upset, and so I need to talk with all of them. I need to find out who is important in order to give the family more support and unity--maybe the priest or the grandmother, or some other person. I just ask and they tell me. I don't feel limited by agency policies, but I do whatever I think will work.

Johnson: I also feel that I can operate pretty flexibly according to agency regulations and relate to clients as I need to in my hospital setting, in spite of knowing the limits of that system. I don't minimize my power and I use my own beliefs and culture behind the closed door, without asking permission from others.

David: Yes. When my client is embarrassed that she has said "Praise the Lord!" in front of me, and that I might think she is some kind of fanatic or crazy person (responses given to such remarks in other legal and drug settings she has dealt with), I can let her know that here, in this relationship, I respect her when she expresses herself like that.

On the other hand, she has been embarrassed, in the first place, because she has responded to the kind of institution in which I work, a private family counseling agency. She may be lucky and I won't stereotype her and will want to build a relationship with her, but I will have to work actively with her to develop that trust, and I can't just take a detached stance.

Azaunce: I have restrictions as to the way I can use myself to link people to resources in my community. In my Carribbean culture, the practice of child-lending is common, according to which, when one family has a crisis and cannot care for the child temporarily, another family close by will care for the child until the crisis is past. This is an informal arrangement which works well and avoids the misunderstandings and tragedies of bureaucratic management. But in the U.S., as a therapist in the public sector, I will not learn about all the informal helping systems in communities because there would be all kinds of legal problems if I linked a family member to an informal resource in crisis. So I need not learn about them: I can just stay over here in my agency, with that gap between what families would find helpful and what I can provide.

Sometimes that gap is tragic. In a family I knew, a girl had stolen and so her father did what was a culturally appropriate thing to chastise her: he hit her with a ruler on the hand she had stolen with. But it left welts, which the teacher saw and reported to the Bureau of Child Welfare(BCW), which placed the child in a foster home. She subsequently ran away from that and subsequent foster homes until she cycled back home again, and then BCW wanted the father to send her back to the last foster home. The father told them to come and get her if they had the power to do so, but that he would not return her. He had never abused her, by his definitions, in the first place, and had never wanted her out of the home. Had anyone really talked to the girl, they would have known that she was temporarily angry with her father due to being punished, but she did not want to leave her home, either, and did not feel abused in any way.

We all know similar stories. My point here is that, had I been the BCW worker, with my knowledge of culture, I am not sure I would have been able to use that knowledge to prevent that tragedy from happening, so that this child had to waste years of her life in a maze of foster homes. It would be good if we had more staff members representing the cultures of their clients, but also if we had them in policymaking positions, so that policies could be flexible enough to allow line staff to pursue different options in cases such as this.

Auerswald: We need to create a worldwide community of difference, fostering connection to each other and listening to each others' stories. To really listen means a willingness to change.

King: We all want change out there, but it needs to start in here,with myself: if I can change, you can change. No one is top dog as a therapist, and in the therapist-client dialogue, both need to learn.

Williams: In the Seneca longhouse, children are taught for years to, first, be quiet and then, to listen to the elders and take things in subconsciously, before they can be taken in consciously. Time and process are important. When things are hard in any relationship, including the therapeutic one, you have to keep on communicating and not run away from the learning. All tribes are welcome, and we have to try to bring out the best in each other: these can be the personal guidelines shaping our work.

When people came here from other countries, if they had assimilated to the Native people here, we would he focused today on sharing together constantly and ritually. We would have Thanksgiving, not once a year, but every day when we come together and acknowledge that, although we need to be on a quest for knowledge, we are human and can't know everything. In our ritual coming together, we would have an intrapsychic sense of belonging, and we could just relax and feel OK. We would also know that spirituality is connected to locale, so it is important to stay connected ourselves, as well as for our clients to do that.

Auerswald: In our professional training, we are not taught about how the history of power imbalances in this society will affect our work; and how we can break out of these assigned power roles with each other so that we can trust each other and develop a relationship. Without closeness and trust, it is expecting too much to think that the client will "bare her soul" to the therapist. Certainly, courses in "cultural competence", "cultural diversity", or "cultural awareness" do not bridge the gap. They imply that we can just get some data on that "other" culture "out there" different from us. Such courses probably widen the gap as they focus on differences in an overgeneralized way, apart from the personal relationship of therapy.

King: When two people come together to accomplish something, they need to ask "Why are *we* here?' This means not only "Why are *you* here for services in which you are getting something from me (you, the defined client)," but "Why am I here and *participating* in this venture with you?" What information do you have? What information do I have? How do we know when we do not have enough information?

Auerswald: Then, therapy is a dialogue, but one in which the participants try to recognize honestly the political effects on the relationship of society's racism, sexism, and classism. This is a tall order, but I think we can train therapists to be able to do it. I spend a lot of my time trying, and with some success, to teach people to think in alternate ways other than either-or, top-down, or other rigid Western classifications of reality.

Dealing With Our Own History of Oppression

Williams: Therapy occurs in a political and historical context. All of us have been colonized, whether or not we come from the client's community. So we need to look at that historical process of colonization before we can figure out the therapist's role. Many of us try to make our work evolve out of our understanding of the history of our people, and this reminds us of the importance of taking action together, not only providing counseling and social services. But most of the history of colonization has been blacked out, so that it is difficult to recognize and talk with the client about the power differential in our "treatment" roles and how we will work with these social definitions. Most of the history of violence in the foundation of America has been blacked out, and so people find it hard to own, and then to deal with, those traditions passed on to them.

Cruz: As a Puerto Rican male born in New York City, I grew up with parents who were trying to assimilate, and a grandmother who constantly told me stories about ways of doing things in my own culture. Both the mainland American and the Puerto Rican ways offered me what I needed for my identity; but the dominant culture dictated that the spiritual leaders in my native culture were not recognized experts because they did not have degrees. People who I had come to respect and who had information I needed were just dispensed with by the dominant culture. This kind of cut-off is an effect of colonization, but creates identity crises in individuals who cannot simply choose one part of themselves over another. If I have such a crisis, I need to consult with someone who has skills from the dominant culture, like a therapist; and someone else who has recognized expertise in my own culture.

Korin: The therapist should be prepared to deal with the history of colonization and how it effects the therapeutic relationship, regardless of the ethnicity or class of a particular therapist and client. All of us have certain cultural expectations and social definitions for the roles of a "therapist" and a "client". What will we expect of each other in those roles, in this particular place? Why are we here?

White: But I think that a person who is connected to indigenous roots would have so much more flexibility as a therapist, access to a broader range of experience. I'm not a therapist, but an educator. But what I do has evolved out of the need to keep developing connections to roots for myself and other Native people. My mother never particularly wanted me to go to non-Native schools, but with the war (Vietnam War)it became a choice of war or school, so I chose school. I felt isolated there without any sisters and brothers, so I started organizing Native students.

When the Attica riot happened (1971), they (New York State)were threatening to take our land and the elders had taught several of us to stand on the road and block them, and be prepared to die. So we were standing blocking the road, but the police were at Attica, instead. It occurred to me that what we were doing was a lot similar to what they were doing at Attica. So I started a program at Attica to teach Native inmates about our history and culture. I would see these men later on, and many of them were not particularly success stories. But one time, a man cameup to me and told me that that course in Attica had changed his life around, and he hadn't had a drink in fifteen years. Even though I'm not a therapist, I work to help Native people turn their lives around like that. I taught the only Native history and social studies classes in the Buffalo high schools, and then I worked to get grants to train social workers across New York State in our history, culture, and Indian Child Welfare. We have to know who we are, and this society sets up barriers to that.

Cruz: In the past fifteen years or so, it has become more and more difficult to feel creative and alive in the mental health field, as more and more restrictions have been placed on our work. I have changed jobs fairly often during this time and came to realize that one sort of unconscious motive in making each change was that in each job, in the beginning, I am always given some sort of leeway to be creative and design program. After a certain "honeymoon period", though, of course, I come up against my institutional limits and can then find out the political reason for my program or position, which has nothing to do with good service delivery but with the organization maintaining itself. Perhaps service delivery and the maintenance of the organizational goals are congruent or in the same ball park, but more often than not in this "era" they are not, and so staff leave. I think that this parallels the length of clients' involvement in therapy in the public sector, about 8-12 sessions, or as long as it takes to express oneself and work together with the therapist before you either accomplish what you came to accomplish or come up against the limits of the traditionally defined therapist-client power relationship.

Korin: We play out our history of oppression this way in relationships when we cannot find ways to deal with that history openly. How can we break out of these social definitions and limitations? First, we have to have questions, which are really ideas. Questions arise where you come together with others and discuss experiences and issues. There has to be a way to come together, a "community". Ideas which can question social definitions come from the times we spend together comparing our lives and our needs, as we are doing now in this discussion. You can't come up with "great ideas" alone, in isolation. No one accomplishes anything in life by himself or herself: we need each other. Brazilian educator Paulo Freire addressed ways of breaking out of our social roles with each other and he came up with a method of self-interrogation which would arise out of shared collective experience. Thus, the presence of non-hierarchial relationships was a prerequisite for the specific questioning of Freire(Freire 1373, 1990).

Goldner: Yes, I'm interested in Freire's questions. I'm not involved in community-based work, so I would like to be a fly on the wall listening to all of you. But some of us in private settings are trying to address power issues more openly also. I do therapy/training at the Ackerman Institute in New York where some of us have been working with families in which violence to women by men has occurred, trying to do work which keeps the moral issues front and center. After working together in the project long enough to have faith that we can offer something solid, we are now going to meet with many other progressive domestic violence services in New York, in shelters and in the battered women's movement, to put our heads together.

Auerswald: We are all politicians. Should the client be at the bottom of the heap in our organizations, the "recipient" of all our expertise and services designed at the top which are deemed appropriate to his or her needs? It would seem that any therapy done with this assumption should be oppressive. Therapy occurs in a power context, not in a value-free void. Avoidance of power issues in our settings often sends messages that therapy is an apolitical process,and that the therapist cannot address racism, sexism, and other sensitive issues with clients.

Thinking About Thinking About Mental Health

Williams: The Perry School of Thought helped me to develop critical thinking, and posits cultural stages of intellectual development whereby, in the first stage, young cultures see new information in terms of dualisms, either one way or another (Perry 1981). That seems to be where we are, at this first stage. Beyond that, the dualisms are there, of course, but they are not the only thing going on. There is much more than that. Educators and trainers need to design training at advanced stages by involving mature leaders of older cultures, and then incorporating thinking from each of the previous stages, so that everyone attending can get something out of it. This means that trainers will need to be from a wide range of cultural, as well as personal, stages--such as you have coming together in natural community settings.

This is really different from our accustomed ways of educating in which we ask students to choose the better way between two options; and then the way not taken is discarded or wrong. Introducing complexity needs to take into account the beginning thinker's need for simplicity, but our educational process seems to assume that everyone is at that level, a homogenous group. When we assemble groups in which there is an obvious cultural mix, at least we will be reminded that simplicity arising frorn homogeneity is not the rule. Diversity can open the way for more complex and creative thinking.

Auerswald: If we want to train therapists to recognize and deal honestly with the client about the power imbalances which affect the "treatment" relationship, then we must redefine what we mean by "treatment". The word implies hierarchy and not mutuality. It would be better to leave it out altogether, and to use euphemisms which satisfy the needs of a system driven by Western linear thinking and insurance monies: to say, for example, that you are going to do "preventive" or "pre-diagnostic" work, and then just never get around to diagnosing. But you can't get away with that any more. Thirty years ago there were fewer strings attachcd to funding, and less rcductionist thinking. Now, though, people are defining tasks in more and more specialized ways, so that we are learning more and more about doing less and less. So instead of one therapist being a generalist who you develop a close relationship with over time, we have many therapists all working with separate problems and different persons in the same family--and all going in different directions. Then, when the many therapists involved are oriented toward finding pathology rather than finding solutions, they really do not look to family members themselves as the experts in their own lives, and as people having valuable knowledge or resources. If we were solution and resource-oriented, we would look to the informal systems of support existing in all communities, and we would *use* these supports and respect their authority. That way we would be lessening the client's isolation, lessening our own isolation and delusions of grandeur and strengthening the natural systems in the comrnunity. This would make it easier for immigrants to identify with both cultures as needed.

King: Information moves some people to get counseling, while others don't. Therapists are not the only ones with information. When I worked with youth groups in the 1950s and 1960s some of the best information that clients and staff got was that it was *possible* to get things done, and as to *how* to get things done. Other youth would see our group in nice team jackets, with good equipment, and they'd feel it was possible to get that for themselves, and they'd ask us how we did it, they'd want to learn our channels. Nowadays a lot of information is needed, so people need to remember the importance of coming together to share--citizens coming together with citizens, be they therapists, bank tellers, waitresses, or unemployed people. We all have some information about how to find resources. How can we affect overcrowded and substandard living conditions? How can we find good legal advice or health care?What are the current eligibility requirements for needed services? Do we know formal services which exist right in our own neighborhoods, so that we can actually afford to get to them and use them?

Auerswald: In our roles as therapists, are we expected to exchange information with our clients about resources, and be linked to local communities, or is there a person with a specialized role who is supposed to "do environmental linkage" while the therapist "does cognitive/affective work"? Is your agency connected to the client's community? Is there any accountability to indigenous communities expressed by who sits on the board, who implements and designs policy, who is hired from the community and at what level? If your agency is not accountable to the community of your client in any way, then it exists in an oppressive relationship to the clients it claims to serve, and that oppression sets parameters to the kind of relationship you can form with the client, no matter how skilled or dedicated you are.

We need to remember that agencies are businesses. In the example given before of the child tossed from one foster home to another, of course Caribbean child-lending or some such informal arrangement could never be an alternative, no matter how much human sense it would make. It would leave the agency open for too many legal problems and lawsuits. An agency is a business, needing to stay in business.

Gaston: Businesses are organized hierarchially, often exerting rigid control. It is difficult to create a climate among staff in which there is real mutual planning, real *experiencing of ourselves as participants* creating something together. When it is so hard to do this, I feel constantly schizophrenic, like the conscience part of me is cut off from the work part of me and the normal way I conduct my life. I can't work that way. There is no joy there and work, like life, needs joy. When I create a climate in my organization which is a real sharing, then clients and staff feel at home together and we all bring whatever information we have to the task at hand. I direct a residence for homeless AIDS patients, so there is certainly enough of a task for all of us to put our heads together.

Saving Ourselves

King: Some issues in our work have to do with how I see myself and some with how you see me. Each situation needs to be put in its place. The history of oppression is one part. Then there are the kinds of information we all have, and not knowing what other people know. The fragmentation ot community and our lack of a sense of meaning dictates that we continue questioning and examining our differences, which can't be done only one-to-one on our own safe turf . We need to get out there, to families in their territory.

Johnson: And our clients can be listened to and teach us something. If I mess up and don't understand the culture, so what? The client can correct me and teach me something, and I can learn from my client.

Auerswald: Yes, stepping out of the role of the omnipotent therapist, taking risks.

But I do think it is important to get out into the community, into the client's turf and out of your own familiar territory. When you are out of your usual definitions of things, a fish out of water, you can really see that your information is partial and socially defined. I remember when I was stationed in Germany in World War II, guarding captured German prisoners in the basement of an old house. When we were in that basement, we spent a lot of time together and got to know each other and became friends; it was like we were far away from the war going on outside. But as the tide turned in the war and that house was captured by the Germans, we had changed from captors to captured. When we had been in the basement not knowing what was going on, we were just fellow human beings. But the context of the war gave us social def initions of each other as enemies .

King: Isolation from the community of self puts you in trouble, and is the definition of mental illness. Oppression is *I*deological, *I*nstitutional, *I*nterpersonal, *I*nternalized, and maintained by *I*solated and *I*ndividual ways of experiencing life (The Six I's of Oppression). Self is not separate from others, and we need to keep renewing ourselves by coming together regularly and keeping our sense of community alive.

I've done many things politically, running for mayor in Boston and serving in the legislature for ten years. But, earlier in the 1950s and 1960s I worked on the streets with youth . Since 1971, I ' ve organized the Community Fellows Program at MIT to give help to those working with youth, to help thern avoid burnout. All of us here need support and help, too. We cannot be isolated within our institutions, but need to create a community together, we need to go back to our different communities and bring our colleagues together for a party. Or have a regular brunch at your house every Sunday, and invite people to change, with a belief that they can... out of their love for one another.

CHAPTER THREE:
LATIN-AMERICAN COMMUNITY
CENTERS IN THREE CITIES

"For me, the really crucial consideration in working with the poor is sizing up the relationship of the family to the key institutions in the community. Does the family know how to get loans? Do they know how to use banks?...And if you are a recent arrival from Puerto Rico or Central America, how do you get your wife to quickly join a group where they train her on the machines so she can get a job?"

--Braulio Montalvo
The Family Therapy Networker (1986)

******

We have authored this chapter from three different cities in the Northeast U.S.: Buffalo, New York; Rochester, New York;and Wilmington, Delaware. In each city, our centers are based in Latin American, primarily Puerto Rican, communities. The similarities in our culture, our migration experiences, and our history before migration give us some assumptions about how to organize and provide services which are different from mainstream social service agencies. In our separate group discussions in the three different cities, we look at those assumptions here, and how they have interacted with factors of economics, mainstream politics, and geography to form unique services in each center.

Hispanics United of Buffalo, Inc, Buffalo, New York

With   Alberto delValle, Andres Garcia, Gilbert Hernandez, Lourdes Iglesias, Carmen Melendez, Jose Pizarro, Raul Russi, and Juan Texidor

Hispanics United of Buffalo (HUB) is a multi-service center located in the heart of the Latin American community on the Lower West Side of

Buffalo, which is home to a preponderance of the city's Hispanic population of 16,446 (5.1% of the total city population in 1991) . It is the result of a merger, in 1989, of three smaller organizations in the community with histories and purposes paralleling the development of the community.

The Development of Leadership and Resources in the Community

We have all been involved in significant ways in the parent organizations which merged into the current Hispanics United of Buffalo and in other organizations in the community, and we were all born in Puerto Rico. Mr. Texidor is the senior member here,and has shaped our organizations actively for the past forty years,since 1953.

Mr. Texidor remembers when there were no organizations in the community, in the first wave of immigration from Puerto Rico in 1950-51, when men came to work for the steel mills and the railroads, primarily. The first organization was begun by Carmen Guthrie at the International Institute, to help new people find resources here: *Ayuda Mutua*, the Puerto RicanSociety of Mutual Help, a "welcome wagon" of older couples helping newer arrivals to get adjusted. Shortly thereafter, her nephew Marcos Lopez founded the Latin American Republican Club, and Mr. Texidor was president of the Latin American Democratic Club. At that time the club functioned like the social clubs in Puerto Rico, helping people to stay together and feel secure in new surroundings. Then therewas no Latin food in supermarkets here, no Latin music on the radio. Coming from a culture with strong extended family values, people mourned the loss of the family and community where they had felt they could operate effectively. Not only was the culture different here, but the necessary godparents, grandparents, aunts, uncles, and so on who would share tasks within the family were gone. There were dislocations, and necessary tasks in the family would often remain undone, as if people were waiting for the old supports to still be there. People often forget how immigration to a very individualistic society effects those coming from an extended family culture, and so how important the social clubs have been in giving us alternative support structures.

Agustin Olivencia had also been active in the Latin American Democratic Club, and was the main force in setting up the Puerto Rican American Community Association (PRACA) on the near east side of Buffalo. We had been advised by Judge Ryan then that we would need to change our orientation from a political and social club to only a social club if we wanted to get public funding. So we changed our name from the Latin American Democratic Club to PRACA, and got money from General

Electric, Westinghouse, a local bishop, and from the proceeds from activities associated with the queen contests we held for three years. With this money, and with community residents all chipping in one dollar and the men coming after work to help build the center, we opened up a new building on Swan Street. We wanted a social center. We had been denied access to the Polish Center which was nearby, and so we decided to have our own center in which to hold dances and meetings. Probably that building cost about $90,000. PRACA also organized the annual Puerto Rican street festival, and this year was our 25th annual festival, still organized by PRACA.

Also on the East Side at that time were the Puerto Rican Cultural Center on Swan Street, which focused on the development of the arts; and Estudia, and Alianza, smaller but influential local organizations.

At that time, in the 1960's, there were Civil Rights marches, the Young Lords, the Black Panthers, and a politically active student organization at State University of New York at Buffalo named PODER("to be able"). Some of these students, such as Albert Cappas, Jose Pizarro, and Michael Rivera, were working for the Community Action Organization, and met at each others' houses to discuss forming an activist organization on the West Side to increase cultural pride and awareness. With some assistance from the organization BUILD, we rented a place on Maryland Avenue initially, and the Puerto Rican Chicano Committee of BUILD (PRCC)was created. It established a library and focused residents on their history and on working together. There was always a little tension between PRCC and the previously existing organizations in the community because the university students at PRCC were primarily from New York City and had more leftist politics. We had ideas which were not in sync with the local mainstream, and had a lot of power struggles within our organization in the early days. But at PRCC we did bring resources to the community from university and state levels. Many in that original group stayed in Buffalo and became leaders here, some splintering off to establish their own power bases in other organizations.

We had heard that Title VII federal Comprehensive Employment and Training Act (CETA) monies were going to be made available, so we formed a comprehensive planning group advising the mayor as to how to bring some of these monies into Buffalo, into the East Side and West Side. Out of this we formed, especially with the help of Gilbert Hernandez, in about 1972, the Consortium of Spanish-Speaking Community Organizations (COSCO) and developed programs which used the resources of PRACA, Estudia, Alianza, and PRCC This does not mean that these parent organizations merged. Each retained its separate place and identity, and leaders did not want to give up their separate bases of power. However, each fed staff and board into COSCO, which operated job training programs out of a building on Main Street, which was not centrally located in the community. Fabio Afant was its first director and Raul Russi its first Chairman of the Board. A lot of money was concentrated in COSCO, which operated for 5-6 years before mayor James Griffin ended it. We did not really develop a strong power base out of that organization, though, probably in large part due to its location and the fact that leadership from the other organizations forming it did not come together there. So, when the city pulled the plug, we had a constant struggle to keep the other organizations going. By 1982, only PRCC and PRACA were left.

In 1979, Julio Martinez had become the Commissioner of Drug Abuse in New York State, and worked with Andres Garcia here as he formed a community support group to respond to several violent acts by addicts then congregating on Virginia Street. Other community leaders prompted the city's support, in 1983, for a state-funded drug treatment program then established on the Lower West Side, La Alternativa. Since the establishment of La Alternativa,and other local culturally-sensitive drug treatment programs, drug abuse had begun to be a little bit better controlled in the community, although complicated by a very high incidence of AIDS in recent years.

Leadership has existed in the community in those who served on the boards of these centers, ourselves, and many others; and also in other organizations such as the *Hispanic Women's League*, which has focused on the promotion of sisterhood and support amongst women in the community and has raised money for educational scholarships for young and often single-parent women to advance themselves. Its presidents and officers have built the organization from a few to hundreds, raising significant scholarship funding in its fifteen years of existence. Importantly, its women have built connections for many in the community. Among the significant leaders have been Carmen delValle, Rosa Aviles, Margarita Santiago, Maria Rosa, Blanca Rodriguez, Silvia Rodriguez; Diane Aviles; Lillian Orsini, and many others. Carmen delValle also served as co-founder, with Emilio Fuentes, of the *Hispanic Health and Human Services Network* in 1983. This organization helped to bring together many professionals serving the community, to help them plan joint initiatives such as a summer camp for children. The *Western New York Hispanic and Friends Civic Association* is composed mainly of professionals who seek to muster political support for community programs, enabling those who cannot have this political role within their own government-regulated centers to stay connected to community leadership. The *Lower West Side Ecumenical Ministry* (LOWSEM) serves to make local church members aware of services and to support services, especially the community centers.

In the 1970's the Puerto Rican population had moved from the East Side more to the Lower West Side, and became much more organized in mutually supported efforts to bring outside resources to its residents here of many ethnic groups. While Puerto Rican culture predominates, the emphasis has been primarily on organization and on increasing resources for all. There are many ethnic groups represented here: Native American, Asian, African-American, South American, and Cuban, primarily. This is a poor community, but also a working-class one with well-attended churches and a small community hospital which we have fought to keep open due to its accessibility and bi-cultural Spanish-speaking staff.

With the advent of CETA programs through COSCO, the focus at PRCC had changed from social action to job training and social services. PRACA still continued as a social club, and also provided some social services. We knew that United way monies could become available to PRCC, and these funds were badly needed. However, all of our organizations ran on very small budgets, and we did not want to set up competition between them for very limited funds, but wanted to make it easier to get substantial funding into the community. We also wanted to be able to administer programs ourselves, without United Way centrally administering programs for us. So, in 1986 we began to discuss merging PRACA, PRCC, and La Alternativa.

The Merger

In 1986, it was obvious that the funding of social programs in the public sector at all levels of government was shrinking. United Way would not have been likely to fund duplicate programs at PRACA and PRCC to help people apply for welfare, access needed services, and find affordable housing; and to get family counseling via referral or linkage with West Side Services of Child and Family Services and Catholic Charities' West Side Office. When United Way's funds were cut, they encouraged us to plan more cost-effective centralization in one center.

Community leaders explored the cost and ramifications of merging PRCC, PRACA, and LaAlternativa informally, and then formally, with several of us having financial expertise. The extensive changes involved in reducing three boards to one, and choosing adequate space and a clear focus for programs raised anxiety in all three organizations. Moreover, there was a history in the community of various leaders each having small separate power bases. To get them to understand and buy into the idea of a merger required a lot of careful attention to process. To cope with this, we met formally every two weeks for eighteen months. In the first nine months, we met with virtually everyone involved in the three organizations in small groups, and encouraged their participation in our bi-weekly planning group. Those participating in the regular planning seemed to self-select, over time, to a group involving Raul Russi, Sara Norat, Olga Mendell, Jorge Reyes, David Rivera, Jose Rivera, Alberto delValle, and other male leaders. Sara and Olga were the only women involved in the primary planning of the merger, even though there were many active women in the community.

During the second nine months, we planned a reorganization into social services, a social center, and administration of both. La Alternativa left its building and its drug treatment services became part of the social programs at HUB, to be located in the old PRCC building. PRACA remained as a social center at its old location. Both buildings and their programs were administered by the newly created Buffalo Hispanic Management Company, which owned the HUB building and leased the PRACA building to its members. Boards were merged into a thirty-member HUB board.

Virtually everyone came to support the idea of the merger. Politicians trying to support the community didn't need to choose between one organization or another. Community residents have one central location which can meet most of their needs. We still hope to develop more specialty services at other locations, to buy another building across from the present HUB location to give us more room, and to develop and invest in housing in the community. But the merger has enabled us to become more financially stable and to administer our own programs, which gives us more control.

HUB Social Services

It is important to remember that those making decisions in HUB and other local organizations are from the community and identify strongly with the people, so that they are serving their own needs as well as the needs of others. There is less distance between service providers and service receivers and less of an attitude of charity or "noblesse oblige" here when common personal experiences inform policy and program. Carmen Melendez, a program director at HUB and previously a director of the VIDA program for youth in crisis at PRCC, remembers how she felt herself as a Puerto Rican high school student who suffered discrimination: when her mother remarried an Italian, Carmen wanted so much to belong that she "passed" as half-Italian to other students,a denial of her heritage which was very painful for her. She has related her clients' experiences to her own. Andres Garcia, president of the community's Columbus Hospital and long active in the formation of drug abuse programs in the Lower West Side, remembers how it felt for him to go to college while learning English watching Sesame Street with his two-year-old son. He knows, from this experience and many others, how difficult it is to progress in a city in which you are poor, minority, and isolated. This affects his methods of administration, and patients and staff feel free to go directly to "Andy" with a problem or complaint. Such "personalismo" (respect for the individual, giving of individual attention) is a strong cultural value seldom finding expression in mainstream social services and institutions.

Staff at HUB,when out on the streets, can hear reactions to their services, and can bring back the gossip to inform services, making them more flexible and responsive to needs. Staff often act as interpreters of mainstream services and policies to residents,and advocate to mainstream institutions for their clients--thus, bridging the gulf between majority and minority worlds. While providing counseling to youth and to families in its domestic violence program, staff see themselves as "informal counselors" not providing clinical counseling on a level with professionals in outside agencies. Yet they do credit themselves with being able to reach people better than professionals who may have more formal training, but not enough knowledge of the community and its cultures, and who are not bilingual or bi-cultural. Counselors are trying to find and develop skills within the organization, and want to increase pay to the levels of state salaries, in order to recruit higher skilled staff. When pay is so low and experienced bilingual, bicultural counselors are few in Buffalo, HUB often loses staff to higher--paying mainstream jobs, after they get basic experience in the community. Staff plans to stop this flow of talent out of the community.

HUB operates a thriving center for senior citizens, with structured day programs and integration of the seniors into many of the other programs. HUB advocates and refers for housing, financial, and health concerns of residents, and is engaged in locating and rehabilitating housing in the Lower West Side, a pressing need. Counselors go into court and high schools to help youth get connected to information and treatment regarding drugs/ alcohol, AIDS and safe sex, and teen pregnancy crises. Counselors go out into the community to meet with many groups and agencies for education and coordination. Specialized programs of counseling for domestic violence link to women's shelters and other mainstream counseling and family services. Youth programs focus on leadership development as well as recreation, and plans are in the works for a general program to develop neighborhood leadership and mutual support of residents by residents. While HUB has has a strong services focus, it is moving now more in the direction of a wide range of community support efforts beyond social services components.

Mr. Texidor feels heartened by the vitality and involvement of youth in HUB and other community organizations, noting that "if we lose our youth, we lose the community". He is proud that bilingual education programs in local grade and high schools, beginning at Herman Badillo School, were fought for by Sonia Davila, David Caban, and others in the Board of Education, with strong support in the community. These programs teach youth respect for their history and culture, and instill in them the desire to preserve it and get involved. "We offer them a way to be concretely involved here, instead of to cop out with drugs, still our major problem", he says. Lourdes Iglesias and Raul Russi call attention to the need for community leaders to come together and learn to compromise better, to decrease territoriality and increase collaborative efforts, as government budget cuts and a slow economy put severe strain on already strained resources here. Lourdes believes that the development here of women's more collaborative sharing style of leadership can assist us in this period to combine our resources, complementing the more independent style of male leadership.

Ibero American Action League, Rochester, New York

With   Lourdes Arvelo, Elisa deJesus, Olga deSamper, Nancy
         Padilla, Gladys Santiago, Fr. Laurence Tracy, Julio
         Vasquez, and Aida Veras

Initial Growth

The Latin community in Rochester is now seventy-three percent Puerto Rican, this probably lower than in late 1940s when people began to come here from nearby migrant labor camps. Then the government of Puerto Rico contracted with the Wayne County Growers Association in Marion, New York, who were short of laborers after the war, when the prisoners of war they had previously employed had been sent back to Germany. Men came without their families, intending to make a lot of money to take back with them to Puerto Rico, where the economy had made a rapid shift from agricultural to industrial (with the U.S. introduction of "Operation Bootstrap"on the island). However, when these contracts ran out, many of the men chose to come to the city to find other jobs rather than to return to low or no employment at home. Others came in the 1940s, not as migrant workers, but simply having made the connections to Rochester in various ways and looking for economic opportunity here.

They gravitated toward the social clubs in which they could come together to relax informally, communicate in Spanish, eat the foods they were used to, and network to find needed resources. The first of these social clubs we remember was at the home of Chito Mon. Men sent for their families and word spread about the availability of low-skilled jobs in Rochester, so that the community was quite sizeable by the end of the sixties, and these social clubs were an important way we organized ourselves and supported each other. Samuel Torres was a prominent leader in the 1950's and 1960's: president of the Pan-American Club, a social club; founder of the Puerto Rican Democratic Committee; founding member of the Puerto Rican Affairs Committete (PRAC), an advocacy organization; founding member of the first Hispanic Pentecostal Church in Rochester, La Iglesia de Dios Pentecostal; and organizer of the first massive voter registration campaign in the Puerto Rican community in 1958 (Vasquez 1994).

The Catholic Church organized us around rituals, dances, summer camps for children, and youth organizations. The churches represented neighborhoods more than ethnic groups as such, so that ethnic predominance in a church changed as neighborhood composition changed. There was the Catholic Brother Association and the Cursillo Movement which promoted the development of lay leadership. Many of the prominent leaders in Ibero's precursor organizations came out of the Cursillo Movement.

One cannot underestimate the importance of the social club and the church in promoting leadership within the community. The practice of coming together informally and regularly to help each other produced many active and conpetent leaders rather than one or two "large egos". Among many distinguished leaders generated through these organizations, the following people are worth special mention. Ramon Padilla was founder and president of the Puerto Rican Republican Committee and a member of PRAC. Also influential in PRAC were Jaime Santana, Pedro Mojica, Saturno Alvarez, Julio Diaz, and Ana Miralba Jorge Colon was an inexhaustible mentor in the community. Edwin Rivera and Pedro Pedraza were political leaders helping us to gain a foothold in the ward politics and party patronage system. Emerging leaders in the 1950s and early 1960s were

Domingo Martinez, Juan Padilla, Pedro Maneiro, Agustin Ramos, and Marcos Santiago--to name only a few(*Ibid.*)

In the l960's the church saw the need to create job training programs but as a religious organization, could not get money for such programs. So the Spanish Apostolate of the church, which has operated in the community since 1967, then formed a lay organization in 1968 with the same director and board, so that the then new organization could apply for government funds for job training programs. This organization was *Ibero* (named for those tracing their heritage to the Iberian Peninsula) *Community Action League*, and, while set up to be a multi-service agency, it focused at first primarily on job training. It was funded first for a summer program, and then for a job orientation project, which was very effective and grew into a $500,000 program.

In 1972 Ibero formally separated from the Spanish Apostolate,and began the growth years of the 1970's. It had become a United Way agency in 1971, which gave it more permanency. Housing was a critical issue in the community, so Ibero built, with low-interest loans from the federal Small Business Administration, the Los Flamboyanes project of 152 units of low-income housing. This project is still operational and strategically located within the heart of "El Barrio". Money was then reinvested from this project so that we have been able to provide low-interest loans to community residents who could not set loans from city banks, with Emilio Serrano having been a long-time Executive Director of Ibero Investors Corporation; and, in the mid-1980s, Isla Housing Corporation came into existence as a spinoff from Ibero, with Elston Hernandez as its Chief Executive Officer. Ibero now has Pueblo Housing Corporation, and we have established a credit union, a day care center, and a drug treatment program (deSamper 1988). More importantly, though, Ibero has played a key part in giving the community a much more stable economic base, and has contributed to creating a web of well-run and solidly-financed institutions. We have managed to keep a great deal of political unity, but without really merging all our resources and power into one organization only. While Ibero is a recognized voice for the community, it is not *the* voice, any more than there is one voice in, say, the Jewish community or the Italian community.

Established political and economic institutions in the city can find qualified personnel and candidates through us, and we can organize voters and consumers, rather than having vague agendas and leadership going off in many directions. We have continued to grow, with 85 staff and a budget of $3.5 million. The separate Ibero American Housing Corporation and Ibero American Investors Corporation, established in the late 1970's, have budgets of $4.5 million and a portfolio of another $8 million.

Puerto Rican Youth Development (PRYD) was born out of the same informal network as Ibero and developed, under the leadership of Roberto Burgos over the past twenty years, significant youth programs and advocacy for Hispanic youth, who remain at such great risk.

Social Services at Ibero

In recognition of the great strengths Hispanics bring to this country, and our respect and reverence for the family as the key to our strengths, the agency has committed resources and staff to maintain and preserve the family,with programs such as:
1)day care and after-school care
2)early childhood disabilities outreach
3)prevention of teen parenthood
4)programs for teenage parents
5)programs for parents with developmentally disabled children
6)El Centro de Oro, a senior citizens' center

For families at risk, we operate non-mandated and mandated preventive services programs, and foster care and adoption services, for which we have recruited many families from the community to be foster parents. We provide community support groups for these foster parents, and assist many of our grandparents and extended families who have become kinship foster homes when parents cannot parent their own children, often due to drug abuse. In our preventive services program we work to keep families together by offering bilingual, bi-cultural trained family therapy to Hispanic families. We have historically hurt in this community for a lack of bilingual Hispanics at masters' levels or higher in the therapeutic community, and our staff's help has often been requested by mainstream agencies who had staff with advanced clinical training, but without language and cultural expertise. Now, we can offer families at serious risk the clinical expertise they need in a culturally appropriate way. This is a tremendous accomplishment, thanks to Lourdes Arvelo, who has gone on for post-masters training in family therapy at University of Rochester.

Our staff also goes out to clients' homes, so that not many families come into the center except for special sessions or groups. We also give many training sessions in the community and out of town. The majority of the requests are for information on providing culturally competent services, although this is beginning to be expanded to requests for information based on our clinical expertise in general. *A key ingredient in good service provision, we believe, is not our ability to translate for clients or to be familiar with particular cultural practices and values in an abstract way. The key is our ability, because of our community membership, to know our clients and to know how to work with them appropriately because of our common ground.* Most Anglo professionals have a hard time understanding the basis of our expertise, but our clients don't. They come by word of mouth and bring us all their serious problems. Generally, agencies fear sending staff out for home visits into poor communities, and so the agencies provide some sort of protection for workers. However, *we rely on our clients for protection: they will call us up and tell us something is coming down in the community that day and so we should not come out; or they will meet us and escort us in a dangerous area. They want us to come to them, and they want our help.* This kind of trust is essential for therapy, and we can train others how to be more effective in their work with this population.

Another thing that is often not understood is the importance of knowing resources for our clients, inside and outside the community. Our clients can talk to us about "espiritistas" and the kind of religious items needed for spiritual rituals which are not widely understood. We can help them make necessary spiritual, economic, and political connections in the community; and we understand the more formal mainstream systems, and can help mediate for our clients to get the resources they need from these systems to survive. We need to work with a view to the whole person and with a wide knowledge of current resources available within our community and outside it. We serve a population with high unemployment, a very high high school dropout rate, political exclusion, and high rates of drug abuse; and they need us to help with real connections.

Community Issues and Concerns

Nationwide, the percentage of Latinos graduating high school has improved from 44% in 1980 to 53% in 1990. Income and unemployment are closely linked to education, though, and we are twice as likely to be unemployed as non-Latinos, and earn only two-thirds as much when employed. By way of contrast, the non-Latino population graduating high school in 1990 was 82%, up from 68% in 1980! (statistics from census tract data quoted in Vasquez 1994). Clearly, we need to concentrate efforts toward helping our youth to finish high school.

To understand why our youth do not complete school, it is important to understand the effects of monolingual and bilingual education on the learning process for Latinos. In states with significant Latin populations, there has been a strong mainstream reaction against bilingual education and a movement to establish English as the only instructional language in the schools (California, New York, Florida). Recent statistics show a total Hispanic American population at 22,354,059, with Spanish spoken by over 17 million people five years and older. Among Spanish speakers, 8.3 million did not speak English well or at all. Spanish speakers represented 54% of all non-English speakers in the U.S. These statistics make it obvious that the Spanish language is predomininantly spoken among Hispanics, and does not seem to assimilate to English (1990 Census of Population and Housing, CPH-L-96, U.S. Dept of Commerce, Economics and Statistics Administration, Bureau of the Census (in *Hispanic American Today*, 1993). Surely language and culture strongly maintain our identity as a people and as individuals, and so cannot just be changed as one puts on a new coat.

When all students, Latin American and Anglo-American, are taught in more than one language, intergroup communication is fostered, as well as full competency in both languages, cognitive flexibility, concept formation, and creativity (Vasquez 1994). While bilingual educators see it as a benefit for all students, those in the English-only movement are well financed, and seem to fear political domination by Spanish-speaking groups in areas in which the Spanish-speaking population is large (perhaps showing their realization that the use of English only in the schools has been a political tool).

In Rochester, many of our Latino students were classified as "slow learners" simply because they did not know the English language well enough to compete in the classroom, and then got tracked into non-Regent or non-academic programs which did not challenge their actual intelligence enough, and caused them to drop out of school before graduating, or to not be able to pass college entrance tests if they did graduate high school. Forty-five percent of Latinos in Rochester live in poverty, and more than half of all Hispanic ninth graders in Rochester schools did not make it through twelfth grade in a city which has a highly technical job base (*Ibid.*), so we have known that, for an action organization, our top priority issue has had to be bilingual education.

It is important to remember that, while Ibero's roots in Rochester came a lot from the leadership development of the Catholic Church's Cursillo Movement, they also came from the grass roots youth movement of the 1960s, when the Latin and African- American communities had pulled together, with help from Saul Alinsky's organization, FIGHT, to form Action for a Better Community (ABC). Leaders Nancy Padilla and Roberto Burgos came out of the youth movement and ABC, and later got the city to fund a demonstration project on Crisis Intervention for the Hispanic Community, which Ms. Padilla took to Ibero to administer, becoming the Director, in 1975, of its Human Services Institute, the foundation for the current programming.

Nancy Padilla remained at Ibero then as Director Of Program Operations and Assistant Director until 1985; then having been elected, in 1981, to serve as Commissioner of Schools for the Rochester Board of Education, where she served two terms over an eight year period, and served as President of the Board, strongly representing the community and influencing the direction of bilingual education in Rochester. The Board commissioned a study which focused on the needs of students in regular programs in Rochester schools (the majority of Hispanic students being in these programs, more than in bilingual programs) and reported on patterns of tracking, curriculum development, teaching, parent involvement, and dropout. This comprehensive study resulted in the 1986 community report, AHORA (*A*ccess for *H*ispanics to *O*pportunities to *R*ealize *A*chievement), which has been used as the basis tobegin to break down some longstanding barriers to education in our community. Ms. Padilla was the first Hispanic elected to the Rochester City Council in 1989, and the first Hispanic elected to any city council then in New York State. After serving on the Council until 1993, Nancy Padilla ran for Mayor of Rochester, but was defeated, in 1994. Her work is nationally known, and has served to bridge gaps of understanding between government and the grass-roots Hispanic community. She has been able to increase the political influence of Ibero at these levels.

She notes that social action has long been a component of services at Ibero, and that many community people have been willing to take strong stands on issues,with leaders following the community will. Early in the 1960's, Maria Lopez had been refused the right to vote in an election because she did not speak English well; so she got an attorney and filed a complaint against the Board of Elections, which she won and which remains on record as a precedent. In 1972, the school district summarily fired the director of *Adelante*, the city's bilingual program, without consulting anyone in the community. The community responded with one of the largest protests ever, and Domingo Garcia, then Director of Ibero, and Edwin Rivera, working with the U.S. Department of Justice, met with Supreme Court Justice Richard Rosenbaum and convinced him to order the Board to appear before the court. The Board was then forced to negotiate with the community to set up a structure for bilingual education which would maintain it within the regular Board practices and structures, but give the community the right to oversee and participate in hiring. This still protects programs from being dispensed with during political changes or budget cuts.

Ibero is named an "Action" League, then, because it not only provides social services for the community and links people to existing resources, but because it creates new possibilities and resources out of effective organization and unity. It is one of several strong community organizations to have grown out of grass-roots *movements* in the community. Education has been a focus of organizing since the 1960s when high school students themselves began to make demands. Students organized as the Puerto Rican Student Union (PRSU) in 1969, and the Puerto Rican Teens for Community. Then, in 1971, PRSU petitioned Ibero to create the Hispanic Youth Council which, in 1972, was incorporated as Puerto Rican Youth Development (PRYD), now a well-established United Way agency with a broad base of funding. Our pioneers in the 1950s sowed the seeds for effective leadership to address our concerns, and *numerous* people have kept the energy of the social movement going. An example of the effectiveness and involvement of ourleadership is to be found in Juan Padilla,who developed Ibero's original crisis intervention concept in the 1970s and initiated the grant for it which Ibero then administered. He also developed the *Instituto de Servicios Humanos*, a five-year CETA demonstration project in the 1970s; formed the Roberto Clemente Little League; and founded the Hispanic Health Rights Coalition, now with 80-100 members. Over the years, leadership *within* Ibero has also been leadership *outside* it: in the Hispanic community, and in cooperation with other Hispanic and non-Hispanic communities at city, state, and federal levels. *A web of strong institutions has developed from social action around issues which have had meaning to residents.*

The Latin American Community Center, Wilmington, Delaware

With   Carlos Duran and Ana Maria Viscarra

Our Beginnings

This year we will celebrate our 25th anniversary as an incorporated center. Hispanics who came to this area fifty years ago were primarily Puerto Rican, but had lived in New Jersey first, rather than coming directly from the island. Originally, a small group followed a Pentecostal minister who had been a leader in the community in New Jersey. Later, in the formation of the center, several young adults got together to respond to the needs of their parents for translators and their children for day care when they were working. Then, 90% of those using services were Puerto Rican; and services soon became extended to include the dispensing of federal FEMA funds (emergency funds for rent and utilities and food, etc.), and employment counseling. These were the services important to residents then, assistance with the concrete practical priorities of daily living.

As we grew and got better known, residents would come to us looking for jobs, so we set up an employment service, job training, and GED classes for those who had not completed high school. Services were provided out of three sites: recreation in one building; social services in another; and day care in yet another. Often, several members of a family would come together to make use of different programs at the same time. But the youth and recreation programs kind of stayed segregated from the rest of the center because they were in another location.

In the beginning, United Way funding was 85% of our budget, whereas now it is much less, about 60%. Many staff were from the community, and served as what you would call case managers, translating and helping people use services which were available, and helping to locate resources which were needed. There was no real therapy component. Our staff has never been all Hispanic. We had a director for a long time who was Anglo, but he had lived in Latin America and knew the language and cultures. Nevertheless, residents felt he wasn't representative of the community, so he was fired and the position was given to someone who had been a case manager here for many years, and who was Puerto Rican. However, then, when he was director United Way guidelines were not being adhered to and our funding was jeopardized, so we had to fire him. He was also a minister in the community with a lot of power, and so there was a lot of negative reaction against the center for firing him.

Our Situation Now

As recently as six to seven years ago, the community was about 90% Puerto Rican, but that has changed to about 60% now, as Colombians, Mexicans, Central Americans, and other Hispanics have moved into the area. About half of the recent immigrants came to escape persecution and repression, and the other half came for economic opportunity, since most of Latin America is getting poorer. With the composition of the community changing, there has been a lot of conflict, particularly between the largest new group, the Mexicans, and the Puerto Ricans who feel displaced. A couple of years ago, there was a fight and a Mexican man was killed by a

Puerto Rican youth. Increased drug availability and abuse increases the likelihood of other violent reactions to such incidents as this in the community.

We reflect the community's struggles. While several of our staff members are from the community, and several are Puerto Rican, some have different backgrounds, and some of the administrative positions are filled by non-Puerto Ricans. Our board is one-third community residents, and two-thirds from outside the community. In 1990, we were able to bring together all our services into one new and very beautiful building, and we have developed a lot of little programs funded from various sources, in anticipation of United Way funding being reduced. Now we have a Center for Home Ownership and a substance abuse prevention program, funded by different federal departments; programs to promote Latin arts funded by the local arts council; and mentoring, tutoring, summer camps,recreation, and counseling for youth, funded some by state and some by United Way funds.

A multiplicity of programs with different funding sources demands much more administrative and clerical time, so you go in the direction of recruiting those who have had experience in program accountability more so than experience in the community. The focus gets shifted a bit, and gets exaggerated by residents who think you have fired a Puerto Rican director and brought in top-level staff who are not Puerto Rican . They see you spending money on a fancy building, while they can no longer get emergency monies in crisis times or transportation for appointments,and they think this means you are building an empire and so are no longer sensitive to community needs. They feel displaced in the center, just as they have felt displaced from such a rapid population shift in Wilmington, and as they have felt kept on the outside from racism here, in general.

Then it gets more complicated . It is hard now to figure out who and what geographic areas constitute our "community". The Hispanic population has grown in nearby New Jersey, Maryland, and downstate Delaware. The census is not accurate for Hispanics in Delaware, but there are about 15, 000 to 30, 000 Hispanics just in Delaware, again with the recent immigrants downstate being mostly Mexican and Guatemalan migrant laborers. We are the *only* Latin American community center providing comprehensive services all the way from southern Delaware and Maryland to Philadelphia, and the nearby Jersey shore! So people hear about us and come here from all over. We cannot turn them away because there is no one else to provide service for them. Most of the area we serve in Delaware outsideWilmington is not as urban as Wilmington, and there are not services in these areas like there are in more urban areas, especially for Hispanic populations. So we need to be sensitive to the non-urban needs of Hispanics elsewhere in Delaware and along the Jersey shore.

When we serve the *immediate* neighborhood, it consists not only of Hispanics, but of African- and European-Americans, so that 40% of our clients are not even Hispanic! The Center for Home Ownership is used by only 20% Hispanic clients; day care has the most diverse population of all the service components; and youth recreation programs have been used primarily by black youth. It is easy to see how local residents would think that we are not sensitive to the needs of the Hispanic population here.

Due partly to the withdrawal of emergency funds, our programs have come to focus now more on prevention and less on crisis intervention. We still have a few funds on hand for crises, but not much. Now we are trying to, as they say, "not give a man a fish, but teach him how to fish" so that he will be independent. A counseling component was introduced in 1990 to help families work out marital problems and issues with children or within individuals which have been impeding them, but that therapist recently left, and has not yet been replaced .

Our thrust now is toward building our youth programs. Whereas these programs used to be the weakest, off in another building, now we have brought them together with the rest of the programs and we are able to offer much more than only recreation: tutoring, mentoring, counseling, substance abuse prevention. Our governor is pro-youth, and we are trying to come together to help youth so that they will have fewer problems when they are adults. Our thrust now, also, is to get more support from the neighborhood and from Hispanic professionals in the community, so that this building does not remain under-utilized by Hispanics in the community. However, our energy is so diverted into management of various programs that this is difficult. There is always, just as in any organization, a handful of people on staff and board who get things done. But then they tend to get burned out and need a private life. We all know this feeling very well!

You know, Hispanics tend not to have the same racial prejudices as Anglo-Americans, but we tend to put our prejudices more in the direction of status and class biases. That tends to get played out here in terms of the new building and more stabilized funding being seen as a sign that the staff is getting more distant and "upper class".

Good News

We are presenting some of our problems and conflicts here because they occupy our minds a lot, how to try to resolve these issues. However, this does not mean that we are not extremely happy with the work we are doing here. We have a wonderful and very dedicated staff. Our services are used, and responses to followup questionnaires given to clients indicate that they are very satisfied with the services received. It is a real privilege to be doing counseling in a place where clients can come to get a majority of their needs met. and everything is right here: one-stop shopping,as in HMO's. It is not like being in an agency in the larger community where I would have to refer a client here for this and there for that, and then the client would feel confused, especially with language difficulties. Also, when therapy is one component in a community center, relationship issues can be dealt with right here in the context of the whole program support system, not by one therapist referring out. That means that a therapist can focus on the more traditional verbal therapy without having to do a lot of linkage. Linkage to practical resources which our families need for survival need not be ignored, but is provided by others on staff right here in conjunction with the therapy.

CHAPTER FOUR:
A BRIEF HISTORY OF PUERTO RICO
CULTURE AS THE BASIS FOR COMMUNITY SERVICES

"...Is it not possible that on a smaller scale Latin politics mirrors American politics? Is it not possible that...all people want personal politics?...that the decline of American political participation since the early part of the century was due, in great part, to...the decline in politics as an interactive process. It may be that what Latinos want from politics is a model for what Americans in general want from their political system".

--Carol Hardy-Fanta, *Latina
Politics, Latino Politics*

******

On the Closing of Gaps

Dominican novelist Julia Alvarez writes about the identity of the in-betweens, caught in the inevitable gaps when living in someone else's country and language. Her fiction is a device to reclaim a stolen aspect of history, and her themes leave the United States, analyzing the role of women under dictatorships in the Southern Hemisphere. Here,the dictator Trujillo is the central figure, an overwhelming shadow in the lives of the Mirabal sisters, who are also, of course, the "real" central figures of the book (Alvarez 1994).

This awareness of the interdependence of the personal and the political aspects of our lives, and of the many cultures we live between, is certainly basic to the work done in community-based organizations(CBO's). The setting which provides counseling for personal and family problems also is a political voice for the community (see Ibero Community Action League in Chapter Three), or is closely associated with other organizations in the community which can develop political support (see Hispanics United of Buffalo Inc. in Chapter Three). Survival needs dictate that those who have been marginalized in this society are always aware of at least two cultures, the native and the majority. So each organization develops a unique synthesis of personal counseling and social action, and finds ways to mirror diverse cultural realities for residents.

When Puerto Rican Americans moved from the island to the mainland U.S., the social club was important in preserving culture, identity, and political power. The clubs were not only "social" but political, and they developed leadership. In Buffalo, one of the precursors of Hispanics United of Buffalo,Inc.(HUB) was the Puerto Rican American Community Association (PRACA), a social club which had officially dropped its political function and changed its name from the Latin American Democratic Club in order to get public funding. The formalizing of PRACA, and then HUB, as places funded to provide services, like other United Way agencies, helped them to take on a more mainstream orientation. It masked, if not actively discouraged, the continuation of political traditions. The concept of a center as a place where neighbors could gather and get information about resources was replaced by the development of specific programs which could be funded by government and private sources.

From Social Club to Service Center

Since the 1970's CBO's have become more stable in their funding, but more like mainstream United Way agencies. The social club functions of institution-building had been, at the same time, dedicated to collegial and personal assistance. With CBO's coming under the United Way umbrella, we might wonder if they would lose the unique social club traditions, and if collegial assistance would be replaced by professional specialists. Majority institutions such as United Way almost always see this kind of transition as progress, when they have not had an understanding of the historical importance of traditional supports for Latin American families. Could increased professionalization be used in a way which could build upon these supports, rather than substitute for them?

In our examples, there are no uniform answers to these concerns, but there is affirmation that the concerns are valid. First of all, in each of the CBO examples, the essence of the social club seems to have survived in programming which meets the normal needs of everyday family life and which families have requested: day care and after-school care of children; a senior citizens' center; and programs for teen parents and parents of the disabled to come together for support and education. In these programs, staff understand culture and language and approach participants as co-residents rather than as clients, from an up-close stance, as equals. This is very much in the spirit of the social club. Moreover; Ibero preserves its identity as a social action voice for the community, in the political institution-building tradition of the social clubs.

Secondly, programs such as substance abuse treatment, domestic violence and sex abuse counseling bring an individual treatment conception of service to the CBO's, long the focus of psychotherapy in private practice and public agencies. These demand clinical expertise of staff which comes from outside the community, from training in universities. Staff at HUB noted their junior status as therapists without this kind of training, and their difficulty in attracting competent professionals due to lower pay ranges; while Ibero staff felt proud to be able to offer *both clinical and community expertise*, generally rare. Since Ibero therapists are in a setting which also has commitments to social action for the population in that community, they are constantly providing therapy according to their agency's mandates. This closes the gap between mainstream therapy and time honored traditions, and helps the therapy be shaped to fit the community, instead of trying to make residents fit the mainstream mold in agencies.

Third, *rapid and significant economic and social breakdown* in already overstressed communities indicates that more majority definitions of what constitutes "service" will be adopted. Counseling services are not generally requested by community residents, but are responses to needs assessed by funding sources and community leaders. When funds are less available from majority channels for primary prevention, community leaders in poor communities tend to go after that funding which *is* available. This has changed over the past twenty years, paralleling changes in society to more of a focus on tertiary prevention, or treatment after there has been significant breakdown. Vastly increased joblessness, homelessness, AIDS, asthma, tuberculosis, drugs and then crime in our poor communities in such a short time has meant that we have had to find ways to treat affected individuals, while offering normal family supports and while continuing to find ways to bring jobs and housing into our communities and keep drugs out through political action. While administrators and leaders in CBO's have allegiance to the latter, they have also been inundated in the past decade with an onslaught of symptomatology which will easily consume every bit of tertiary program funding available. The challenge is to accept and use funding from all of these available channels, but then use it in a way which, at the same time, will enhance social action and regular supportive programming. This is a tall order for administrators, but is missing in mainstream agencies, in addition to Spanish language fluency.

In Rochester, Ibero's primary focuses prior to United Way funding were of an advocacy nature: job training, advocacy for youth, and bilingual education. Subsequent preventive service programs, foster   care and adoption services, and professional counseling to families at risk seem not to have replaced the primary goals of economic development and advocacy, but to have enhanced them. In Wilmington's Latin American Community Center, provision of services under United Way was the initial focus and seems to have stayed the focus, when the organization has tried to meet concrete needs of faimilies in a wide geographical area beyond the local community. However, as ethnic group composition changes in the immediate neighborhood, residents seem to be putting pressure on LACC to provide a place with more of a community identity, perhaps expecting the CBO to function more like the Puerto Rican social club. In both Buffalo and Rochester, CBO's provide a central focus for the community, but not its "single" voice, as a web of effective organizations in the community and many grass-roots leaders constitute "the" voice. Neither Buffalo nor Rochester communities seem to want to pull the varied strands of leadership together into one conforming group, even though there maybe confusion and lack of clarity at times with diverse leadership. In Wilmington, though, when the "community" covers an extremely diverse and geographically spread- out area, local leadership expects LACC to be its one representative center.

In all three centers, the provision of bilingual bi-cultural preventive and counseling services to individuals and families are at the core of what defines CBO's. Ibero's service provision seems to target residents outside the walls of the agency, with staff going out to peoples' homes; while LACC offers "one-stop shopping" more inside the center itself. All CBO's are aiming to increase the clinical skills and salaries of bilingual bicultural staff who docounseling, and Ibero has clearly done quite a bit in this area. While LACC seems to be going in the direction of more direct service provision, HUB is going in the direction of programming which will bring families together in ways which will build community and ease personal problems simultaneously. Limited funding will make it difficult to both increase counseling skills and provide a wider range of political and economic supports to resident families.

Community Organization and Social Action

In more or less the same time period of the beginning of United Way funding of CBO's, civil rights and youth movements had a big influence on CBO's, too, in terms of their social action and advocacy functions.While LACC in Wilmington does not mention much of an advocacy function or locate its roots in those movements in the 1960s, it was established then, at a time when the needs of minority communities were being given much more attention than at any other time in recent history. In Buffalo, the Puerto Rican Chicano Committee(PRCC), one of the precursor organizations of HUB, was formed directly from the social action of Puerto Rican/Chicano university students, supported by BUILD, an organization designed to bring white, middle-class resources to minority-controlled community-building. Similarly, Saul Alinsky's organization FIGHT, assisted in the formation of Action for a Better Community (ABC) in Rochester, which, along with the youth movement and the Catholic Church, encouraged a base of well-organized leadership to promote needed changes there. When CBO's promote community-building around a common cause, such as bilingual education in Rochester, *one sees clearly the common bonds of staff and client, all residents in the same community and working toward the same goals.*

It seems, in all of these centers, that the organization will be more oriented toward social action/advocacy when its leaders are united with other community leaders. When they are opposed by the community's leaders (LACC) or there is fragmentation and competitiveness among community leadership, as has sometimes been the experience in Buffalo, the organization will have less political power. Since Puerto Rican culture has already been marginalized in the larger society, Puerto Rican CBO's attempting to increase the power of residents in their communities need to find ways to develop leadership which will help people pull together. A recent study of political development in the Puerto Rican community in Boston suggests that a key to developing this needed unity can be found in women's leadership styles (Hardy-Fanta 1993). Latina politics tend to work more from the bottom up, developing a broad base of involvement and sharing, contrasted with the male style of achieving individual stature and control. When male leadership is complemented by significant broad-based active political female leadership, as in Rochester, perhaps more unity is encouraged.

Buffalo and Rochester CBO's are closer to each other geographically and serve a more clearly Puerto Rican population with more similar migration histories than in the Wilmington CBO. The Puerto Rican population has tended to come to Buffalo and Rochester more directly from Puerto Rico, and has tried to promote the same sense of community felt on the island. Initial Hispanic migrants to Wilmington were also Puerto Rican, but came at a later time and indirectly, from New Jersey. They seem to have relied on the Pentecostal church and the minister who had led the move, for many, to

Wilmington; and then to have organized around common needs for services, rather than social and political organization *per se.* While all centers now target a population of about 16,000 people, those populations constitute more compact urban *barrios* ("neighborhoods") in Buffalo and Rochester. In Wilmington, this number is made up of many Hispanic ethnic groups in many different locations spanning three states, and with many degrees of urban to rural life.

At the time the author met with each of the groups in the preceding chapter, each CBO wias grappling with different kinds of internal and external struggles. In Wilmington, the stress was pretty straightforwardly stated to be a growing sense of alienation of the Puerto Rican community from the staff and programs at the center. Since we talked, though, the Latin American Community Center has hired a new, and very administratively experienced Puerto Rican director, Idalie M. Munoz, who has moved to Wilmington from New Jersey, and who is making direct efforts to heal old rifts. A new spirit is ernerging. In Buffalo, the initial settling-in process after the merger into Hispanics United of Buffalo has been accomplished, with regular programs in place. HUB has hired an Anglo director, Sheila Smith, with some initial negative reactions within the community, but with respect for her administrative skills and likely ability to pull programs together in a more cohesive way. In Rochester, the directorship of Julio Vasquez is stable, and much cohesiveness has been built. However, as Ibero and other Hispanic organizations and leaders have significantly increased the economic competitiveness of the community, those in the mainstream threatened by this power will try to unseat it, particularly as we face now a much smaller economic "pot" for all in our cities.

Participants in both Buffalo and Rochester talked about their histories in terms of names of specific leaders who they felt had done a lot for the community, rather than more generally in terms of the unfolding of events, as with the Wilmington participants. I was reminded of the way of understanding what happens in life, in Puerto Rican culture, according to "personalismo", the respect for individual persons. *History is not an abstraction or a progression of linear events, but a recording of relationships and an opportunity to give respect to those who have contributed to the community, It differs from Anglo reporting in which only a few very great leaders would be named, and the goal would be to keep the focus "objectively" on the linear progression of "true" events.*

In meeting with these groups, the author was struck with the sense of a personal relationship to history as Puerto Ricans in the U.S. since migration and before it. I was repeatedly reminded of community residents' need to be treated with respect, this meaning that staff would show affect and relatedness to them, rather than the more distant detachment which might mean respect in some other cultures. It occurred to me that, since CBO's are organized by their cultural connections to residents, readers should have at least a sketch of Puerto Rican history in order to understand the significance of the CBO.

Aspects of Puerto Rican History

It is common for Puerto Ricans to conceive of their immigration experience as an "air bridge", different from the experiences of immigrants fleeing from South and Central American despotic regimes, in which one never expects to return home (Inclan 1991). Puerto Ricans, as American citizens, have, since the Spanish-American War, belonged in this country, whether in Puerto Rico or on the mainland, *and* have always belonged uniquely in Puerto Rico different from other U.S. citizens, a uniqueness understood not only by realizing cultural/language differences, but by understanding the history of Puerto Rico. This history is consciously or unconsciously understood by the groups in the preceding chapter, and it serves as a basis for program planning and activities.

Spanish Colonization

Accounts from old Taino Indian records from the 16th century indicate that after Christopher Columbus claimed Puerto Rico for Spain in about 1532, Spaniards were welcomed until they hoarded gold and enslaved indigenous people. In about 1538, Taino people declared war on Spain. While Spain defeated the Tainos, new laws were passed by the Spanish Court in 1542 prohibiting Indian slavery and the *encomienda* (plantation) system(Barriero 1993).

Both Puerto Rico and Spanish America had been conquered by Spain during the 16th century, but they were not equally developed nor used for the same purposes. Puerto Rico, unlike Spanish South America, was primarily used as a military outpost until the end of the 18th century (Jimenez de Wagenheim 1993). Its size and strategic position in the West Indies made it possible for Spain to fortify it and use it to patrol the Caribbean and protect the colonies to the South. Spain did not then develop the island's economy or educate the population in preparation for commercial agriculture, as in other colonies. A Spanish agent visiting in

1765 reported only 44,883 persons on the island, of which 5,037 were African slaves; and people preferred to live far away from each other in the countryside, coming together only for church (*Ibid.*). This has meaning in terms of the survival of indigenous ways. The Taino Indian indigenous population, even while previously enslaved, could initially resist colonial diseases and abuses.

While other Spanish colonies had been clashing with various "reforms" introduced for two centuries, Puerto Rico was just beginning its colonization at the end of the 18th century, and collected in 1797 a mere 60,000 pesos in revenues, not enough to cover the costs of the colonial administration. In 1812 Alejandro Ramirez was appointed the island's first Intendant and, until 1836 he introduced many incentives to transform the rural economy from subsistance farming to commercial crops for export. Then, when South America was fighting Spain for its independence,the Crown showered Puerto Rico with favors, due to its strategic importance militarily. This launched a period of prosperity.

After the loss of Spanish Anerica in the 1830s, Puerto Rico reverted to a highly militarized colonial status, the economy stagnated, trade was in Spanish hands, and the bureaucracy of administration grew. These were harsh setbacks, after having had free trade with Spain, protected trade for exports of tobacco, rum, sugar, and molasses, and reduced tax on imports. Prices had increased and there was a growing demand for the island's coffee, met by increasing land cultivation, farming having been encouraged by the dispensing of free parcels of land. Then, with labor regulations imposed after 1848, free laboring classes were coerced to work for large farms or face punishment. With more land reserved for coffee production, less land produced food crops and the nutrition of the people suffered . Small farmers were indebted, and the island became dependent on overseas trade, importing more than it exported. A hurricane in 1867 intensified the economic stress, with many persons left homeless and destitute.

By 1865, 43% of the island's budget was spent on the military. Five militia units had been added in the 1860s after the restoration war in Santo Domingo and the abolitionist movement generated in Puerto Rico by the emancipation of slaves in the Carribbean and the United States. Moreover, in 1866 Spain had made Cuba and Puerto Rico responsible for paying the interest on her war debts from unsuccessful colonial wars, which the governor exstracted from the coffer as "contributions", leaving the coffer empty; and which were exacted by income tax, church tax, special project taxes, and state taxes on municipalities. In 1869, the population had doubled to 600,233, of which 96% were born in Puerto Rico, 2% were born in Spain, and the rest were foreign-born, with 5000 of these being slaves. Eighty-four percent of the population was illiterate, with citizen requests for more schools and better paid teachers having been ignored.

Such were the conditions setting the stage for *El Grito de Lares*, the revolt in the town of Lares in Northwest Puerto Rico. Ninety-three percent of the 551 suspects ultimately charged for inciting rebellion there were born in Puerto Rico, and 97% of these in Northwest Puerto Rico, disputing the claim made by Spain that they were ungrateful foreigners. Most of those arrested were propertyless agricultural workers, slightly more literate than the general population, and in their late 20s to early 30s. Leaders were Ramon Emeterio Betances, Segundo Ruiz Beluis, and Ana Maria Bracetti Cuevas, who, among other intellectuals, were exiled. Motives for rebellion were to see the island independent from colonial rule, and to protest unfair colonial practices and taxes. *El Grito de Lares* was a brief insurrection, with the 600 to 1000 participants easily put down by the Spanish militia, since the island had been used as a center for the military for all of the Carribbean (*Ibid.*).

Yet *El Grito de Lares* stands as a symbol of Puerto Rican identity. Forgetting its history, many have stereotyped Puerto Ricans as passive and easily accommodating to colonialism, without the insurrections occurring in other Latin Anerican countries. Many forget that Puerto Rico did not have an economy developed for colonial purposes until two hundred years after the colonization of the rest or Latin America. However, *El Grito de Lares* rerninds us that, once colonized, Puerto Ricans arose to protest its abuses, even though the land was not mountainous enough to hide guerrillas and it was impossible to approach the size of the Spanish militia and arms housed in Puerto Rico. The rebels did make an impact on Spain which, in 1869, extended some liberal reforms: Spanish citizenship; elections, and the right to organize into political parties; and the beginning of the abolition of slavery (*Ibid.*). Most importantly, *El Grito de Lares* marks the beginning of a liberation struggle toward a national Puerto Rican identity which continues in the United States.

In this chapter, the struggle for bilingual education has been important in both Buffalo and Rochester, and has seemingly been a major issue which has unified Ibero and the community. When we can understand the difficulty of maintaining Puerto Rican identity, we can understand better the importance of this issue; and the intensity of the conflict between Puerto Ricans and "newcomer" Mexican-Americans in Wilmington.

Colonization by the United States

The Monroe Doctrine of 1823 had established a unilateral principle that the Western hemisphere was not for European colonization; and the U.S. Secretary of State Richard Olney, in 1895, spelled out its implications: "The United States is practically sovereign upon this continent, and its fiat is law upon the subjects to which it confines its interposition"(Jacobs, Landau, and Pell 1971). In the 1890s the U.S. had established dominance or intervened militarily in Cuba, Santo Domingo, Haiti, and Puerto Rico. There was debate in Congress between imperialists who wanted to catch up and compete with Eurpoean colonization and those who wanted to avoid the expense of colonial administration. The depressed economy then seemed to demand expansion, but policy in Puerto Rico came up with a unique compromise for those congressmen wanting to control the expenses of administration attached to colonial expansion. Military governor George V. Davis published an explanation of U.S. policy in Puerto Rican newspapers: "...(to provide)the Territorial forrn (of government) heretofore applied in the Unites States to those portions of the national domain in a transition stage or one preparatory to full statehood and membership in the National Union" (*Ibid*.). But the Foraker Act of 1900, which formally set up the form of government under U S. rule, gave Puerto Rico less autonomy than under Spanish rule, and was unwilling to grant self-government to an "inferior" people. Government under the Foraker Act consisted of a governor and an executive council appointed by the president of the United States, who also appointed all of the justices of the island Supreme Court. The executive council functioned as the upper chamber of the lesislature; the lower chamber, the House of Delegates, consisted of thirty-five members elected by Puerto Ricans, but all legislation had to be passed by both houses and could be vetoed by the governor. Thus, no legislation not favored by the governor and other U.S.-appointed officials could pass(Clark 1975). This form of government was, in fact, unconstitutional in the U.S.

The Foraker Act set in place the essential framework for the U. S. connection: while the political framework might be enlarged in the direction of home rule in an attempt to remove the stigma of colonialism, the economic bond worked against any final severing of permanent political union with the metropolitan power. While Puerto Ricans were denied American citizenship, Puerto Rico was not considered a nation in international law. The Puerto Rican became a wo/man without a country, waiting to be deemed worthy of statehood and offered assumilation without incorporation (Carr 1984). Ironically,this harkened back to the American colonial experience in which settlers resisted rule by English governors, and recognized the tyranny involved. Whereas the Foraker Act was amended to offer Puerto Ricans citizenship n 1917, commonwealth status continues. Laissez-faire economics has meant the rapid growth of great absentee-owned sugar corporations, absorbing much land formerly belonging to individual growers. While this has encouraged investment by corporations, it has meant that Puerto Ricans have had to import most food staples previously grown there, paying higher prices due to import tariffs. Appointed officials have come from the mainland, not often even speaking Spanish. Historically, English was the imposed official language in the schools, even though students spoke only Spanish (Jacobs Landau, and Pell 1971).

In the Carribbean, Puerto Rico is often billed as a "showcase of democracy" avoiding the problems of its Third World neighbors because of U.S. protection and magnanimity. The standard formula for analyzing Latin American development, in general, is 1) to point out the problems of poverty, inequality, underdevelopment and injustice; 2) to contrast development in Latin America with the development of "healthy Western democracies"; 3) to identify the villains in Latin society and contrast them with the efficient heroes of the Western world; and 4) to proclaim the need to emulate Western elites or suffer the torments of Totalitarian Revolution (Petras 1970). Puerto Rican economic development shows the fallacies in this analysis. Its first stage of capital importation and export processing after the Second World War did not essume the development of local- or state-owned industries; but was based on attracting U.S. capital in export-oriented light manufacturing industries (the"macquiladora" .model, inducing economic dependence on the U. S.). Rapid agribusiness transformation displaced *campesinos* to New York City and other U.S. cities as cheap labor, and alleviated the island's high unemployment ¡Lopez 1995). While industry in Puerto Rico had provided a pool of cheap labor for the U.S., by the 1970's minimum-wage laws there and globalization, which opened up cheaper sources of labor in Asia and elsewhere eventuated in many of those industries relocating. In 1986 the employment rate in the U.S was 61%, while for Puerto Rico it was 35%, one of the lowest in the world (*Ibid.*) The encouragement of economic dependence on Europe and the United States by these powers is the definition of colonialism in Latin America, so that this kind of developnent in Puerto Rico is similar to other Latin American countries. However, the citizenship of Puerto Ricans adds a new twist. Since the 1960's the U.S. has essentially subsidized the failure of development strategy in Puerto Rico in the form of veteran's benefits, Medicare benefits, Social Security pensions, housing assistance, nutritional assistance, assistance to families in disaster areas, and others. The total of U.S. transfers n 1931 was $4.958 billion; the gross national product for the same year was $5.674 billion, a one-to-one ratio between production and subsidies. This lends credence to the unconfirmed notion that only ten percent of the population does not receive some sort of subsidy from the federal government (*Ibid.*).

Puerto Rico's commonwealth status, and its colonization and resultant poverty, have altogether changed the meaning and possibility of work there. The possibility of work propels many more Puerto Ricans to urban areas in the United States in the past decade, even when they have heard from relatives here that the likelihood of work is slim. In a society in which males have been respected as heads of the household who have the responsibility to provide for their families, this kind of "redefinition" of work has been totally disruptive to family life, with "government benefits" instead of salaries going straight to the women to maintain households. Youth turn to alcohol, drugs, and the protection of gangs when they no longer feel a strong male role model in the home. Men may understand that their disempowerment is systemic and political, but take out their anger on their women.

However, history also provides models of Puerto Rican leaders who have made significant attempts to change imperialist practices, such as Pedro Albizu Campos. He had begun a career in journalism in Puerto Rico after World War I exposing imperialist practices in the U S. He traveled throughout Latin America, wrote and spoke for popular audiences, and developed a following. After he gave a fiery speech in Puerto Rico espousing independence, nationalists assasinated the chief of the Insular Police, an American. A few weeks later, Albizu Carapos was arrested for sedition, even though in Puerto Rican law there was no such crime as sedition. His conviction led to an atmosphere of tension which exploded in The Palm Sunday Massacre in Ponce on March 21, 1937, in which the police fired into a Nationalist parade and indiscriminately killed all men, women, and children, and even other policemen in the line of fire.

In 1947, Albizu Campos was released from prison and returned to Puerto Rico where, again, he espoused the cause of independence. After several Nationalist Puerto Ricans fired shots in the U S. House of Representatives n 1954, Albizu Campos was sent back to prison for inciting revolt. He died in prison in 1965 (Jacobs, Landau, and Pell 1971).

Albizu Campos became a symbol for resistance. In 1959, Puerto Rican and Black college students at NewYork's City College burned down some buildings. This riot particularly shocked those who were not aware of any Puerto Rican resistance beyond the 1954 terrorist attack on the House of Representatives by a few individuals. However, 60, 000 Puerto Ricans had refused to register under the Selective Services Law during World War II; and 1300 nationalists were in prison in 1947 (*Ibid.*). Political parties in Puerto Rico are organized around the issue of independence. The Popular Democratic Party in Puerto Rico espouses statehood, the fulfilling of the original promises made at the time the U.S. acquired the island from the Spanish, to improve its poor economy. The Puerto Rican Independence Party counters with reminders of the disastrous effects of dependence on the U.S. not only economically, but culturally and politically. Elections maintain an impasse between the two positions, as both are right and independence is not likely to be economically feasible at this point in history, so that the choice is between commonwealth status and statehood.

Puerto Rican values respect the elders and remember their struggles to maintain awareness of Taino, African, and Spanish heritages. Even when real choices seem to be between commonwealth status and statehood, assimilation is not desirable, largely out of respect for those who have gone before. In the 1960s and 1970s when the Young Lords were continuing to resist policies of U.S. domination, much of the social action in the above CBO's resulted directly, at least in part, from college organizations similar to the Young Lords.

It is helpful for counselors to understand the larger political and economic context when working with youth, families, and symptomatic individuals. When this context is not known, therapists only see the obvious abusive and avoidant behaviors of symptomatic persons, and so may tend to offer solutions which only scapegoat the male even more. Counselors may take the aggressive seeking of entitlements by the Puerto Rican client to mean individual laziness or unwillingness to work, not understanding how work has been replaced on the island over the past two decades by government benefits. Child Protection staff may not understand how child neglect in a family may be a response to the loss of extended family caretakers during migration. Hispanic families need to be offered a protective holding environment in a setting which understands, and can also treat, the economic and social nature of their trauma. Such is the primary role of the community-based organization, with its secondary role being to educate mainstream agencies about the contexts in which community residents' problems have occurred.

Importance of Community-Based Organizations for All Communities

Ema Genijovitch, speaking as an immigrant and from her work with immigrant families in New York City, explains that therapists have often thought of helping these families to "adjust to the new culture", as if they must then leave behind the "old" ways and be helped to "take on the new". In this either-or kind of conceptualization, immigrants must choose one culture or the other, and are not, then, well-adjusted when they cling to the old culture. Genijovitch reframes this into a "both-and" way of thinking in which the immigrant needs to think of him/herself as having a leg in both the old and the new cultures, permanently in both places and never completely in one or the other. This not-belonging and dual-belonging carry with them many difficulties and identity struggles, the moreso the more different the two cultures are from one another(Genijovitch). While immigrants may not have the Puerto Rican "air bridge" in terms of U.S. citizenship/commonwealth status, they often do return to their countries of origin and/or keep the dream of returning "if politics or the economy improves". Some choose to come to this country much more than others, and this control or lack of it will affect their adaptation, as well as others' acceptance of them here.

Indeed, since the United States is a land of immigrants and frequent internal migration, rnost of us experience the stress of "relocation". In this post-industrial period, we are confronted with such rapid social and economic change that there seems to se a time warp between generations, and it is more difficult than ever before for youth to respect their parents and other adults in authority. With the rapid shift in the economy from an industrial to a service base, unemployment of large sectors of the population is likely to be a permanent condition, and we are confronted with "colonization" similar to the experience of Puerto Rico and other Third World countries. Since community-based organizations have emerged from an identification with these struggles, they show us ways to build services when the primary need is to preserve community. They are living laboratories of community-designed therapy, meshing the individual counseling needs of individuals with the social action and advocacy needs of the community. Therapy done in the context of the community-based organization has the potential to correct many of the abuses of mainstream therapy which split into separate categories individual, group, and community work; and then give more status to work with individuals, ignoring the importance of community and economic development in the lives of poor people of color. When therapy occurs in a context which normalizes the difficulties of immigration, such as community-based organizations, it stands a better chance of helping families move past a stuck place in the transition. Mainstream agencies often unwittingly design services geared to helping clients assimilate or become more like the "dominant" culture, forgetting the culture of origin. This sets a bias toward conformity instead of diversity, and encourages the labelling of personal difficulties in this process as "resistance" or "regression", rather than normal responses to biculturality when old and new cultures are very different from each other. The pressure to choose one important tradition forming one's identity *over* another equally important tradition usually exacerbates symptoms and further complicates the life-long transitional process.

Many therapists, especially family systems therapists, base interventions on their knowledge of the immigration process, beyond only the more static and abstract knowledge of cultural profiles or content (e.g., Hernandez 1996). While immigration is never, of course, the single determining factor in the problem presented, it, like poverty, is a powerful contextual variable shaping identity and the supports available to help individuals with further change and loss. In the context of the community, however, the immigration process is interpreted in the light of current social contradictions. One client who addresses personal contradictions in therapy in a setting which is community-based is automatically, at some level, putting those personal issues in the context of larger social contradictions (i.e., historical issues of identification among Puerto Rican people). When Hernandez wonders why he does not grasp the cultural issues involved in a client's dilemma sooner, he remarks in passing that he might have been prompted to reflect sooner if he had wondered why the client was coming to his setting which was strongly identified with culture. All settings are strongly identified with culture, and community-based organizations speak to the need to have one's specific culture reflected and serving as a basis for action.

Eliana Korin writes about her work with Puerto Rican women in the Bronx, using Paolo Freire's problem-posing method (Freire, 1973 and 1990). According to Brazilian educator Freire, there is no merit to personal change when it is divorced from change at the social level; and there is no legitimacy to social action without a corresponding concern with personal issues. The personal anh the social are inextricably linked. Therefore, therapy is not a useful process when it splits the two and focuses only on the personal aspect, coming out of European traditions which split the two. Korin uses a particular circular questioning adaptation of Freire's problem-solving process to achieve greater social and political awareness in both therapist and client as they examine the client's concerns; and she points out that Freire's method has not been as successful with clients who lack a sense of community; perhaps, critical consciousness is difficult to promote without a basic sense of connection among people (Korin 1994). The more one's agency, then, promotes community connections for its residents, the more the therapy in such a setting can bring together personal and social awareness which will eventuate in action meaningful to the client, the therapist, and the community. Such is the potential of therapy which happens in the community-based organization, in which general concerns of residents from a particular culture and community are the main focus, and therapy is a small part.

Many times professionals in mainstream organizations do not know how to recruit bilingual, bicultural qualified staff for positions,and are sincerely perplexed when told that their programs do not reflect community needs. Community-based organizations can also serve the functions of training and linkage for mainstream organizations, when mainstream agency administrators seek out the CBO's in their areas for help in recruitment and in understanding more clearly how to design therapy to meet the needs of the community. The community-based organizations discussed in the preceding chapter probably are fairly representative of the goals and operation of hundreds more such organizations in various locations around the country.

CHAPTER FIVE:
TREATING ADDICTION AND BUILDING
COMMUNITY AT THE SAME TIME
Cumberland Diagnostic and Treatment Center, Brooklyn

"Alcoholism; drug addiction, and nihilism are diseases of the soul. To turn soul
around, you need folks joining at the local level, together, to strengthen those
institutions still vital enough to promote self-affirmation."
                                                    --Cornel West (1991)

                              ******

With Barbara Carr-Eubanks, Teresa Grant, and Ann Solomon

We are part of the Health and Hospital Corporation in New York City,
a small chemical dependency treatment clinic serving addicted persons in
the Ft. Greene, Bedford-Stuyvesant,and Red Hook sections of Brooklyn, and
nearby neighborhoods, pretty much by catchment area. We follow the basic
format for all chemical dependency and alcoholism programs which are
state-funded, so that we work in interdisciplinary teams and review cases
every threemonths. Programs can be short- or long-term, and Cumberland
tends to be on the longer side, with most clients enrolled in the program for
well over a year. We are located in a section of a closed hospital, and, in the
larger facility here, our clients receive complete medical care and vocational
education. There is also a shelter in another wing of the facility, occupying
eight floors. People tend to think of our clients as the most difficult to work
with, not only because of their multiple addictions, but because of their lack
of resources, being poor and minority in communities in which drugs and
crime are everywhere and there is little financial security .

Our Clients, Our Selves

We, of course, recognize the difficulties of living in this neighborhood. Most of the staff is also from the area, and some of us have lived here between 25 and 40 years. We have seen the neighborhood change, and a lot of the old informal supports disappear, so that other people on the block no longer look out for your kids when you have to be somewhere, and don't feel free to chastise them and help you keep them in line. It used to be that children had to account to the whole block for their behavior, and parents had some help. Now you never know exactly who your neighbor is, and you are afraid he might get an attitude if you chastise his child. So people stay more to themselves. However, there are still a lot of good resources here, organizations and churches who will help out. If you are from the area, you know these resources and the people involved in them, and we encourage our clients to develop communication with them and help out.

Our clients tend to know us from seeing us on the streets and at AA meetings. There is no "them" vs. "us" here, as in so many social agencies where the client gets treated rudely, from a distance, like one more number having Blue Cross insurance. While we do keep appropriate professional boundaries, we operate with our clients as peers from the same community. We are not afraid of them. We speak the same language. We are not put off by a man with gold teeth and his hat on backwards. Many of our staff know from personal experience the difficulty of kicking an addiction, and have been clients themselves. Clients are involved in the running of this place, providing clerical help for us and staffing our canteen. There is a mutuality here, a cooperation between staff and clients to keep things running. As you can see, there is a lot of warmth, emotion, and conversation going on in the hallways; it's not possible for an outside observer to really tell who is staff and who is patient.

Just as clients are actively involved in program with us, so too are we all involved in the community together, familiarizing ourselves with procedures in the borough and in the city by which we can access power and resources. In a large city, you have to know how to get things done, who to connect with. Addicted persons have lost touch with this whole world, but yet many of them know channels we don't know about. We put our heads together in a lot of groups, to figure out how to get what we need to stay straight and stay together with our families, if possible--e.g., education, job training, jobs, shelter, food, clothing, day care. Let us give you some examples as to how clients actively advocate for themselves in the community.

Advocating for Ourselves, Building Community

When you have few resources, you cannot isolate yourself from others. You need connections. Our clients just do not realize how isolated they have become while doing drugs. It is shocking to them to begin to wake up and see how the world has changed and left them behind. A therapy which does not help them rebuild relationships and skills to reconnect just is not an effective addiction therapy. Many therapists pay attention to relationship skills with husbands, wives, parents, and loved ones. But therapists treating poor people and people of color need to realize also what a broader informal and formal system of connections is necessary in order to help that client survive. Otherwise, it is just not possible for the person to make it politically and economically--and so relapse to drugs is a simpler, if pseudo, way to survive--or, rather, to take control of at least killing yourself. Therapists who are outside the client's community just do not know the web of informal helping connections there which must be established. But let's get back to the examples of our clients getting active in the community.

When the Auburn shelter was turned into an assessment center, plans were being made by the city HRA to send residents to Queens, near JFK Airport where residents couldn't receive treatment any longer at Cumberland, and would have been cut off from their social networks. The residents protested. They went to the Brooklyn Committee on Alcoholism, which has information from state and local agencies regarding resources available for addicts locally. They sought information about affordable housing in the community and how to get it. Residents were advocating for themselves as consumers, becoming politically active, exercising their power as participants in society again who didn't only have to settle for shelters. Residents wrote letters to politicians, with some help from staff; but many of them already knew where to write and educated staff. It was a mutual process between staff and clients. Patients took over all planning, disseminating information, faxing, and so forth.

Each catchment area in the city has a community planning board, like an elected block association, which can initiate program planning which residents want or stop plans we don't like. Our Community Planning Board is used by residents in the community a lot, and by politicians, congressmen, police, and fire departments; so that people can come together and get action, for example, regarding drugs and crime in the community. Initially, the community planning board resisted the Auburn shelter in this community, but once they saw reduced drug activity in the community as a result of the drug-free floor, they listened to the residents. Residents were able to block the move to Queens, and recently moved to a wing of a new facility in Bushwick which has really beautiful apartments for families and a community room for AA meetings. Residents also petitioned for transportation from Bushwick to Cumberland for their treatment in the program, and for transportation of children to day care. There is now van transportation for these purposes.

Then the Child Welfare Administration (CWA) responded to this active advocacy by developing certificate programs in private agencies, to train local mothers in good babysitting practices and to monitor adequate space and safety in their homes. CWA could see that our clients were serious and competent, which meant that they could also imagine local mothers, some of them ex-addicts, as competent to be certified to provide day care. This addressed the problem of women hospitalized for detox with no place for their children to go by keeping families together in the community and giving employment to local mothers who could babysit.

These positive results might seem fairy-tale. On the contrary, the real getting things done was very hard and conflictual. It took a long time and there were many set-backs. We often did not know what to do next, but we bolstered each other up to keep trying. The process of working on issues together for the benefit of all of us in the community cut down on some of the stigma in the neighborhood associated with addictions and with chemical dependency treatment. Those who had never had a drug problem could see that those who had were working *competently* with them. They could see that the drug-free floor we established in the shelter here reduced levels of crime and made the environment better. We were allies.

But, most importantly, involvement in the process of getting things done again in the community taught addicts survival skills which they could never learn in a class, segregated off with only other addicts. It skipped right by their tendency to be passive and got them involved before they much had a chance to think about it. Years of individual therapy can't do this, and we think that this change in the client's responses and activity is the single most important predictor to his or her ability to stay straight and make a new life. AA is very important. We have AA and A1 Anon meetings here, and we encourage clients to attend all the meetings they can at various locations. Note that AA works on the community concept: building new systems of support and challenging the myth that you can just recover all by yourself and "pull yourself up by your bootstraps", like many think in this society. However, our treatment program attends to a gap between therapy and AA, which neither of them attends to. This is the client's natural neighborhood and community, not only the community of recovering people, but the real world system of supports which must be developed. It is rare that AA or therapy has connections to this world of the client well enough to be able to help the client re-connect. But we think it is crucial.

Bringing Resources to Clients

Our focus on active participation helps clients to move from reacting to a crisis in their lives to being knowledgeable about resources so that they can prevent crises. In order that they become knowledgeable about resources, we bring in the Board of Education to give daily classes in reading, Spanish/ English, and courses required for the GED. We also have an after-school adolescent program to help children with homework; and, for kids of 9+ years who have dropped out of school, we provide all-day activities. We have parenting skills classes for teen mothers who have gone into parenthood unprepared and for parents who have had their children removed by the Bureau of Child Welfare(BCW). We work with monitors from BCW and their clients here, and BCW provides 16-hour courses off-site on parenting. Just as we serve as facilitators for BCW monitors, we also follow up parole mandates with clients and invite parole officers to attend our interdisciplinary meetings every three months, and to attend our Achievement Day. We have a full complement of dental, eye, gynecological, and other medical services available in the medical section of Cumberland here for our patients, and we use food pantries and meals provided by local churches. We use our sister hospital, Woodhull, for detox, and also use Brooklyn Hospital, which is nearby. Involving local and larger city services and institutions in our actual work here on the premises serves to provide a bridge for the addict who needs more support than referrals out to various parts of the city.

What does "community" mean to us? It means functioning and being able to live and have access to needed and desired facilities and socialization so that you don't have to feel isolated. It means identifying with this community, taking a personal pride in watching the program grow and develop services for the community in response to felt needs--for example, AIDS testing, a portable hospital van. It means really helping people, which is very rewarding personally. This is different from the distant perspective taken with clients in agencies in the community in which staff come in from outside to work rather than being community-level people. Here, I already know my clients. I don't have to adjust to know them. There is none of that professional edge where we don't know each other and stay our distance. A lot of staff has been in recovery, and so share the personal pain of their clients. The language is the same between staff and clients.   My two-year-old grandchild says "What's happening, man?' I can walk into a room of clients and get respect for who I am as an older woman in the community who knows them. Respect is automatic and connected to traditional values and morals we were all taught. We are accustomed to certain behaviors and things here, so when we go out from the community we have to readjust ourselves. Many professionals out there act like you're a name on a paper but not a person who bleeds, sneezes, coughs and has feelings. Our staff show feelings to clients, show who they are as people, make the human connection. Here we establish trust which does not easily happen outside the community where you are not sure how people will treat you. Our staff is very good at this and sometimes argues wlth medical staff who don't do this as easily.   We are role models to our clients and professional friends.

Drugs have become a substitute for family and community so we have to rebuild family and community if we want to change drug habits.This is the crucial difference in healing and recovery. Our clients have no idea that they have isolated themselves as much as they have on drugs and that they have lost touch with their families due to the disease. Treatment here begins the family connections again if possible. Sometimes it is not possible. But we work to make clients aware of where they came from and what happened in the famlly to get them to this point. We do not define "family" in the sense of white nuclear family but in the sense of peers and street connections as well. We help clients to begin relationships again making connections between themselves and one or two others to start peers in the recovering community. We put them in touch with things they needed in childhood which they still need. They made the mistake of thinking that drugs and alcohol could be a substitute for all those needs and connections, denying their humanity the way this society often teaches us to, substituting quick fixes and technology for spiritual connectedness to your past in preparation for your future.

****

Expanding on the Themes in This Work

In the work done with alcohol and drug addicted clients at the Cumberland Diagnostic and Tr:eatment Center in the Ft. Greene community in Brooklyn, staff seems to work consistently on *lowering barriers and reducing distances,* i.e, reducing the social distance between themselves and their clients, reducing the distance between addicts and their families and community, lowering barriers between addicts and non-addicts in the community, and between clients and large bureaucracies such as parole and the Bureau of Child Welfare in New York. In work with populations who have been communicating primarily with the substances to which they have been addicted, it is formidable for clients to get in touch with the barriers and the distances between themselves and others when they stop the substance abuse. They need to trust others to help them traverse the distances and Cumberland therapists do this up-close, as "professional friends" from the same community.

Perhaps, *when the contexts in which we work and live are distant from those of our clients we need to respect that distance and its limitations. But when the contexts in which we work and live are close to those of our clients (community-based), our interventions will be developed out of that close relationship.* Structural and ecological models of family therapy (e.g., Aponte 1981) treat symptoms such as drug addiction as reflections of the under-organization of the family and its immediate community supports, but do not also address the patterns in the larger society which maintain the family's under-organization. Addiction also lessens a person's motivation to change an oppressive political environment (described by Halleck 1971); and solutions powerful enough to curb addiction would then have to address the political and economic patterns maintaining the addiction in the larger society, as well as in the client and his/her family. Such is the incredible power of addiction, and the difficulty of treating it. Cumberland staff, by virtue of their community membership, provide an example of both micro- and macro- systemic interventions, working with clients as peers to develop hard-to-find resources (i.e., social action).

In this way,they also discourage an over-dependence on therapy, the goal of the transitional therapy model of J. Landau-Stanton (1986), which is based on the belief in the system's inherent competence, and teaches brief interventions with large family systems which help them to move past unresolved losses and cut-offs. This model often works well with extreme symptoms such as addiction, when clinicians need encouragement that they need not "replace defective" families or "babysit" those with serious symptoms from cradle to grave. However, it seems to presuppose adequate resources from the larger society or not to address that issue. In the author's work in mainstream agencies removed from the communities of poor and minority families seeking treatment for very difficult problems such as addictions, she has used models similar to that of Landau-Stanton, *in conjunction with* connections to community-based therapists and leaders, who could inform about practical political and economic channels available in the community for clients which the author did not know about . Of course, there is no easy solution to tough problems, and no model of therapy can ever be complete. The author has found the above structural, ecosystemic, and transitional models to be of tremendous help in maximizing family resources to deal with serious symptoms such as addiction, which seriously threaten not only the individual addict, but the family's ability to support the addict to live without the addiction. While the family may protest the addiction, it has served to organize their relationships in ways which prevent them from having to deal with other toxic issues which sobriety threatens to bring to the surface. Structural, ecosystemic, and transitional family therapy approaches are important in the treatment of addiction because they help us to interrupt the family's patterns which have been organized around drugs; and they help families to deal with toxic issues in new ways, so that they do not have to unwittingly undermine the addict's individual drug treatment. *When such treatment happens in community-based settings such as Cumberland, it becomes much more powerful and able to address, with addicts, through social action, the larger societal imbalances which maintain the family's organization around addiction.* Community resources enhance the power ofthe therapy, and help it to more adequately tackle those problems in families which are maintained by power imbalances in the larger society.

Indeed, Alcoholics Anonymous (A.A.) and Narcotics Anonymous (N.A.) are community-like movements. A.A. declares three legacies (Alcoholics Anonymous World Services, Inc. 1957): recovery from alcoholism; alcoholics staying together in unity; and actively carrying messages about the organization to those who need it. The goal is to foster individual change by developing a community-like context for the individual. It is not a question of whether to treat the individual or the group, community, or society. *One must do all of the above, in order to effect change in an individual's addiction.* Its leaders preach out of their own experiences in a spiritual quest which is shared by the congregation. People come together to heal each other and to receive the wisdom of "Shaman-like healers, like shamans because *the essence of what makes them healers is their membership with the "masses",* understanding their illness from experience. As reflected in the influence of Carl Jung on the founders, personal experience is collective experience. The absence of separation between "them" and "us" makes the A.A. experience different from therapy.

For staff at Cumberland, community identification and participation come from traditional African-American values and from a history of difficult survival in the midst of oppression. David Berenson, a family therapist recognized for his work in the treatment of addictions, notes what he calls the numerous "paradoxes" built into the A.A. program: putting sobriety ahead of all else, yet caring for others; ending dependence on the bottle or others, yet accepting the power of the group and a Higher Power; and accepting alcoholism as a disease beyond one's control, while participating in treatment which makes amends for the damage one's behavior has caused (Berenson 1990). It seems to us that, in large part, these "paradoxes" rest on Western assumptions of the dichotomy between individual and collective realms of experience, and that application of non-Western scholarship to alcoholism treatment, such as that done by the staff at Cumberland, makes both-and acceptance of such paradox commonplace.

Cultural Traditions as the Basis for Drug Treatment

Therapists at Cumberland were all at different educational levels, and with lower educational levels and much lower salaries than therapists in private practice and many public sector settings. Clinical skills were filtered through their experience in a fairly cohesive African-American community with its own history, and an understanding of that history in terms of longer cultural traditions.It seems to me that it is *when cultural traditions take shape in regular community relationships and rituals, individual lives have meaning; and when therapy participates in the community it has relevance and power.* Cultural traditions cannot maintain themselves in the abstract, in a vacuum, any more than individuals can. Drug and alcohol addiction eat away at these connections, and so are quite powerful and frightening for the future of our society, and especially for the future of minority communities, when individuals have less access to mainstream resources and constant access to drugs.

Nathan and Julia Hare note that the oppressed often feel too weak to fight their oppression; and so turn away from social combat to patch up their battered selves in therapy, a diversion to the personal which often serves the same function as addiction. They note that the black child is five times as likely as the white child to be counseled, and psychological, chemical interventions are promoted by the mental health establishment as a way to deal with oppression, at younger and younger ages (Hare and Hare 1984).This kind of linkage with the white mental health establishment can never satisfy the need for social relatedness which has healed in

African-American families and communities (see also Thomas, Milburn,Brown, and Gary's study of depression in black clients 1988).

The intense healing power of social relatedness, while dimly appreciated by all of us in this alienated society, is hard for those of us who work in majority institutions not strongly identified with a particular community to appreciate. But African-American traditions have been available to inform clinical work such as that in the Ft. Greene example above. Kwame Nkrumah explained that European colonists had presented African history as an extension of the European, as if "primitive" cultures were propelled into history by European contact. Such presentations of the collapse of traditional societies justified the practice of slavery (Nkrumah 1964).

However, African societies can be understood to have three broad features: the traditional way of life; the presence of Islamic tradition in Africa; and the infiltration of the Christian tradition and culture of Western Europe into Africa, using colonialism and neo-colonialism as primary vehicles. The traditional face of Africa regarded man as primarily spiritual, endowed with integrity, dignity, and value, as opposed to the Christian idea of original sin and the degradation of man. Clan structures underlined the equality of all and the responsibility of many for one. No sectional interest could be regarded as supreme, until colonialism introduced new sources of power through individual education, status, and wealth. Christianity reinforced Western capitalism, while Islam offered a deconstructive function, a system of morality eradicating personal behaviors and social barriers to *communal* fulfillment (*Ibid.*). Notable black leaders have reinforced the need to preserve traditions destroyed by colonial practices. Malcolm X recognized the value of Islam in this process (Haley and Malcolm X 1964). Marcus Garvey understood that the affirmation of the African cultural heritage was necessary for the liberation of Diasporan Africans; and saw the relationship of continental and Diasporan Africans as variations of one people. He outlined a cultural project to unite all Africans (Asante 1988). W.E.B. DuBois, having had early life experience in new England town meetings, saw their similarity with African traditions:

> The meaning of America is the possibilities of the common man. It is the refutation of that wisespread assumption that the real makers of the world must always be a small group of exceptional men, while most men are incapable od assisting civilization or achieving culture. The United States proves, if it proves anything, that the number of men who may be educated and my achieve is much larger than the world has hitherto assumed (Franklin 1990, 69-70).

African -Americans have created a kind of Christian church here which models the African community, and organizes for the economic and political concerns of the body as well as the soul. While James Baldwin and many others have criticized the church for a conservative tendency to focus on rewards in the next life instead of fighting racism in this one, their criticisms are those of loving insiders; the Civil Rights movement was church led and financed, with leaders such as Martin Luther King, who were ministers.There are over 75,000 black churches in this nation, and every black neighborhood has at least one church as a major institutional presence, providing for the concrete needs of the community: housing for senior citizens, small business and home loans, day care, block club organizations, and gospel music which has preserved traditions (Billingsley 1992). The black church is powerful, able to organize thousands quickly around a cause or a vote. It is an example of religion which does not separate physical from spiritual realities, nor individual deliverance from communal and political participation.

Dorothy Haight explains that self-help has been necessary in black communities for survival. Black entrepreneurs built up businesses to serve black needs. The community nurtured children and fed them on next to nothing, valuing the experiences of older people in the process, and respecting many kinds of family composition beyond the nuclear family. The National Association for the Advancement of Colored People(NAACP) was founded in 1909 for blacks to protect themselves from lynching. In the 1930's and the 1940's, black women's clubs offered services which traditional agencies didn't have enough of, networks of assistance which could take in young mothers. The National Council of Negro Women has sponsored the first Black Family Reunion Celebration in 1986 in Washington with 200, 000 attending (Haight 1989).

Jomo Kenyatta stated: "children learn this habit of communal work like others, not by verbal exhortations so much as by joining with older people in such services....the whole thing rests on the principle of reciprocal obligations"(Kenyatta 1965: 109). Joanne Martin and Elmer P. Martin feel that this black helping tradition, with its elements of mutual aid and class cooperation is plagued by a cool street ideology which rebels against helping, protest, and religious traditions. Ahistorical street perspectives portray conning as the norm of black life in this country, a street ideology compatible with the detachment which accompanies addiction (Martin and Martin 1985). As economic resources in a community get thinner and thinner, the likelihood seems to increase that the aid you extend to your brother may not be mutual, and that you had better look for other ways to sustain yourself than to look for mythical jobs or depend on mythical mutual aid. This is similar to the reminder of Lindblad-Goldberg and Dukes, after their research of the support networks of poor urban black single-parent families, that the traditions of social support in the black community do not necessarily play out in individual families. Networks can consist of many persons who are overwhelmed and without sufficient resources, not able to relieve each others' stress well (Lindblad-Goldberg and Dukes 1985).

For these reasons social action approaches which strengthen community support networks at the same time that they are engaging high risk populations and increasing individual competence have been found to be extremely effective in the rehabilitation of vulnerable persons . Vera Paster gives a rationale and model for a social action approach with high-risk youth and adults (Paster 1986) . A study of leadership patterns in ten buildings in a housing project in Harlem which had transferred management and ownership to tenants via the Tenant Interim Lease Program in New York City, was a surprise to the psychologists who interviewed thirty-seven acknowledged leaders. They found the leaders to all be women, and to be so not necessarily because of their personality characteristics, but because of their membership in longstanding social networks in the community, and their reli ance on these networks for survival. The social glue of *kinship* in the projects predicted to the success of the projects, with successful buildings being the ones in which tenants took action on repairs, senior citizen tax abatement, and Section 8 rent subsidies. Those in which the project failed were those in which tenants depended on outside advice and help and did not see themselves as powerful (Saegert 1989) .

Nancy Boyd-Franklin is an African-American family therapist who sees the need to bring together groups of black women in her practice, noting that, whatever the class a black woman belongs to, she generally suffers from significant stress and isolation from others who can understand her stress in a supportive way (Franklin 1987). These groups provide an experience of sisterhood which has been lacking, and which can encourage individual change in ways the family system cannot do.

Often in treatment, or in self-help groups, when the focus has been on helping individuals to mature in ways different from those previously learned in their families, this has meant labelling the family "dysfunctional" and placing the client in the uncomfortable position of seeming to replace a "faulty" family with a "better" treatment system. Unfortunate results from this have often been feelings of disloyalty on the part of the client, an increase of his/her anger to justify the disloyalty, and the discovery that the treatment system is unable to deliver in the way it seemed to promise, as replacement for family. When the therapist and client are grounded in a community which has flexible family roles and extended family traditions, as in the Ft. Greene example, many related or unrelated "family" can help out without there needing to be such loyalty conflicts . Clinicians and clients are encouraged to join together to look more closely. also, at the effects of oppression and hierarchies of power in our society based on race, class, and gender, beyond just their immediate families. This sets the stage for social action, instead of putting us in the uncomfortable position, as therapists, of defining symptoms only at the individual level. Marianne Walters, in an article in *The Family Therapy Networker,* reminds us that the addict's immature and manipulative anger, having been co-produced and reinforced in a certain context; must be resolved in that context (Walters 1990) .

"Power" and "Addiction"

Family therapy literature addresses the integral role of power imbalances in society in maintaining symptoms, particularly addiction. MacKinnon and Miller (1987) remind us that therapy can inhibit social change by its focus away from the political struggle necessary for a healthier world (MacKinnon and Miller 1987;see Ritterman 1987, and see Miller 1983 for similar positions). The work here in Ft. Greene is an example of how therapy encourages social action, while therapists keep clear goals for change in the addiction of individual clients.

But addiction literature also focuses our attention on the more generic role of power in addictions. Systems therapist Thomas Todd reminds us of Bateson's paradox: in a society in which persons are to analyze situations and control themselves rationally (the "dry" alcohol state), relief from this extreme comes in the letting go of control (the "wet" drinking state); and the addicted person oscillates between these two poles to get a balance necessary in his/her life which s/he is not getting normally (Todd 1991). Elkin and others have noted that people get drunk in order to be more powerful in their interpersonal contexts (Elkin 1984). Bepko and Crestan explain that alcohol either permits the expression of or allows the suppression of impulses, feelings, and behaviors which violate traditional sex role norms, so that norm violations need never be directly acknowledged and people can stay together easier,with all the attention going to the alcoholism. Bepko and Crestan are concerned with sex role norms, in a society in which it is difficult to deal with the imbalance of power allocated to men and women (Bepko and Crestan 1985). It seems that the same construct can be applied to race and class imbalances in terms of aggressive and self-destructive behaviors of addicted poor people and people of color.

It has long been recognized that residential treatment for substance abuse needed to be organized with attention to the reduction of hierarchy and power imbalances. The Northfield Experiment in 1946 tried to decrease the hierarchy and power of doctors in a community "milieu" where patients were active participants in the treatment of other patients. Synanon was based on individual choice and responsibility to the community, not diagnosing the patient mentally ill but believing he/she had choices and would change in response to confrontation and teaching by others of that which had not been taught in the patient's family (Bratter, Collabolletta, Fossbender, Pennacchia, and Rubel 1985).

Self-help literature often portrays Americans as generalized addicts, addicted to eating, work, TV, and other habits. While this tends to pathologize us as victims or potential clients (Kaminer 1992), it also points the way to an understanding of the control issues involved in addictions of all sorts, and of the *normal societal* contexts which encourage addictive patterns in Americans.

Josephine Martin, in commenting on the mental health profession and social action, notes that we attempt in the work of therapy the amelioration of illnesses but do not well address *prevention* of these illnesses in our present cultural and political climate (Martin 1991). Since non-Western cultures do not separate as much the individual and social levels of experience, and de-emphasize individual control over self and environment, examples of non-Western approaches to addiction should be helpful in informing our treatment of addictions. Van der Velden, Ruhf, and Kaminsky (1985) have written about the use of *network therapy* wiith substance abuse. In this process, therapists convene about 25 people, including immediate family and more distant family and friends to help the addicted person with some current crisis in his/her life other than the addiction. They are assembled to support the immediate family, to offer different opinions from those who have been so close and involved in the relational "rut", and to participate in a powerful healing ritual. The idea of convening community to help with emotional problems and participate in ritual has come to us particularly through Native American tribal traditions However, such tribal healing is also a part of the African Yoruba religion and, undoubtedly, has contributed indirectly to the strong belief in the healing power of community connections in addiction treatment in the Ft. Greene African-American community.

Avoiding Polarities in Treatment

M. Duncan Stanton and other family therapists have reminded us of the need to understand family patterns (seeming to refer to "nuclear" family) and cycles in the family which maintain the addiction of a family member. However, rather than to focus on these patterns as dysfunctional in the system he urges us to look at the function the addiction serves, typically distracting from other family tensions or serving to keep the addict from growing up and moving on, away from *vulnerable parents with unresolved losses* (Stanton 1985). With this understanding of substance abuse, it is clear to see how networking or community-based approaches, which bring support from "outside" to the immediate family; can be quite useful in helping the addict to focus more independently on his/her own issues *and* put back into the community as a productive citizen, without depriving his/her family of needed support. This avoids the either-or thinking often involved in substance abuse treatment, which advises recovering addicts to separate and focus on themselves *first* and *then* on family later when stronger. We think that conceptualizing "family" as "community" provides a context for *both* distance and closeness; and provides a way to approach the patterns and cycles maintaining substance abuse outside the family without avoiding individual issues.

The treatment of substance abuse particularly tests our ability to expand our thinking and come up with *"both* this *and* that" solutions, rather than those which limit us to "either this or that" (see Sawatzky and Lawrence's discussion of dualisms inherent in substance abuse treatment, 1989). For example, there are excellent reasons for lengthy treatment of substance abuse, when we consider the grievous stripping away of self-esteem and relatedness to the world which happens in addictions; complicated even more by the need to work through the family's reactions to the addict's recovery; and by the poverty and lack of political power which many convince themselves they have "escaped from" while addicted. However, brief interventions (e.g Fisch 1986) can be especially helpful in combatting the stereotypical thinking which classifies recovering addicts as dependent and disabled. In stages of recovery from addiction, it is helpful to think of the huge task in terms of manageability from the self outward, so that one does not introduce family work until later on in the recovery process. It is also helpful to think of recovery as an immense task without natural supports, so that it is good to bring as much support to bear on the recovery process as soon as possible.

We think that substance abuse treatment *within the community context,* as in the Cumberland example, helps us to manage what appear to be irreconcilable differences in these approaches to treatment . When supports come from staff who are members of the same community as the client and who can then carry with them familiar ways to nurture and to connect to others, the recovering client can get quick support from both staff and community without having to assert her/himself before s/he is ready to actively seek supports; and can feel the familiarity of family before having to actually deal with the complex family issues which may have helped to maintain the addiction. *Conceptualizing "family" as "community"provides a context for both distance and closeness. It also provides a way to address those patterns which maintain substance abuse outside the family, in the race and class oppression in minority communities, without scapegoating the family for these abuses, and without treating the recovering person as a passive victim of larger abuses. The recovering person can be immediately active in social action, while not without substantial support.*

CHAPTER SIX:
TAKING THE "COMMUNITY" OUT OF COMMUNITY MENTAL HEALTH
Morrisania Mental Health Center, The Bronx

"In this poor community, if you took care of peoples bread and butter issues in treatment, a lot of the craziness disappeared and people went home fine. When we had people from the community on staff, they knew the clients and could normalize and make them feel at ease. But, as time went on, new staff became more analytic and lost that feeling. They wanted to focus only on emotional issues, without the bread and butter."

-- Velma Thomas

******

With   Martha Becker, Donald Brown, Hector Coll-Ruiz, Lawrence Dyche, Luis Garcia, Steven Goldstein, Michael Jones, Elsie Maldonado, Raphael Pagan, Myrtle Parnell, Velma Thomas, Jo Vanderkloot, and Winifred Wells

Staff reflect on the early days

Beginnings

The magic about Morrisania then was the people. The use of family systems frameworks, which so closely paralleled the family values of the cultures here, and the emphasis on training everyone on staff in these frameworks, was very important to our functioning. But we had an unusual mix of people and the people made the place.

Residents of this community were responsible, in large part, for the creation of Morrisania Neighborhood Family Care Center(NFCC). There was a gap in mental health services here. If you were discharged from in-patient treatment at Bronx State Mental Hospital, you could go to Bronx Mental Health Clinic for your out-patient treatment, or you could go to a clinic at Morrisania Hospital. But if you were discharged from any of the New York City in-patient psychiatric facilities, there was no nearby out-patient clinic in this community. When the city tore down several houses across the street from Morrisania Hospital and announced plans to build a parking lot there for the hospital, residents got together and signed petitions to use it, instead, for a clinic. And so, at the inception, in 1976, patients felt that Morrisania was theirs.

Velma Thomas served on the search committee to find a Director of Mental Health, along with several others from the community. We were looking for someone from the community, preferably a minority, but we liked Dr. Don Brown. We were impressed with his thinking. He espoused a participatory management model, with much less hierarchy than was customary in the New York City Health and Hospitals Corporation(HHC) of which we were a part, and with staff interviewing prospective job applicants. Our focus at Morrisania was on primary care more than outreach, but we did go out into the community in teams to help those who were in crisis and to help connect people to resources. There was an effort to bring in more people who represented the composition of the community, and paraprofessional views were important internally. This involved a lot of different cultures, classes, and viewpoints, and presented us with struggles around power and hierarchy. While such struggles promoted tension, they also were real and related to the struggles our clients faced. Morrisania was a passionate place to work. You cared about each other and about your clients, and you would stay late to get the job done right.

Structure

Morrisania NFCC was the last community mental health center started up in New York City (and maybe in New York State) with federal money, before that money was shifted into city block grants where it competed with other city-wide services and where mental health monies were no longer earmarked according to community need. The intention of Congress, in creating CMHC's was to have them be economically self-sufficient in time, which was ludicrous due to the poverty in most communities, especially here in South Bronx. The South Bronx was particularly victimized by New York City housing abuses. City policies protected landlords who could charge excessive rents, warehouse, or set fire to properties to collect insurance money. So you had a situation in which people were doubled up in inadequate housing, and the area looked like a war zone from so many fires. When Co-op City was built in the northeast Bronx, many middle-class residents left the community and moved there, taking a lot of services with them.

By the time Morrisania began in 1976 it was probably beginning to be clear that poor communities could not support their CMHC's, and so the federal government got out. We continued as part of the city hospital system, structured according to HHC policies, which were hierarchical, with physicians in positions of power. Each HHC facility has a medical school affiliate, ours being Albert Einstein College of Medicine/Montefiore Medical Center, with some staff being paid by the city and some by Montefiore, the latter higher paid and generally having more status due to the teaching function of the private facility.

Shortly after we opened, Morrisania City Hospital across the street was closed. That meant that our NFCC needed to have a strong medical, as well as mental health, department, and a day treatment program.While we are talking here only about the mental health clinic, we need to remember that mental health was not the whole of Morrisania and that we were trying to work together with the medical staff in holistic ways. Some staff were hired on a line for one department but also consulted for the other; for example, Velma Thomas ran groups for staff and clients in both departments on accessing community resources. Our staff consisted of nurses, social workers, psychologists,mental health aides, and psychiatrists; and many students in these various disciplines did placements or internships here as part of their training. It was, and is now, a busy place.

Caseloads

Then, large caseloads were as high as 75-80 and there was a lot of focus on getting out into the community and on continuity of care. Our clients had been sent from one service to another over and over, experiencing more frustration than help. We wanted to break this cycle for them, so clinicians had what we called "uninsulated caseloads" in which we had no waiting lists. Staff would be there for their patients who returned and we would see people when they needed help in our Crisis Room. There we used the crisis positively as a focus for change, and were eventually able to do very good work in ten sessions or less. Word got out in the community, and clients began to come at those hours in which they knew we would be working that way in the Crisis Room; and so clients selected treatment models. Generally, the more you could work with crisis, the busier your caseload. If you took a more laid-back approach, you ended up with fewer, and longer-term, more verbal clients. So clinicians, of course, "selected" their caseloads, also.

Language played a large part, Elsie Maldonado explains:" Sometimes I would have a hard day and I would be tired. I would be speaking to a new client on intake who did not know I spoke Spanish. So she would have in her mind a simple explanation of her problems prepared to tell me so that I could understand, and so that at least she could get one thing on her list taken care of that day. I would watch her speak very slowly and logically, but then I would give in and say *'Ay, senora, digame que paso'*. Well, then would come the flood, the whole laundry list of problems, the feelings; and we would have to take a good deal more time to get this all understood and prioritized a bit. Had I stuck with English only, my clients would have tended to be calmer and would have only presented me with one problem at a time". Elsie continues:

> We did not treat mental illness in isolation, but in regard to the effect it was having on the whole family. I remember once when myself and a psychiatrist went out to evaluate a client in her home when she refused to leave it. Her husband had come to the clinic for help when she had regressed to childlike behaviors and was hallucinating. When we got there she chased us downstairs with a pipe, and would only calm down when we played house with her. She needed to be hospitalized, of course, and the police needed to handcuff her for safety's sake; when the adrenalin got going, that 90-pound woman became very strong. But she did not need to be handcuffed in front of her four little children, so we arranged with the police to do it discreetly, while we talked to the children, comforted them, and explained a few simple things.
>
> The father was working all day, and could not take off work to care for the children without losing his job. They had no family here to help out. They had moved recently to New York from a rural area in Puerto Rico, and the wife did not speak English and was afraid of the city. The husband had tried to help her in the only way he knew how, by keeping her at home and going out and getting everything for her. The children had not even been registered in school. The more the wife was confined to the apartment, the more childlike and afraid she became, having no adult dialogue all day (completely unlike the extended family company she had had in Puerto Rico).
>
> *CWA could have placed the children in foster care. We could have stabilized the wife on medication and then put her back in the same system, but we changed it.* We made a report to Child Welfare Administration(CWA), but then helped CWA to go to the neighbors and

enlist their help to care for the children temporarily while the wife was in the hospital, and then in the day hospital. Mental health aides Luis Garcia and Velma Thomas helped the father to take the family to the park and on outings as tasks. By the time the family was together again full-time, they had learned to use a lot of staff support and would continue to share with other adults in the neighborhood. They continued to use our support in getting to know how to get what you needed for your family from bureaucracies.

This family needed a lot of concrete support to help them through a painful transition. Hospitalization, medication of the patient, and placement of the children would only have slowed the process: *the family's relation to its environment needed to change.*

There were often a lot of situations in this community which professionals with a lot of reliance on books, but very little exposure to the community, would find hard to understand. So behaviors seemed a lot crazier than they were when you understood the context. For example, in the South, many people had had no refrigeration, so they ate leftovers from the night before for breakfast; some thought that was crazy food to eat for breakfast, especially when they had moved North and were still used to eating that way, even with refrigeration. In a lot of families, they all slept together, too. Now everyone worries about incest, but many in this community don't think of sleeping together in terms of sex, but more in terms of cuddling and nurturing: if you pushed children out of bed too soon, they didn't do well. They didn't have enough security.

Staffing and staff support

At Morrisania the goal was not to label, but to understand multicultural meanings of behaviors and to make services fit the needs of our clients. Staff was encouraged to innovate more than to follow formulas, and to talk to other staff about cases and problems with cases. The motto was that you should never feel alone with a case you had a question about. Just as clients' problems were complex and needed a great deal of support, so did clinicians need to rely on a team of other brains to pick. No one understood everything. Some staff had had specialized training in family therapy. Some spoke one language, some others. Some knew the community well, some did not know it at all. Some had had years of experience in certain bureaucracies, some in others. We needed to pool all this knowledge to be able to help clients effect the changes they wanted to make.

With an administration which did not reinforce rigid hierarchy, but which encouraged team structures, a climate was created which was conducive to listening to each other, across our various fields of specialty, race, ethnic, and class backgrounds. Frequent staff socialization and staff training decreased inevitable tensions and misunderstandings. We celebrated birthdays, and had many informal luncheons in which staff shared incredible food with each other. At holidays our patients would sometimes give us small gifts and bring in food for staff. There was a feeling of good energy, and treatment given for and with the community, rather than to it.

Training according to common family systems frameworks increased our communication, and helped to prevent burn-out. Even though salaries were not high, staff tended to stay. Each staff person had about seven hours a week of individual supervision, team supervision, or staff meetings in which administrative issues were discussed. This placed a high premium on discussion and face-to-face contact among staff, and on, again, nurturing each other. Training was done in two teams. While the content in both teams was family systems approaches, this, of course, got interpreted to fit the training and life experiences of the trainers. Myrtle Parnell, Don Brown, and Elsie Maldonado ran a family-of-origin seminar in which staff presented their own genograms and social backgrounds relative to work agendas; and over the years two thirds of the staff participated in this seminar. When trainers came in from outside the community, with academic training and majority middle-class life experience, they tended to need hierarchy in which they could feel more in control of the process; needing data about cases ahead of presentations, so that there could be adequate time to reflect on interventions by the trainer before advising trainees. This method of training is certainly responsible, but teaches trainees not to take risks and to keep a certain detachment. It teaches that there is a right approach, and calls upon *"universal principles"* from books, from which to decide what will work. This discredits the life experiences in this community, which were not the data from which the books were written; and ignores the solutions which have worked for our clients: connections with others, not detachment.

Myrtle Parnell focused on creating a certain context for training which was congruent with the emergency problems and the community solutions used in the community (Brown and Parnell 1990), such that teams of staff members were helped to work with each other in such a way as to develop trust. You couldn't be sitting there alone, stiff upper lip, with a case which perplexed you. You had to consult with someone, but, to consult, you had to trust that colleague. To trust, you had to get to know others, talk to them: a private practice model didn't help you to do this sharing. Nor did the idea of going to only one person, your supervisor for consultation. What if she was busy? When you worked in a middle-class community with resources, things such as supervision and thinking about solutions could wait. Here, to stay calm and prevent burn-out or false "super-woman" grandiosity, you needed to share with several people. So we built community within Morrisania, and this process was as much the content learned as the family systems frameworks and terminology.

Pressures

Just as family systems training was done differently by different trainers at Morrisania, we never had been without a certain dynamic tension. While the core of our program was a commitment to treatment of patients within the real contexts of their lives(in depth), we operated within a city system which ignored this context and promoted hierarchy and efficiency in terms of numbers of patients seen (superficial). Then the Medicaid fee-for-service system required a psychiatric diagnosis, which said to HHC that payment dictated conceptualizing patients' problems in terms of individual deficits/disease. In this system there is contextual invalidation of a systems point of view. And so we were always "swimming upstream". The folks at Einstein just could not see the efficiency of bringing in "lay people" from the community to treat people who were diagnosed mentally ill. It was hard to orient new staff to ways of operating which seemed so counter to the mental health norms they had been taught. This is why training and staff support were so important to us. We mirrored the minority power/resource dilemmas of the people we served, with accompanying higher stress levels.Then we began to feel the effects of federal budget cuts on our mental health services strongly around 1985, when there was an increased push to document contacts with clients to justify funding. We had contact sheets, monthly sheets, and computer sheets to be filled out with #2 pencils--wlth hours of time spent in lessons as to how to do the forms right. When we were busy trying to meet the demands of a lot of families needing service, it was often hard to locate those #2 pencils...just when you really needed one!

Last straws

Admittedly, we had been much too loose with our recording. It was irresponsible not to record notes in charts. When you were out, others would need that information, perhaps, to help your client through a crisis better. We needed to be accountable, and could not afford to be prima donnas who were above recording. However, with that said, it became clear that outside sanctions were more for keeping us in business than for giving clients what they needed. It was a big shift for us. Morale was low. Then in 1985 there was increasing social distress in the community due to the advent of crack cocaine, and it became harder to get families in for training. While families had loved the friendly atmosphere at the clinic and lingered in the hallways to get some of that "extended family" support, when crack impacted the community, folks were just too scared to come out of their apartments any more than they absolutely had to. Staff felt overloaded and didn't want to do training any more. Staff parties were discouraged, with the increased time pressures of recording and the focus on efficiency. When, in that same year, HHC decided to save money by reducing social work vacation time from four weeks to two weeks each year, something snapped. Some staff went out on strike against these changes for a while. Many quit.

By 1988, Director of Mental Health, Don Brown; Director of Training, Myrtle Parnell; Crisis Room Coordinator Jo Vanderkloot; and Community Resources Consultant Velma Thomas had resigned, along with many others not included in this discussion. Those who had been on staff and resigned before 1985 remember it often as the best place they have ever worked. Jo Vanderkloot, who originally joined the staff as a volunteer for the first year just to have the valuable experience, looks back at her four years there as having "changed my life."

Persistence

Myrtle, with her focus on training as nurturance and team-building, and Don, with his trust of shared power, have left their imprint. A handful of us have remained from the beginning, almost twenty years, and we are tough. Elsie Maldonado, during that time, worked her way up from a paraprofessional position to Director of Social Work, after obtaining dual masters degrees in social work and administration. In this position, she has been able to help staff adapt their professional skills to the needs of the community she knows so well. She has not given up the "old" clinical goals, but insists on attending to the practical survival needs of the clinic. Our new staff sound a bit more practical than passionate. Yet the community's cultures are still reflected in staff composition. Luis Garcia has combined over fifteen years' experience on staff with a lot of knowledge of the community. Administrators pay special attention to ways in which they can attract and retain staff: while training in family systems approaches is no longer done on the previous scale, staff are encouraged to get whatever training they need for their own growth and stimulation. In general, the old community mental health philosophy is now more alive in primary care medicine and family medicine, than in mental health. As we have reverted to the need for more focus on hierarchical administration, physicians have more authority than previously in our settings, and they have less of a systemic orientation than other fields. So the systemic orientation, while still remembered and encouraged, is not taught to all as a unifying framework.

Demands on administrators are more complex, with more attention needing to be paid to brokering therapy to external forces. Administrators now tend to have more specific business goals in management. Hector Coll-Ruiz, as the present Director of Mental Health, is a psychiatrist who understands clinical perspectives and uses them as the basis for his work. In his training in public psychiatry, he was supervised by Don Brown and he was born at the old Morrisania Hospital; so he feels he can bridge the "old" and the "new" worlds for staff. However, he concentrates on knowing the rules of the game with the many external forces having influence at Morrisania: the New York City Health and Hospitals Corporation; the federal Office of Mental Health; the State Department of Mental Health; and Einstein Montefiore. These provide program parameters, first and foremost, for what it will be possible to do.

Administrators speak about practically accepting limitations, while not giving up the vision. Mr. Pagan, as Director of Outpatient Services, notes the difficulty now of assuring that the same clinician will continue with a family when a case is reopened after having been closed: we try to maintain this continuity, but staff often just do not have openings. With less team support for brief, crisis approaches, and with new clinicians hired who work from many psychodynamic models, there is a tendency for the length of therapy to be extended: thus, fewer openings. The Crisis Room now operates to triage and make sure that more critical cases are seen immediately. With the change from crisis management to triage, the focus is put more on suicidal, psychotic behaviors, and there are more hospital admissions, without as much attention being paid to the person-in-environment.

It is difficult to recruit and hold good staff: There have been so few minorities graduating from schools of social work, especially since cuts in financial assistance to minority students seeking graduate and undergraduate education during Reagan's term. We try to find good people from the community and give them all the encouragement we can to go back to school and to advance. But we have so many fewer options for staff now than before. Staff instability, disruption in services and budget cuts are the norm, just as constant and chronic lack of resources are the debilitating norm for our families.

Our families have changed now, too. Not only are they poorer, with more crises, but there are many new ethnic groups represented. We have people from many different countries in Africa, and from India. This is complicated for service delivery, when you realize that there are twelve dialects of the Hindi language represented, for one thing. Who on staff knows all these indigenous languages? Drugs are just pervasive now, and AIDS. Velma Thomas lives in the community and is now Director of Operations for her tenant association. She often works with people behind in their rent to avoid eviction, but still gets calls for help from many in the community who have heard of her by word of mouth. She has a sign on the door of her apartment listing the hours she is "in" to consult with those needing help: two hours in the morning for those not working, and two hours in the evening for those working: "I'm almost like an agency,but without pay."

At Morrisania, now, there is an air of quiet determination, planning to continue and to survive, within narrower options. As ever, Morrisania is about people who innovate, improvise, and keep on creating for a community badly in need of services.

****

Family Therapy and Social Work Themes

Swimming upstream

In the 1980's Reagonomics increasingly took from the poor to give to the rich. Tax cuts for those with high incomes reverberated in poor areas such as the South Bronx on, particularly, the housing policies and landlord practices referred to earlier here. At the same time, the federal Omnibus Budget Reconciliation Act (OBRA) of 1981 eliminated the formal community mental health care system, as mental health funding became part of a block grant program which returned responsibility for mental health initiatives to the states; and over 90% of all state-funded outpatient and residential care was then provided by private vendors through contract arrangements with states (Wade 1993). This privatization meant that policies for the allocation of mental health funding in poor areas would be determined even more by those with very little understanding of the needs in poor communities. Moreover, areas in the state with greatest (but more unrecognized) mental health needs should compete for funds with more middle-class areas with more political clout (*Ibid.*) . This is an example of institutionalized racism in action.

OBRA reversed a trend set by the federal Community Mental Health Centers Act of 1963. Then, with goals to treat and rehabilitate the mentally ill within the community and to promote mental health generally, centers such as Morrisania were set up in poor communities and mandated by the federal government to provide 24-hour emergency service, inpatient services, special programs for children and the elderly, followup care,transitional services, and alcohol and drug abuse programs, as well as outpatient counseling, in the community. Morrisania, in 1976, was one of the last in New York to be established under this funding. With OBRA, non-reimbursable services such as consultation/education, prevention, evaluation, and indirect clinical functions such as case management were cut back, and/or centers concentrated on serving those clients with insurance coverage (Jerrell and Larsen 1986). *In this policy shift, that which became non-reimbursable was that which distinguished community-based from traditional mental health counseling: 1) training of staff from the community, creating new models of service which both those staff from outside the community and those from within could relate to; 2)evaluation, a focus on the clinical effects of the work, as opposed to the traditional psychiatric practice of focusing on diagnostic labelling of the client; 3)staff getting out in the community, and defining clients more broadly as the well members of the family, as well as the diagnosed client(prevention); and 4)staff, again, getting out in the community enough to know its resources, informal and formal, with which to link clients, focusing on empowerment ("indirect" case management).*

Staff at Morrisania who had been hired under CMHA policies were hired because they had a commitment, and some skills, in the direction of community-based work. By 1985, as the about-face in policy of OMBA had sifted down to day-to-day operations, many of these staff members felt bound and gagged, in terms of being able to do the kind of work they considered relevant for their clients.

However, those staff with least connection to the community and most connection to traditional university-based training and higher salaries based on this training were less able to see the severe effects of this shift. While they had learned more about the community from sharing with each other under the much less bureaucratic direction of Don Brown, the staff from outside the community also had allegiance to radically conflicting ideas of treatment. They had more access to money and status based on their previous out-of-community paradigms of treatment. When official federal policies changed in the direction back to the traditional, it forced "bi-community" individuals to revert to their original paradigms, albeit unconsciously. Since most of these persons were white physicians or psychologists, and most of the staff from the community were African-American or Latin American lower-paid staff dependent on their bosses in the previous group, *the federal policy changes encouraged tension and splitting among staff along race and class lines, impeding their ability to learn from each other across these lines, and markedly increasing individual staff members' stress levels.* As in dysfunctional family systems, both "sides" end up pointing the finger at the other, diverting a lot of energy into anger, quitting, and *failing to locate the source of their dissension outside themselves,in the policies which needed to be changed.* This is an exact replication of the power dilemmas in poor and minority families.

In the discussion by Morrisania staff it seems that the locus for their frustration, the point at which these changes were felt, was in dilemmas around efficiency and record-keeping. It seems that, according to traditional bureaucratic definitions, good work was efficient, focusing on the production of good records and away from the immediacy and unpredictability of crisis work with clients. This meant that record-keeping needed to reflect "direct service" with individual patients, or that which was important and paid for according to the medical model was contact with the "real" client, the one "having" the mental illness. This focus directed the therapist's thinking and seemed to tip the balance, at Morrisania, in the direction of individual, more than family and community, treatment. It seems that when recording requirements changed and the system-ically-oriented staff became more in the minority (about 1985), they began to experience a lot of frustration and many staff had resigned by 1987. This left less family-oriented staff there, and new staff hired did not have a family focus. The identity of Morrisania had shifted from community-based work with families in crisis to a more traditional community mental health center.

An article by Walfish, Goplerud, and Broskowski (1986) talks about the importance of consensus on values and goals between top and middle management for weathering cutbacks in community mental health centers,with resistance and inefficiency disrupting service delivery when consensus is not there. While we can concur that in the experience at Morrisania services suffered from the split, we need to point out that the authors here seemed to miss the point of the inherent value and goal differences between different levels of staff when programs are to serve communities whose needs are best understood by those line and middle-management staff more often from the community; and when those in power are brought in from outside without much experiential knowledge of residents' needs.

Utne Reader (1994) reported on an Oakland physician actively advocating at the state level in California for the needs of a large population of suicidal/homicidal teens. In May 1993 teens and their advocates from all over the state were waiting in Sacramento to testify about their problems; but the hearing was abruptly cancelled because legislators were busy downstairs grappling with a state budget that was $9 billion from balancing. This article reminded me of our initial meeting at Morrisania planned for staff discussion for this chapter. We had scheduled a meeting for this chapter with Morrisania staff in January, 1994, just as the new Guiliani administration had announced cuts. We were able to meet with only one third of the originally planned staff on that day, since many managerial staff were in an emergency meeting planning which ones of them should lose their jobs. Other line staff presumably did not attend then due to the general low morale that day. Staff have expressed previously here how morale was affected by the cumulative effect of all these cuts. The emergency nature of the cuts has been particularly destructive. When money needs to be saved quickly, decisions for what kinds of services need to be saved are made by administrators, without time for comment from clinicians, let alone from the customers who are to reap the "benefits" of the changes.

Robert Alford (1972) elaborated on the health care "crisis" in 1972, before the establishment of Morrisania, as, not a crisis at all, but the continuation of forty years of inadequate services, insufficient funds, and understaffed hospitals, maintained by patterns of superficial changes in response to emergencies, but a balancing of physician and corporate bureaucratic interests which have shielded the system from structural change. As physicians had moved away from poor and rural areas and solo practice, corporate "rationalizers" challenged their monopoly on health care provision and moved in to coordinate them, adding a layer of new costs to the system and demanding that clinical staff keep more intricate records to keep track of patient data and billing. Increased record-keeping justified billing, but did not focus on quality of services or who uses them. Alford's analysis, predating Morrisania, is something staff were reluctant to return to, knowing its dangers.

The excellence of the program

Loren R. Mosher and Lorenzo Burti have spelled out, in their thoughtful and well-researched *Community Mental Health: Principles and Practice,* some good administrative and clinical guidelines for the practice of community mental health. They suggested some clinical principles (1989, 105-108):

1. *contextualization,* keeping clients in as close contact with their usual surroundings as possible;

2. *preservation and enhancement of personal power and control,* involving the client with non-mental health resources and helping him/her with doing rather than doing for the client;

 3. *normalization,* using the most average ways in the community to help the client get needs met first, before trying exceptional ways

Suggested administrative principles which could support these kinds of clinical principles were several (92-101):

1.*absolute responsibility for a catchment area,* with boundaries conforming closely to natural ethnic, religious, and geographic divisions;

2. *multidisciplinary teams,* working together to insure continuity of staff for clients;

3. *decentralized horizontal authority and responsibility,* with teams making their own day-to-day decisions;

4. *capitation payment,* a flat amount per resident to cover all mental health needs;

5. *use of existing community resources,* not duplicating anything that could be accessed in adjacent areas;

6. *multi-purpose center,* open long hours for other community non-mental health purposes such as recreation;

7. *non-institutionalization,* staff being required to provide in-hospital staffing for their clients when hospitalized; this tends to cut down on the use of the hospital for crises;

8. *outcome-based bonus system,* for cases best-served, not least-served, as in HMO's;

9. *citizen/consumer participation,* such as a citizens advisory board, self-help groups, NAMI (National Alliance for the Mentally Ill), all overlapping

Traditional mainstream principles of organization are wedded to hier-archy, efficiency, and business outcomes (e.g., Blau 1987). Mosher and Burti's principles, above, delineate how these traditional methods of operating need to be changed to suit the provision of good community mental health. What has made it such a joy to visit Morrisania, of course, has been the obvious strengths of the client population and of the staff, working together effectively *despite* so many insurmountable odds, internal struggles, and continual fighting for even minimal resources.

Some staff have written about how it has accomplished what it has

accomplished. Previous Director of Training Myrtle Parne.
Director Don Brown have described the southwest Bronx
which Morrisania is located in terms of a rapid 10-year shift
in which more middle-class Jewish families left in "white f.   ⌐ for the
nearby new Co-op City housing complex (Brown and Parnell 1990). Poorer
Blacks and Puerto Ricans escaping worse housing or no housing moved into
the area, and they could not afford the previous rents. There was an
epidemic of arsons, as landlords got their profits, instead, from insurance
companies. Small businesses collapsed in the area, and drugs and crime took
over. Morrisania Neighborhood Family Care Center was established to
provide services appropriate to the needs of the population, and continuity
of services, so that clients could maintain contact with one regular therapist
over time. A typical case seen in the clinic could be a single parent of
several children living in a deteriorated building and receiving inadequate
public assistance from which she would have to borrow from the cash
allowance to have enough to pay the rent. The presenting problem would
most likely be the mother's "nervousness" or the children's misbehavior in
school. Children would generally be kept indoors after school due to the
danger in the neighborhood. There would be a strong kinship network,
including father and extended families on both sides, godparents, and
unrelated friends. The family might believe in a Pentecostal, Espiritismo, or
Santeria religion, non-Western traditional religions more popular with the
poor, in addition to the middle-class Roman Catholic religion. Twenty to
thirty per cent of patients would have drug or alcohol abuse problems,
secondary to mental illness (30% chronic or episodic, with psychotic
symptoms; another 30% with longstanding disabling anxiety or depression
due to severe stressors; and another third with demoralizing chronic family
or relationship problems).

*Staff were taught a model of family therapy which emphasized family
strengths, bolstered support systems, and used present-oriented pragmatic
interventions with clients.* They worked in interdisciplinary teams of six to
ten staff each, sharing work-related problems and learning from each others'
cases hands-on. *The experiential nature of the work and training kept it
close to the community* and gave paraprofessionals an opportunity to
perform as excellent therapists. However, bureaucratic fragmentation,
inadequate resources, large numbers of clients, and lack of control of
program limited effective ecosystems work(*Ibid.*).

In spite of the frequent crises of both staff and clients, Morrisania
attracted those who had a high degree of systems expertise and provided
community- and ethnic-sensitive applications of systems work not taught in

many other places. Steve Goldstein, a previous supervisor, described exquisite interventions with families designed to involve uninvolved fathers in the therapy (1990), and to calm and focus a seemingly chaotic family (1986). Lawrence Dyche and Steven Goldstein wrote from their experience in the day hospital at Morrisania about work with schizophrenics who also were dealing with surviving racism and poverty (Goldstein and Dyche 1983): their ecological approach focused on how deficits in organization in the person, the family, the network, and the community sustained the symptoms of schizophrenia. Therapy in stages first tended to the family's priorities of survival, to help create a stable living situation and some leadership to get things done. Then, in middle stages therapists could expand adaptation options beyond the extremes of either enmeshment or isolation, and in the third stage could contract with the schizophrenic long-term to help with good decisions about his/her life.

Morrisania continues to thrive. It straddles two worlds, as do all programs in minority communities which do not have control of funding and decision-making. Because of this duality, it is a study of both how a program can closely approach the principles outlined by Mosher and Burti and how it can operate in the community and provide mental health services in ways which are not community-based. Psychiatrist Matthew Dumont (1992) has written in an impassioned way about efforts to similarly blend two radically different paradigms in a community mental health setting in Chelsea, Massachusetts . He describes the angst he felt at the demise of the "community" aspects of this work, such that "community mental health" became "public psychiatry", a definition of practice defined by economics, what remained after all the profit had been skimmed by the private sector. We can feel that angst in the staff accounting of experiences at Morrisania, as noted. But we can also be reminded of our limits, our vulnerability, and our need to organize in sophisticated ways at grass roots levels to prevent and protest further policy changes which encourage race and class separation, and which prevent active participation of community residents in the formation of clinical interventions to be used in their mental health center.

Maybe we watch too much T.V. and we forget our own power when we come together. Knowledge of the histories and persistence of the various Latin American cultures represented in the population of the South Bronx can teach us better our place in the world and our ability to come together for more than just survival, to create mental health services for the unique needs of specific communities. The strong, upbeat feeling of joy you get when you enter Morrisania, even after all the changes, is constantly nourished by the histories and persistent organization of the residents of the South Bronx. Examples of some historical and cultural contexts represented in this communi ty are as follows.

Rigoberta Menchu tells about her life story, and that of Guatemalan peasant cultures, after the authoritarian Lucas Garcia regime came to power in 1978:

> My father was our community's elected leader, and so was my mother. My father used to say, 'We don't do this so that our neighbors can say, what good people they are! We do it for our ancestors. ' . . .We also had the example of my grandfather (who) used to tell us many bits of his life: he said that years ago he'd lived when there was slavery . . . He told us about many parts of his life . And it was like an education for us....It was like a political discussion every time we talked to him"(Menchu 1984, 188-189).

For her, the personal was political, and present strategies were informed by intimate knowledge of past struggles, with family closeness the vehicle for change, rather than an impediment to personal freedoms envisioned in Western cultures.

In El Salvador, 1980 witnessed mass demonstrations of unity and strength, followed by an all-out war against the people which took the lives of more than 43,000 people since 1979, and in which even the funeral march of the assassinated Archbishop Oscar Romero was fired on by government troops. On January 10, 1981, the political-military organizations of El Salvador, united in the FMLN, launched a general offensive throughout the country, and, since then, the strength of the FMLN has increased in spite of the U.S. government's massive military aid to the junta (Rodriguez 1983).

Our people bring with them to this country, a personal understanding of politics, traditions of struggle and persevering, and clear voices. We know that development in Latin America according to Western European models is no longer conceivable, and that services for Latin populations in the United States must be designed according to Latin values and traditions, and staffed by Latin Americans. Almost no one is interested in a selfish policy any more, and the majority is looking for a more human alternative structure(Dumont 1970). Marjorie Agosin advises that the present agenda of women and the human rights movement in Latin America is to restore among ourselves and our countries a sense of growth, a sense of connections between our individual selves and the collective trauma that our countries have suffered; and to speak the unspeakable about public atrocities which have been committed (1993). Gonsalves talks about the need to promote the formation of new support systems here in work with Chilean refugees, supports which can experientially understand the trauma recently experienced; thus, the support of those peers in the community.

Many immigrants to the South Bronx have suffered debilitating loss, torture, and trauma. However, those who have lived through such experiences, such as those writers just mentioned, seldom write about the experience as an individual phenomenon, or as one which can be helped by individual therapy alone. Just as individuals must connect to collective trauma to heal, so too must analyses of personal problems suffered by immigrants from Latin America relate personal change to the economic and political changes in the histories of Latin American countries (See Barry 1987; DeSoto l989; and Jimenez deWaggenheim 1993). If we spend time in our local Latin American communities, we will not be able to avoid learning these histories and engaging in political discussion. Flores-Ortiz and Bernal(1990), in an article about family therapy with Latin drug abusing clients whose families were marked by a high degree of disconnectedness from extended family in both country and culture of origin and in the new society, noted the importance of reconnecting family legacies, which would lead to:

1) a firm rootedness in history serving to challenge cultural cutoffs;
2) acknowledgement of the interconnectedness between social and family legacies;
3) liberation from the revolving slate of victim and victimizer through the recognition of social processes larger than the family;and
4) developing the ability to distinguish between family and social events.

Michele Klevens Ritterman writes of her increasing involvement, over a period of years, with a political prisoner in Pinochet's Chile,as she tried to understand the sources of his ability not to be controlled or repressed by state terror and torture constantly experienced (Ritterman 1991). As Daniel Rodriquez spoke passionately about his family, the author came to understand the power of family support and relationships which could survive terror by means of solidarity and love. Such reminders give us hope to get through a much different period in our history and hope that our skills as family therapists can be useful in promoting such solidarity. An important paper examines countertransference between therapists and their client victims of political torture and repression (Comas-Diaz and Padilla 1990). These authors who worked in the repressive political climate in Chile found that therapists needed to take special care to avoid hopelessness and despair; and that teamwork, mutual support and continued reflection shared with a mental health team were indispensable as well as an active sense of doing something to help. This agrees with the emphasis on team-building taken at Morrisania no matter how inefficient and time-wasting it might have seemed to some.When family therapists experience burn-out they will not be able to develop the empathy needed by immigrant families who need a bridge from their extreme suffering to the "freedom" experienced in the U.S. (Domokos-Cheng Ham 1989).

Family therapy trends affecting the work at Morrisania

A trend in the field of family therapy parallels changes at Morrisania. Family therapy has refocused on the individual over the past decade and promoted itself as an extension of individual therapy (See Wachtel and Wachtel 1986; Scharff and Scharff 1987; Kirschner and Kirschner 1986; and Nichols 1987), with the reasoning that family systems approaches have too zealously swung the pendulum in the direction of "system" and now need -to move out of this immature focus on dramatic differences to a more mature integration of old and new. Integration of individual and systemic approaches to treatment has indeed been the buzz word in family therapy literature over the past decade and it does sound reasonable, apart from economic considerations. But it seems to assume an actual split in experience between individual and contextual change which needs to be integrated:

> We all know that some family patterns are enormously resistant to change. *What we forget, sometimes, is who changes. Systems don't change. Couples don't change. People change* (Nichols 1987, 38; emphasis mine).

This is similar to the assumption of Menand quoted in Chapter One, which denies reality beyond that of the individual and is very much in the tradition of European and American individualism. Braulio Montalvo perhaps influenced by his Puerto Rican traditions of both family/community and respect for the personal ("personalismo") offers an integration which would not invalidate the kind of community work attempted at Morrisania:

> It's nonsense to say that the only way to get change is by attending to the family--- look at Wolpe's behavioral work with phobias or Aaron Beck's cognitive therapy with depression. But we need to do more than go back and salvage traditional theories of personality that never understood the individual in context (Montalvo 1987, 85).

It is true that in the early days of family therapy we were just a little too elated with "new" discoveries. We had managed to train many people in agencies which would then pay for their staff to get postgraduate practicum training because agency administrators saw the need for approaches which were less individualistic and more attuned to the minority world-views of their client populations. To be marketable *then*, we pinpointed the *differences between traditional individual approaches and family systems approaches.* A master in the field, Jay Haley, offered explanations as to the ways in which systemic paradigms were radically different from traditional mental health paradigms (Haley 1976). These *are* radically different ways of organizing data which our clients present, and our responses to that data; and Morrisania provides an example of the conflict between systemic, wholistic, non-Western approaches and Western medical models. *Now, marketability supports our identification with the medical mainstream,but does not support community paradigms.* This tendency to shift back and forth from one trend or "right answer" to another, particularly in the U.S., has a lot to do with our history, in which we have not been *inclusive* of differences. It has disastrous effects on our clients, particularly when we know that Morrisania was not just an interesting "experiment" or showcase of opposing paradigms, but an effective service for people needing it and supporting it.

Joel Feiner, in a review of Dumont's account of the changes in Chelsea (cited earlier in this chapter),notes the extreme difficulties of community mental health work in times such as ours, but offers that we can often succeed more readily as therapists when we use broad interventions aimed, not only at therapy with the named client, but at building relationships with other elements making up individuals' contexts (family, religious groups, cultural dimensions, the political process). He reminds us of the large system family therapy focuses still alive and well, but also of our tendency to do therapy, even in a community-based setting, with narrow, rather than broad strokes.

Bureaucratic accountability and paperwork focus us more on the large system of the organization than that of the community. When therapists must satisfy increasing internal demands of the system in which they work, their sensitivity to the broad strokes of systems work is not increased. It is almost inevitable that therapists will deal with their own increased stress by focusing smaller, on whatever part of the whole will ensure their jobs and seem to promote less confusion and conflict for them. It becomes easier to just focus on *my* job and *my* clients; and the mental health clinic itself becomes less of a community, with less interaction, creativity, and pos- sibility. Social service organizations need linkage with the community and its cultures; and community involvement on the part of the therapist is essential, for self as well as client, and for work which has meaning.

Brazilian educator Paolo Freire advises us that individuals are taught to transform the world through a *dialogical encounter* with others who are not separate from them, but who share personal and social realities in such a way that *the realities can be examined together and criticized* (1990). When we have therapeutic relationships with our clients which enable us to dialogue in this way, we seem to build a basis for social/political change, and our mental health services are less "crazy-making" for poor people and people of color.

CHAPTER SEVEN:
PREVENTING PLACEMENT BY
COMMUNITY SUPPORT
The Lower East Side Family Union, Manhattan

"One is born through the conditions of parentage; his body is nourished by food, his spirit is nurtured by teaching and experience. Therefore, both flesh and spirit are related to conditions and are changed as conditions change. As a net is made up of a series of ties, so everything in this world is connected by a series of ties. If anyone thinks that the mesh of a net is an independent, isolated thing, he is mistaken. It is called a net because it is made up of a series of connected meshes, and each mesh has its place and responsibilities in relation to other meshes.... It is the everlasting and unchanging rule of this world that everything is created by a series of causes and conditions and everything disappears by the same rule; everything changes, nothing remains without change."

The Teaching of Buddha
Bukkyo Dendo Kyokai, 1966

******

With   Alfred B. Herbert, Jr., Paula L. Liranzo, Denise Martinez, Esther Morales, and Fan Wong

Our History

In 1971 an advocacy group for children throughout New York City had been concerned about inadequate, fragmented services for children here, and published a report calling for "new locally based services" and "reorganization for a family focus". In response to these recommendations, the executive director of the Henry Street Settlement House brought together four other settlements on the Lower East Side: the Educational Alliance, Hamilton-Madison House, Grand Street Settlement, and University Settlement. Together, they presented a proposal to the Foundation for Child Development creating the Lower East Side Family Union, which began operation in 1974 (Beck 1974). The major goals of the Family Union have been to rehabilitate hard-pressed families for whom disintegration is an immediate threat; and to prevent out-of-family placement of children. A primary assumption upon which service is based is that such placement most often happens because other supports are not available to help the family deal with problems which may beset it. Our mission here is not mental health or substance abuse diagnosis and treatment, but to build supports for normal overwhelmed families. Our focus is Preventive Services, to prevent the placement of children in foster care. Programs are funded primarily by the city's Child Welfare Administration(CWA); and also by other grant funding.

The Family Union and the Neighborbood

To achieve our goals, the Family Union structures services in one outreach and four ongoing service teams. Each team consists of a professional social worker and several social work assistants, generally B.A.-level staff selected for their familiarity with the neighborhood, its cultures, and the kind of problems commonly experienced in families. All new staff are oriented to neighborhood resources by going out into the neighborhood, and then they are given in-service training in the service model we use with families. Teams 1 and 4 consist of bilingual (Spanish), bi-cultural staff who work with families in the primarily Puerto Rican and Dominican Lower East Side neighborhood from 14th to Water Streets. Team 2 consists of bilingual (Chinese)bi-cultural staff located in the Canal Street office and working primarily with families in Chinatown, but also with Asian families in any of the five boroughs who are referred. Team 3 is the Living With AIDS Project, serving the Lower East Side, but also all boroughs. The Outreach Team does initial assessments and contracting with families who are referred in the Lower East Side community, and goes out to the neighborhood's schools, churches, agencies, and other institutions to educate them about services at the Family Union, and to hear about their problems and resources, promoting coordination of neighborhood resources and referrals of families who might need services but who would never come to us through more formal channels, due to their isolation.

We are quite well-known here, and families come to us by word of mouth or by knowing us as we are out and about in the community. This is an area in which everybody knows everybody, and where most people do not venture out beyond this familiarity. Most are recent immigrants or their families once immigrated here and passed the housing on to the next generation. There is a lot of cultural and historical stability in this neighborhood, and this brings with it pluses and minuses. On the one hand, people could never survive this city as poor strangers not speaking the language, and, as with the Chinese, coming from an extremely different non-Western culture. The neighborhood is a known entity, strangers are spotted, you are easily understood, you can buy the kinds of foods you are used to eating, and you do not have to feel so cut-off from your past. You can often run into someone from your same village in China. Chinese families who do move out to other areas and boroughs still stay in touch with Chinatown, their home base here.

However, the area is changing. Gentrification is encroaching on already sparse HOUSING...the big problem, HOUSING, HOUSING, HOUSING. As housing has become so expensive in other parts of the city, artists and those seeking relatively inexpensive housing develop this area, crowding out the poor people who have nowhere to go both because they cannot afford higher priced housing elsewhere and because they are afraid to leave such a womb-like enclave. Many people here could not tell you what exists above 14th Street. It has been earth-shaking to many families when they become homeless and HRA finds them a place in Staten Island or out in Brooklyn: the home may be nice, but the disruption caused by such a move is immense. It is like immigrating to a new country all over again, and New York is too huge to process without a smaller reference group or neighborhood.

This is why services need to be based in neighborhoods, and why we need to go out of our offices to meet people and enable them to be familiar with us and recognize us as part of the community. It will be hard enough to ask for or receive help from outside the family, but it is easier when you can go to someone who you think may understand you--who speaks your language, knows the same places and people you know here, and has respect for where you have come from. We can easily chat with Puerto Rican clients about where our families have come from on the island, and that creates a common bond.

However, we are not friends with the families we serve. We are careful to maintain certain boundaries. We do not accept food or gifts from clients and, while often invited to certain family functions such as weddings or baptisms, we decline such invitations. Families need to keep a clear idea about the Family Union and its function for them. Because we have common ties in the community, this would be too difficult if we also socialized with them. We respect the "personalismo" of our Puerto Rican clients, a warm person- to-person attachment which is culturally accepted, and which is a bit warmer than the distance used in Anglo-American relating. While we decline gifts, we can still maintain this expected person-to-person respect.

Social workers and other counseling professionals often make a lot of mistakes in beginning to work with Chinese families when they ask family members to divulge or discuss feelings. This then becomes very awkward, when family members want to work on a concrete task which will help the problem, and expect the clinician to work on concrete issues; but do not want to insult the clinician by disagreeing with his or her suggestions. We frequently need to mediate these kinds of misunderstandings between family members and other agencies serving them.

The service model: task-oriented and time-limited

Our role at the Family Union is specific, designed to increase family supports and connections to resources, and then to leave. We do not provide long-term intensive counseling, but refer clients out to this when it is needed. Often it is not. We find that when families get, and learn how to access, needed resources, and take charge of this process to solve problems, they become empowered. Our goal is empowerment, with families strengthened so that children can remain in the home.

Our Outreach Team is the first step in the process, receiving referrals from service providers, friends, or family members in the community and outside it. We do not simply take referrals in the office, but go out to local hospitals, schools, etc. and make ourselves available as resources on the spot. We spend a lot of time getting known in the community, and give presentations about our services. This is the way that trust gets established here, by being part of the community and being visible and involved. Generally, families are referred to us who are in crisis or seen to be at risk, and so we contact them within 24 hours. If a client does not connect with us well at the time of referral, we get in touch with the referral source and go out and meet jointly with the family to try to engage them.

The outreach worker does a lengthy 2-3 hour assessment wlth the client, using it as a tool to help the client identify strengths, resources, and ways in which the family has coped with crises to that point. We do not underestimate the family, but assume that they have been able to hold things together in some way, and want to learn from them how they have done it.

We do not assume incompetence, even though many families are dealing with substance abuse, mental illness, and domestic violence. We use the assessment as a way to look at the total picture with the family, and have them prioritize for us their most immediate concerns and needs. We get a good developmental history of each child, and may discover that a child with special needs may qualify for certain services available, for example, from OMRDD, which he or she could not receive without the special needs assessment. We get an idea as to the family's familiarity with resources in the community and the city, and their ability to use these resources. Often, family members lack some very basic skills: they may never have used the subway, and may not have let a potential employer know that this was an impediment to a specific job; or may have accepted a referral to counseling outside the community which they could never follow through with because they have never been out of the area. The assessment helps the family focus on the range and the connectedness of the issues in their lives.

Sometimes the client does not need or want ongoing work beyond a referral or help to interpret for and negotiate with existing services. Chinese parents often sign papers for their children to be placed in a special class in school or to have medical treatment, but they do not understand what the class or the treatment is for, or the diagnosis or prognosis for the childen. Often children can get lost in the system or parents do not follow up properly with a medical regimen because they have not understood what they are signing or how the system works. They need for someone to take time with them and track the process in the system, making it understandable to them. This can be quite time-consuming, considering that this is not just social services, but housing, legal, financial, ernployment, job training, medical, etc. Moreover, Chinese clients who move to other boroughs still come back here for assistance and do not find Chinese-speaking services elsewhere, so that our Chinese staff really need to update themselves on so many services all over the city. However, this service is invaluable, educating clients as to how to use the system, how to get what you need in an urban Western culture yourself. Children can see that their parents are not powerless here, but are able to learn and to take control. This is very important, in that so many family problems are created when children seem to be wiser in the world than their parents. We learn, also, from clients updating us on resources they have found. It is important to keep your ears open and be creative: resources and supports are scarce, even though they are somewhat better in the Lower East Side than in other areas.

Most often clients do not just need help with the system or a referral, but ongoing work with one of the teams. The assessment serves as the basis for ongoing work, and is given to the team leader who assigns a case worker. Then the client, case worker, and outreach worker meet to provide continuity of services as the work transfers from one worker to another. Continuity of service is something we really pay attention to at all stages in the process with the client, making sure that things are understood, taken in, and agreed to. When our primary goal is empowerment of families, then they must feel in control of the process as much as possible, and must understand why and how changes occur.

The caseworker and client make a work agreement or contract together, which spells out what the client will do to address issues which are top priority, and how the caseworker will help. This is specific and time-limited, assuming that the family will not need a lengthy relationship with the caseworker, who serves as a case manager, linking the client to resources and strengthening the family's internal and external supports. Family members are often referred to groups. There are structured parent education groups with specific topics and speakers brought in. There are two groups for clients with AIDS: the more structured Friday group with an educational format from which clients can graduate into the less structured and more supportive Wednesday group. There is a teen group and a young mothers' group, the latter run by the women themselves, who often plan outings and activities they are interested in. Since clients come from the same general area, they often form friendships which can continue after the particular group experience ends.

The service model: expanding the provider's range

Our model seems to be quite simple. We focus clients on manageable tasks which help them to resolve crises, and we link them to necessary resources and supports so that they can experience success. It rests on some basic assumptions which may be different from those of many service providers. First, we operate in the client's community and we are part of *this* community context, making the services flow from the ways of life here. This means that we take our direction and pace from the client, and so may seem to be less efficient than other standardized services. We are not funded on a case-by-case basis, and so do not have to achieve certain set goals within "X" amount of time in case records. We are funded in a grant according to the numbers of clients we serve, and the funding source requires that we serve those clients whose children are at high risk of placement, following the mission of the agency. The methods we use involve a lot of creativity and sensitivity to the unique needs of each family, and require us to think in a broader range of possibilities than if our work were organized by charting requirements. *Success will depend on who we are able to involve in the solutions; how much we and the family are aware of in the community; and on political and economic realities in the city which we cannot control. From doing the best we can together, knowing resources and not assuming pathology or deficits on the part of clients, we will bump into snags which tell us that the family's problems are social problems needing economic and political change.* In this community, residents often come together publicly to press for such change. We hope that our work enables this kind of change, as well as internal *relationship* changes in families. Traditional agencies which account to governmental bureaucracies more than to defined communities are more prone to target only internal changes within the family, and do not help clients to develop the kind of supports which are necessary for other levels of change. In this way, they tend to scapegoat families and focus more on their deficits than strengths, often fostering dependency on the system.

Our focused and short-term work with clients demands that we know how they live and how they cope; and how the systems they must interact with function; and how to bridge the gaps between these two worlds. Thus, the burden of a wide range of knowledge falls on us, involving complex skills which the title of "caseworker" does not quite capture. In placing this burden of a broader orientation on us, we can share with the client some of the difficulties of bi-culturality and poverty, rather than offering a narrow service which it will be up to the client to understand and fit into his/her own life experience. Often therapists outside this community do not know how hard it is to make the services they offer understandable to poor people of color. Without extensive bridging, such services will not be usable and will be rejected. Clients in crisis already have too many daily pressures to then be expected to bridge service gaps. Some of this work must be done by service providers, and knowledge of the community gives them guidelines.

****

Settlement House and Home-Based Preventive Service Themes in Social Work

Cultural Need for the Neighborhood

While understanding that the term "Asian" encompasses a wide range of diverse cultures, Tsui and Schultz (1985) enumerate some common cultural characteristics: deference to authority; more restrained modes of emotional expression; strong family bonds; well-defined social and role expectations; communal responsibility; and a pragmatic view of life and interpersonal relationships. The unacculturated Asian client expects that the therapist will offer advice on how to rid him/herself of symptoms; and will provide structure and orientation as to what to expect from the therapeutic process. He/she will defer to authority, and be uncomfortable with a nonstructured amorphous "therapeutic" encounter. A crisis-intervention approach of emotional- environmental first aid, with the therapist in the role of a health educator or practical family friend works far better than a non-directive approach. The therapist should avoid focusing on issues of individual achievement or growth (seen to be selfish) but should involve family and community, since the integral role each member plays within the Asian family dictates a focus on family in treatment(*Ibid.*). The ideal is the endurance and stability of the *social order*, maintained by the durability of roles played by individuals. A concept of individual morality based on universal ideas of right and wrong, outside the context of prescribed social roles, is foreign. Work with a therapist will be less intense and peripheral to the more intense involvement with family (Tung 1991). This is very different from Western American experience of very little environmental stability and social structural support, in which each new relationship involvement and the relationship with the therapist are intense.

Asian values, as opposed to Western values of individual experience and feelings, inherently link the mental health of the individual to the social system. Puerto Rican non-Western values also defer to authority and strongly respect the family and community, expecting help to be family-focused and practical. It is easy to see how these cultural traditions in the Lower East Side of New York have informed the work of the Family Union in its family- and community-centeredness and its practical and informational services.

We need to remember that many who have immigrated in the past twenty years to Asian American communities, as to Latin American ones, are refugees from terrorist regimes. They may have suffered years of famine, bombing, imprisonment, and physical torture such as the experiences of Cambodian refugees. A recent study of the psychiatric disturbances of Cambodian Americans ten years after their resettlement here found many severe symptoms of post-traumatic stress disorder and depression, at levels still as high as those Cambodian Americans who had more recently experienced such torture. The need for treatment was great and individuals were not sleeping or remembering much at all of recent or past events or identities. Availability of treatment was poor, with a paucity of personnel who could understand their culture and speak the language(Carlson and Rosser-Hogan 1993). The community context, such as that in Chinatown, offers some *much-needed* beginnings of security and structure. However, the extreme need of populations like the Cambodian, as well as the lack of Asian personnel in other boroughs or areas in New York, underscores the inadequacy of treatment for Asian people. Asian staff at the Family Union number only four, and they cover all boroughs, as well as Chinatown There are more numerous Asian social services in Chinatown to which Family Union staff can refer than in other areas, but there are also tremendous gaps in service, so that residents rely heavily on their communities for support and nurturing. As at the Family Union, services need to find the existing patterns of support in the community, and build on them. This is especially important when we realize that community *structures* have the *resources* to help families reorganize, restructure hierarchy, and reconstitute boundaries; and the *culturally appro-priate group experiences within which refugees can process their extraordinary experience and reduce their sense of isolation and powerlessness.* Chambon (1989) points out that research on the needs of refugees generally deals with the effects of trauma on individuals, but does not look at the needs for families, who are living as pieces of families or frag-ments, and who do not identify primarily as individuals. It is important to remember that therapists who know the community and speak the language can, by connecting refugees to informal neighborhood structures, do a lot to begin the healing process (as staff at the Family Union are in a position to do) without necessarily referring people to therapy.

Lin (1984) notes in the Chinese a disinclination to face squarely the question of mental disorder, but comfort in seeking general primary health care in neighborhoods. Many emotional problems are experienced somatically, so that attending to practical physical concerns in the neighborhood will allow for the topic of psychiatric symptoms to come up in an atmosphere of trust. Lin suggests that we need to make a concerted international effort to understand non-Western-based psychiatry which can underscore the importance of the neighborhood context as well as the individual, and the somatic as well as the emotional .

The Settlement House and the Neighborhood

Price *et al*, in an American Psychological Association Task Force, set out to identify effective prevention programs across the life span, and found a number of features which these programs had in common: careful targeting of the population; capacity to alter life trajectory; the provision of social support and the teaching of social skills; strengthening of existing family and community supports; and rigorous evaluations of effectiveness (Price, Cowen, Lorion, and Ramos-McKay 1989). The emphasis on social support and community assumes family strength rather than weakness, and roles in which knowledge is shared between professionals and parents, without the paternalism of traditional professional-client realtionships (Weissbourd and Kagan 1989). *Good family support and preventive programs understand the child in the context of family and community, and have an ecological orientation with goals to improve the context as well as the child.* Antecedents of the family support movement were the self-help movement of the 1960's, parent education and rights to information, and the settlement house movement at the turn of the last century, with its emphasis on advocacy. Reminiscent of the settlement house, family support programs are *locally* focused and designed, propelled by internal principles, rather than conforming to external bureaucratic regulations (*Ibid.*) This seems like the kind of preventive services offered at the Family Union.

By way of contrast, family support programs have been introduced also at state levels in Minnesota, Missouri, Maryland, and a few other states, stimulating local programs which are family-focused, rather than the traditional focus on the poor, neglected or mistreated child, with family seen often as obstacles to the child's well-being (Weiss). These programs, unlike the Family Union and other locally developed programs, originate in state government, with family support as a unifying philosophy permeating preventive programs. Funding is in grants to diverse areas which each design their own programs under the general state guidelines. They particularly encourage cooperation among state institutions (schools and other agencies) and the family; but then compete with other social services for funding, and are subject to political shifts occurring at levels beyond the local community. This trend seems to bureaucratize, and possibly destroy the benefits of, a local grassroots movement. We tend to want to universalize something which works well in one cultural context or in one community. Whereas we might see that treat-ment should, and can, benefit both individuals and community, when we legislate it, or build treatment models which can be applied or taught anywhere, we negate the particular mix of need, culture, politics, economics, and geography which is community.

Community is a living, particular, interactional mix from which should evolve ideas for programs. The ideas need to come from the people who will use services, not, as is usually the case, from social service practitioners, administrators, or bureaucrats at state levels. For, no matter how much we may use the language of mutuality and empowerment, it is only so much rhetoric if impetus and funding come from outside the target community, without community members or leaders having conceived the process. Programming which is conceived on a grand scale and is intended to be applied in many different kinds of community contexts often calls itself "community-based" in that it intends to adjust interventions to fit local needs and to involve local staff in the secondary local planning and delivery of services. This kind of programming may, of course, have merit, but it needs to specify the "community" in which the primary planning took place (was "based"). All too often, the life experiences upon which paradigms for services are built are those of white middle-class males in urban areas and university settings, not identified as such and so assumed to be applicable to poor, rural or minority communities. It is later left to line staff, who appreciate the greater power and experience of their supervisors and agency executives but who know the community more, to sort out their confusion when being asked to make a square peg fit into a round hole. Particular communities need programs constructed from the thinking and experiences of those in the community. This is certainly not radical thinking, since most of us would not welcome citizens from, for example, Scandinavia, coming into our country to set policy, no matter how educated. Ideas are not abstract or universal, but reflections of personal experience and partial truth.

As far back as 1890, Jane Addams established Hull House, the first settlement house, in Chicago. The commitment then was for social workers to "settle" amid the people who were their concern and to reduce the distance between the social classes (Brieland 1990). It emphasized neighbor-to-neighbor helping, and focused on showing respect for the heritages of different immigrant groups. Addams also worked with residents to address problems of housing and sanitation in the neighborhood. What would later be called "group work" was the core of the program, as a kindergarten and a variety of activity groups were organized, with residents, to make up for deficits in the public schools(*Ibid.*).

Social work historians contrast the settlement house with another tradition, the friendly visitor, who at that time was a well-off volunteer coming in from a "better" neighborhood to assist the poor under the auspices of the Charity Organization Society. The role of the volunteer was not that of a helper, but a gatekeeper who determined who deserved assistance and who did not. Charity Organization Societies were the forerunners of modern casework, with the guiding philosophy that poverty could be cured by personal rellabilitation of the poor(*Ibid.*).

These conflicting traditions in social work have influenced the development of the field, as we have maintained a precarious balance between the idea of the social worker as a consultant connecting clients to supports which will enable them to build on existing strengths (the settlement house philosophy which is obviously still the foundation of work at the Family Union); and the idea of the social worker as one who locates social problems in individual clients and then attempts to cure their pathology from a one-up, now paid professional instead of volunteer, stance. Often, those social workers paid to do individual therapy in medical or mental health settings wedded to individual treatment paradigms are paid far better, and are better educated, than those in more generalist or community settings. It would seem that social work traditions have been biased in favor of the Mary Richmond casework model.

However, in 1981, a task group of social work leaders developed a statement of the social work mission with six objectives which should characterize professional practice, as follows (*Ibid.*):

1. help people enlarge their competence and increase their problem solving and coping abilities
2. help people obtain resources
3. make organizations responsive to people
4. facilitate interaction between individuals and others in their environment
5. influence interactions between organizations and institutions
6. influence social and environmental policy

It seems that if we want to get an idea as to how these general principles could be applied in actual practice (all of them) we can look to the work at the Family Union. Perhaps we need not think in terms of polarizing the disparate traditions in social work, but of finding ways to locate the strengths in both models. This book contends that community provides a training ground for staff who know it well to learn more advanced clinical methods which have arisen out of work with minority and poor populations (see Chapter Nine). Staff who know community can advance relevant clinical skills. The work of Insoo Kim Berg is important to mention in this context.

In her book, *Family-Based Services: a Solution-Focused Approach,* Ms. Berg gives clear guidelines for staff in child welfare and family service settings as to how to do productive assessments with clients and how to contract with them in such a way as to positively build from their strengths in brief time-limited work (Berg 1994). She is a well-known family therapist and trainer, and so bases this work on significant practice experience. Moreover, the concrete practicality of her approach, its emphasis on strengths, on the family and social system, and on the social worker as a consultant to be involved briefly rather than in depth over a long period of time, is congruent with the needs of Asian clients, as recognized by staff at the Family Union and referenced above. It has been interesting to the author to read her book after meeting with staff at the Family Union. I learned a great deal from the staff about reasons for the difficulty of my work with only a few Asian families. The primary difficulties seem to have come from my favorite up-close stance and slow building of relationship with clients. Ms. Berg helped me, as a family therapist, to call upon some old contracting traditions in my social work background which may help me expand my range. While Ms. Berg's work is certainly applicable to a wide range of cultures, problems, and settings, her Asian culture definitely informs the work in ways that I would not have known prior to my contact with the Family Union .

This family-based work focuses on problem-solving, rather than assessment and diagnosis of the "problem". In this way, the process of counseling/therapy need not be led by a therapist in search of causes or cures for pathology. Instead, the therapist can focus, with the client, on strengths and possibilities. Strength-based social work practice avoids the barriers inherent in problem-based work: ignoring social variables in assessrnent; ignoring variables which may retard change within the treatment system itself; and setting the stage for client passivity/professional authority (Weick, Rapp, Sullivan, and Kisthardt 1989). Moreover, when the client is a child dependent on his/her social context, the clinician needs to assess a broad range of interpersonal and environmental resources available for the child: when planning in child welfare persists in noting only family deficits, planning for particular children will most likely eventuate in placement (Proctor, Vosler, and Sirles 1993) .

The mission of the Lower East Side Family Union is prevention of placement of children outside their homes and communities. This work comes from the settlement house tradition which implies a partnership with clients and a focus on their strengths and their empowerment by means of community connections. Salvador Minuchin points out the importance, when working in foster care or in the prevention of placement, of using clinical models which respect the devastating effects of separation on children, and so which can emphasize foster family, natural family, and other supportive persons working together to meet crises and ease transitions, rather than emphasizing the severing of connections in the interests of protecting children from problematic interactions in families (Minuchin 1994). This is especially important when we realize that child-rearing problems are usual in immigrant families. Kyung-Hee Nah (1993) reported on the results of in-depth interviews with 90 Korean families who had lived in New York for less than ten years. During this transition time, families experienced high levels of stress, anxiety, and conflict particularly focused on child-rearing, since much more independence of children is encouraged in this society and since bonds with family are difficult to maintain due to financial pressures to work long hours. Conflict and family difficulties could seem to necessitate placement, and further exacerbate the difficulty in maintaining a close family in the U.S. On the other hand, as at the Family Union, when we understand the cultural conflicts, and understand that rnost adults in the family are working twelve to thirteen-hour days, we will try to help the family make some internal shifts to support everyone better, and bring in some support from the community to help the family over the transition.

Coming into the Family Union from outside its community, the author did not know the turf and felt a little anxious, but was relieved to find a similar atmosphere as at Morrisania and Cumberland facilities, a down-to-earth friendliness and warmth. After having trained and supervised many people over the years, one gets better at spotting those who seem like they will be good therapists, in that they have an ability to reach out and connect with people. Perhaps this ability cannot be trained in, but one can create a community climate in one's agency or training facility which reproduces the community existing outside the it. In minority communities, small size and few economic resources relative to the mainstream, as well as an often hostile majority community, contribute to interdependence and getting to know each other. And so the community can help to train in that quality of empathy, important especially in work with immigrant families (Domokos Cheng-Ham 1989). When we are empathic we reach out to meet and welcome someone, to try to fathom his/her experiences, and to share with him/her that experience. Emotionally and cognitively we are present, attending to subtle indirect communication and nuance between family members and ourselves in a process of mutual consultation and collaboration.

CHAPTER EIGHT:
CHARACTERISTICS OF
COMMUNITY-BASED AGENCIES

"The choices we make concerning how to deal with our power and our agency's power are crucial. We may choose to keep our power and use it in behalf of clients, or we may choose to work on policy, agency, and interpersonal levels to transfer power to clients. This is not a trivial choice, for to take the second option commits one to radical change in service delivery systems and in our practice".

--Ann Hartman
"The Professional is Political"
Social Work

******

Down-sizing and Streamlining the Bureaucracy

Social service agencies provide the context for therapy for poor and working class people in the United States who cannot afford to pay higher private practice rates. Since poor and working class people are disproportionately people of color, agencies most often set policies determining therapy for people of color. These policies provide the philosophical parameters within which clinicians operate.

Such policies and philosophical stances become institutionalized and provide continuity and stability in service provision. They reinforce and depend upon a certain structure of relationships between clients, staff, middle management/supervision, executive staff, and board. These internal relationships are reinforced in relation to other agencies, services, and institutions. Some agencies are international, with internal functioning strongly influenced by very distant authority. Particularly in the last fifteen years, when agencies have had to grapple with sharply reduced budgets, middle management has become thinner, and hours of clinical supervision of the work of staff have been fewer. This is just one of many structural changes in agencies which have occurred in response to funding cuts, and it is often viewed in a positive light, in terms of increased independence for clinicians and trust in their clinical competence.

Those who operate in the public sector using private practice models generally envision therapy to be a private contract between the individual client and the therapist. From their standpoint, less clinical supervision of the therapist's work would seem to be an advantage, like less "babysitting" or interruption of the therapist's independence. However, while supervisory "interference" in individual practice may have lessened now, time spent in accounting to non-professional representatives of managed care companies outside the agency's standards and control has increased. Administrators must attend primarily to the survival of the agency, and so cannot afford to keep "unproductive" staff who do not generate money, whether they do or do not do effective and creative therapy. Time must be spent primarily on proving the agency's efficiency, more than its expertise; and on coordination with other agency administrators around more efficiently dividing up an ever smaller funding pie, more than promoting those services needed by clients. *When programs must first of all, generate income for the agency, programming is driven by the assumptions about services held by funding institutions.*

Even the language we use in agencies flattens to fit our accountability to business "supervisors" and the accompanying computer technology, and becomes a kind of supposedly universal linguistic "prefab", but misses the depth of historical specificity or roots, ambiguity, paradox, wit, irony, subtlety, and emotional insight common in our relationships with real people (Poerksen 1995, Birkert 1994). Clinicians and their clients increasingly speak different languages when speaking English, one using words like "relationship", "communication" and "information" and the other silenced by the greater status and supposedly greater education of the expert. When the gulf increases between client and clinician, it is just one more rift between self and services in a system which has long been insensitive to the needs of the poor and people of color. But the clinician more intent on proving his/her own productivity is not likely to locate the "cause" of the rift in the changes in accountability within the agency; when clinicians are directed away from looking at their own relationships with clients, and at *changes in those relationships being maintained by both partners in the relationship, the client and the therapist.* There is an increased tendency to attribute a rift to resistance or low motivation on the part of the client. Neither the clinician nor the client is likely to realize that, for them to remedy their missed communication, they will need to address the structures and policies in the agency. When agencies are structured hierarchically and both the client and the clinician tend to be at the bottom, neither of them has enough support to call attention to problems. In Chapter Six, however, when many of the staff at Morrisania had evolved very effective systemic ways of meeting the needs of their clients, they could see effective treatment becoming impossible and quit their jobs, while many of their clients stopped coming. But, a decade after those changes at Morrisania, staff and clients have fewer alternatives if they quit, and so they try to evolve a treatment milieu which can do justice to philosophies and practice standards which are polar opposites.

Those who fund services are far removed from the life experiences of agency clients. Their membership in more privileged groups makes it hard for them to want to change a system they profit by. While clients experience reductions in already low financial assistance, social services and normal support services for families, incomes at higher levels of government/private investment have increased dramatically. In fact, structural changes in social agencies over the past decade give us a stage upon which to see social problems played out and maintained. When administrators are caught between the demands of those of privilege, who do not define client dilemmas as symptoms of serious social dislocations, but solely as evidence of individual or family dysfunction, programs reflect class, race and gender biases. Staff are paid by insurances to "treat" those who are mentally ill in some way, or, by block funding, to educate or control those individuals with character or intellectual "deficits". Community organization available thirty years ago brought normal community residents together to *demand* social change, according to definitions of client problems which included power structures in the larger society and institutions providing therapy. Clients were then demanding a voice as to how monies were spent for their benefit, and it took *social* action to influence the supposedly *private* therapist-client relationship in the public sector. Now that relationship is more controlled by business interests, with less emphasis on the agency as a social system *participating* in client problems and solutions.

However, we can assume that a client in an agency has the power to voluntarily contract with a clinician for service, because that seems to be true, at least superficially. The client need not sign an agreement for service, and can shop from agency to agency to find a compatible therapist when experiencing a crisis. Many clients do not trust the system, and so do shop around (perhaps then labelled "manipulative"); but most try to relate to whoever they are referred to, pressed by the felt urgency of their current crisis.

Ultimately, of course, the client can reject the service offered, and need not show up for the appointment. Indeed, failed appointments generally account for about 30% of staff time, even though schools, legal authorities, and child welfare/child protection often pressure poor and working-class clients to attend. When staff must fulfill a quota of direct service hours per week, they must then attract clients; and so it seems that the need to market to clients in order to keep them should ensure client power. While it may not be the same kind of power as that which controls resources and can make demands, it is power, and bears closer examination here.

Marketing to Clients: the Power of the Consumer

The Lower West Side of Buffalo, New York contains five neighborhood women's health clinics within ten blocks in this relatively small community. While it is difficult to find enough physicians, nurses, and nurse practitioners who understand the cultures, community resources and languages of the community, each clinic has slightly different options and barriers to service. When services are designed to capture insurance dollars rather than to meet community needs in a rational coordinated way, patients often go to as many of the clinics as they can, overcoming the barrier of one clinic at another and availing themselves of third and fourth options at others. Such fragmented health care is the result of marketing strategies which teach residents to shop for health items as one would shop for a new wardrobe. It has nothing to do with developing relationships with regular health care providers, nor with health care related to the whole body and whole person.

In mental health, when agencies try to attract insurance dollars, they tend to offer services, again, for more specialized problems. Thus, we see clinics specializing in eating disorders, Attention Deficit Hyperactivity Disorder, anger control. encopresis, post-partum depression,school phobia, agoraphobia, etc. All of these categories describe real human difficulties in behavior, perception, emotion, cognition, but they are diagnoses meant to be determined within an evaluative process which would place them in the contexts of the whole personality, family/work/school ecology, and historical, cultural, and social milieux. When problems are defined in terms of each individual's unique contexts, "treatment" has meaning and a sense of direction which is just not replicatible in the exact same way with any other client. However, when treatment assembles those supposedly versed in one particular behavioral problem or another, it encourages potential clients to go through a reductionist process by which they take a particular problem out of context and go to one specialist for one problem and another for another, etc. This is the American system of medical care, and it exaggerates the need for professional intervention, while undermining self-care and prevention (see Chapter One).

Before counseling was funded so much under medical "mental health" auspices, clients could go to, for example, generalist family service agencies for a wide range of family problems. Family members related to only one professional, and came to understand the connection of one family member's problem to another's, or to a family loss or crisis. The tendency was to normalize problems, so that family members had more understanding and control. If more than one therapist was involved, the usual practice was to convene all involved with the adult clients and coordinate so that the client was not overwhelmed by different opinions going off in different directions. Such coordination and normalization characterized services in Chapters Five, Six, and Seven here, but mental health services paid by insurances are not reimbursed for this kind of work. Normalization of problems would increase the client's self-care and reliance on normal community and family supports, and does not increase direct service hours. While managed care might appreciate the short-term nature of therapy which normalizes problems and treats them in context, it would not pay so readily for the tasks involved. Coordination is not categorized as direct service and, therefore, not paid for, so it has generally been continued in many agencies by a different person than the therapist, a B.A.-level case manager who specializes in coordination, and is not the therapist. This coordination can tend to promote more confusion, unless middle-management spends a good deal of time building relationships between staff members, so that their work toward specific goals with clients is "on the same wave-length". Cuts in middle-management staff and time, and a management focus on efficient use of time which discourages socialization and the building of work relationships make such internal coordination between "specialists" extremely difficult--let alone coordination with other agencies! Such are the ethical and management dilemmas in mental health settings over the past decade.

The marketing of services according to specific complaints or diagnostic categories makes sense in terms of capturing the attention of prospective clients. It starts with where the client is coming from and disseminates information which encourages clients to think in terms of symptoms as separate categories of reality, rather than what they might be symptoms *of, what they might be pointing to.* This process leads persons to seek many kinds of specialized help for many different kinds of problems; and discourages wholistic, problem-solving thinking, and preventive strategies which build on strengths and natural supports. It is much more akin to Western individualistic ways of thinking than non-Western . In the three previous chapters, those agency staff members who were members of the client community understood that services needed to reflect the predominant cultural orientations in the community. Asian-American, African-American, and Latin-American cultures cited in these chapters temper Western individual, scientific, rational orientations with spiritual, family and community understandings of reality. It would seem to follow that counseling in these communities would respect the basic cultural orientations of clients, as in those agencies cited in the previous chapters, rather than trying to convert them to European orientations.

When treatment imposes strictly European categorical thinking, it demands too much of a shift in the client's basic assumptions about reality. When the client has faith in the expertise of the therapist and is feeling vulnerable, he/she will try to adopt the assumptions underlying treatment, but will feel confused, put-down, misunderstood, and not valued. He/she will have more problems than before "therapy"; and so many clients with traditional values try to stay away from therapy, leaving it to the white middle-class clients for whom categorical thinking is natural.

But we can see from the examples of services in the three previous chapters that agencies are able to counteract the powerful pull of finances and marketing. The agency settings in the three previous chapters addressed different problem areas such as addiction; mental health; and prevention of child placement) but designed services according to the predominant cultural orientations in their communities. When agency staff and board reflected strong membership in the community, a third party was introduced into the relationship between the funding bodies and the agency, tipping the balance to allow for more culturally-appropriate services. When agency staff and board belong to the communities of their clients,the cultures of the clients have a bit more opportunity to inform services than otherwise, as in the examples given in the previous chapters. *We call these agencies "community-based" because of that common membership and the opportunity it can offer agencies for organization which is less hierarchial and less driven by marketing concerns.* It is no coincidence that non-Western cultures kept out of the mainstream historically would have preserved alternative ways to meet the needs of residents in their communities. Now these alternatives are needed by all of us in order to counter the excessive confusion and fragmentation in our services and in our lives. The benefits of cultural diversity will not be available to us through academic studies of the cultural profiles of one group or another, but in lived community relationships.

Expanding Options for Agencies

In times when funding distribution has shifted our priorities, as now, agencies with little representation from clients in their funding sources, boards, or staff are hard pressed to be sensitive to the needs of the clients they serve. Clients who do not pay fees and are not organized to demand services designed according to their cultural assumptions about reality cannot be equal partners in therapy. However, when agencies are driven to the extremes of survival, staff members can begin to experience for themselves the anxiety of threatened loss of jobs and the effects of power imbalances in society on agency structures and services, and so we *could* be better able to glimpse larger contexts for symptoms. But this glimpse is often frightening, and professionals feel caught between "either" racing after dollars to preserve their own middle-class standing "or" sticking to their ethical guns and either leaving the field or becoming as poor as their clients. *Both extremes are untenable, but we tend to see only the polarities of either power or lack of power, and not the power of social organization to effect change.* Hierarchy and Western culture teach us to understand power as a commodity which some folks have and some folks do not have, rather than inherent in each of us and magnified when we come together. We get to be in a rut in terms of the way we think about power, and so need a third party outside hierarchial and Western orientations to help us out of the rut. When an agency joins with natural community leadership to realize certain goals for its clients, the use of the community as a third party helps to avoid polarized ways of dealing with power and encourages creative thinking.

But how will mainstream agencies serving a whole city or a large rural area become members of the many communities of their clients? It must be remembered. that agencies are not community-based organizations. Community-based organizations do often provide services similar to more mainstream agencies, but are different in key respects:
1) the dominant culture(s) in the community drive the services there. This
  is exemplified by the model of the Puerto Rican social club influencing
the forms services took in our three community-based organizations;
2) the clients design services with and through their community ' s leaders
     who dominate the board membership of community-hased organizations;
3) staff are recruited primarily from the community;
4) with lower budgets, services are more often spontaneous responses to
 community concerns and more often involve community residents as
volunteer staff;
5) community-based organizations are generally formed in response to the

needs of normal residents for resources and corrections, more than from outside diagnoses of problems in a given population;

6) the primary purpose of the organization is to serve a small geographic area. Difficulties could be seen in Chapter Three when the Latin-American "Community" Center stretched its definition of community to include parts of three neighboring states

Agencies are not meant to be community-based organizations. Historically, government and private United Way/Community Chest would research the needs of a given area such as a city and would be charged with the responsibility of maintaining a balance of services to meet those needs. Different agencies had different functions, but each function was made available to all in different sections of the city through the establishment of catchment areas. These were often regional pie-shaped wedges not established according to culture or history in an area, but according to management requirements involved in administering duplicate facilities in different areas. Agencies have generally provided services from a "main" office and then several "branch" offices in different catchment areas which were to offer the same services across the board. According to this plan, cultural differences in different areas could be seen as only a different "twist" on the usual mix of services, rather than primary determinants of practice.

Since agencies extend over large geographic areas, they employ larger numbers of people according to more "objective" professional criteria established in educational institutions. They can afford to pay higher salaries,and to recruit needed skills from outside the region. Their boards must consist of powerful persons with access to the substantial resources required to run a large operation. And so agencies have always been more-or-less consciously run *by* "the majority" *for* "minority" poor and working-class, disproportionately women and people of color. Agencies have attracted great resources to meet the needs of large and diverse populations.

At this point in our history, it is obvious that we can no longer assume the prominence of one majority, the European-American. Moreover, as men have become increasingly detached from women and children in families, it seems that we can no longer contribute to their alienation by treating only the women and children who come to our offices for problems experienced in families which include men. Our class structure seems to be undergoing a radical shift to that of a Third-World dichotomy between rich and poor, so that reduced numbers of middle-class staff in agencies cannot by themselves bridge the gap between board and clients; yet agencies need to preserve their identity and ability to serve varied and large populations.

All of the agencies above, but especially the Cumberland Diagnostic and

Treatment Center in Ft Greene, operate from Africentric world views which place African-American clients at the center within their primary contexts of collective identity, kinship, and spirituality. This puts the social work practice imperative of beginning where the client is in the context of his/her community and culture (Swigonski 1996); and directs both clinician and client to "other" sources of power, beyond money and hierarchy. Clinicians in Ft. Greene, and in other communities with similar non-Western values *had mandates from their administrators to empower themselves and their clients through linkage with community, kinship, and spiritual groups.* Clinicians were not coming up with "creative" or " individual" ideas, and were not "bucking the system". They were following normal practices of empowerment in both their agencies and their communities, passed on by Africentric traditions. This does not imply that Western thinking regarding empowerment is "wrong", but that it is partial, and less useful during times of economic hardship, since it is more tied to individual wealth and status.

Agencies with Africentric as well as Western assumptions about service tend to: 1) empower staff and clients *together*, from their shared membership in community, with less separation between the two groups. This implies mutuality between staff and clients, and less "charity" or "expert" hierarchy; 2) combine expertise in the community with that in the agency--e.g.,church religious leaders or supports; 3) search for the help of extended family and kin in the clinical work; and 4) direct efforts at social change,automatically, as well as individual change. This is not from a desire to confront power (although that may be an outcome), so much as from a world-view which does not separate individual from collective reality.

Staff and clients in such agencies participate in rituals together and in the community which celebrate their history, help them grieve loss, or simply reinforce their own identity as a group, as at Morrisania. Agency administrators are connected, not only to the boards of their agencies, administrators in other agencies, and funding bodies, but also to the local organizations which enable the community to get its business done, as at Lower East Side Family Union.*The agency then becomes connected to the community's normal operation and begins to contribute to its efforts to improve*. In such agencies one sees notices or flyers about fund-raisers and local events, beyond only counseling resources. Apart from ethnicity *per se*, this participation tells residents that the agency is part of the community, belongs to them, and may be better able to understand them. Non-Western values frequently guide agencies to develop a community identity and a community base for services. This can give the agency more options when the economy shrinks.

This way of understanding how culture affects the structure of agencies through community membership is an entirely different conception of culture than the cultural profiles popular in the last decade in agencies. Many agencies have employed fewer people of color and distanced themselves from minority communities over the past 15-20 years, as federal funds have been withdrawn which encouraged inclusion and connections. Then, from a position of such increased distance, it has been easier to view non-Western cultures as "other", as categories or topics about which one can learn objective content. We have not then sought to change our personal experience or agency structures in such a way as to expose us more to these groups of people or communities, but to take certain courses in "cultural competence" which generally give us content on specific cultures *without changing the process between cultures, or exposing us to actual community structures and rituals*. These courses tend to perpetuate the status quo distance between agency and community, and between clinician and client, while offering an illusion of understanding. Generally, agencies offering such courses are not community-based, or consciously connected to the supports, resources, and cultures in the community. Alternatives or followup to these courses might be inter-agency seminars with community-based agencies, or shared projects which lessen the distance experientially.

Of course, it would be nice to know that we do not know that which we do not know. Ignorance is ethnocentric, and we tend to think that our world is the whole world. Educators are always faced with the challenge of changing ethnocentric thinking, even when the subject matter has nothing to do with ethnicity. Constructionist clinical focuses are concerned with helping us decipher, with clients and within our work settings, the ways in which our process and thinking has been constructed within a certain social context which has given us certain information about ourselves and others, and not other kinds of information. As we understand that our reality is not objective truth, but contextually based, we are encouraged to understand problems and design solutions in context (Greene Jensen and Jones 1996). The way we see our clients, and they see us, will be shaped by the ways our family, community, and agency teach us to see each other. When we understand the *limits* of our own thought and perception, we *expand* our own possibilities: we connect to our own unique ethnic and cultural heritage, beyond ethnocentrism; and we realize the importance of connecting to other cultures with other perspectives and solutions, in order to resolve serious problems in our communities and in society. This sense of self-esteem and connection to others which comes from knowledge of our roots is important to positive mental health, a way of seeing *personal power in connection to social, political and economic power, and spiritual resources in conjunction with political and economic ones* (Pinderhughes 1989).

United States history is one of oppression of the poor and people of color. However, it is also a history of the attempts of many people of diverse backgrounds to live together peacefully. In communities, diversity is expressed and available for social agencies to tap into and learn from Communities can help in concrete ways: agencies can link to community-based organizations in various communities at administrative levels, coordinating their efforts in joint programs; and at line levels, doing co-therapy with some cases or running groups together. Agencies and community-based organizations can train each others' staffs, share information about effective clinical frameworks to use with community residents. Agencies can share larger economic resources with commun-ity-based organizations who have much smaller budgets; and community-based organizations can link agencies to informal networks which support residents, but of which formal agencies are seldom aware.

Residents can be enlisted as trained volunteers in poor communities, running agency groups, locating resources for clients, and performing other valuable functions. This gives unemployed residents a chance to develop a service background which could increase their employability, and it helps to focus those who do therapy on the normal social and economic needs of their clients. Agency board and staff members can offer to participate in volunteer efforts in the community, such as fundraisers or ethnic festivals. Such participation fosters relationships and the social organization which is basic to an increase in power and effectiveness.

None of this is "new", just as our agency examples are not unique or rare. Social work traditions have linked agencies to poor communities for generations. However, with few resources and greater class, race/ethnic, and gender divisions as we end this millenium, it is more difficult for agencies to connect to the communities they serve.

Support for Administrators

It is not a new problem that those in agencies who have knowledge of the community served are those at the bottom of the hierarchy, case managers or aides who have less professional education. If these staff members want to increase their salary and status, they must then get more education in therapy fields which do not understand their knowledge of community to be a clinical skill...and so the prospective clinician must start all over and learn new skills which do not build on the old ones. If clinicians want to increase their salary and status, they must move into super-vision/administration. These positions do not require either knowledge of the community or significant clinical experience,but more management experience/education...and so the prospective administrator must start all over and learn new skills which do not build on the old ones. Levels of hierarchy value certain skills *over* others, and each level has a knowledge base *separate from* the other levels. This system discourages a high level of expertise within each level. Case managers are not paid to go back to school to increase skills in case management with higher salary; social workers are not paid to go back to school for doctorates or to take advanced clinical training so that they will stay clinicians at a higher rate of pay.

So much of what we accept as natural in the structuringof our agencies is geared to maintaining hierarchy and the accumulation of significant expertise (thus, power) at lower hierarchial levels, among line staff. This limits clinical expertise and helps us to think of effective solutions in terms of good solutions *for the organization*, respecting administrative power. While this accepted structure promotes loyalty to the organization, it can become too geared to the upper end of the hierarchy when resources are severely limited and lower level staff fear for their jobs. Administrators need to find ways to keep clinical work rewarding and rewarded for the clinician in the public sector, and often use training for this purpose.

It is difficult for administrators of agencies serving large areas, and without a lot of prior community or therapy experience, to have and maintain a vision of services which is really based on any concrete experience of client needs and solutions. Administrators will listen to middle-management carefully, but with an ear attuned primarily to existing resources. While administrators do, of course, also get information from direct service staff, this information cannot be heard in the same way in hard times as it is when financial survival is not top priority. Moreover, direct service staff does, and should, rely on those in positions of authority to give it clear mandates for service. When direct service staff are left "on their own" to interpret as they see fit, this will work only so long as their work falls within the unspoken but nonetheless real service priorities of the agency. Agencies need particularly strong administrators now, but this means those who use *extra supports* to enable them to stay in touch with the experience of clients' needs without becoming overwhelmed

When agencies serve poor people and people of color, their policies and staff perceptions must be wide enough to encompass many values. This makes agencies very interesting places in which to do therapy. Conflict and contradictions will be part of the work, and administrators will tend to deal with it in several ways. During times of retrenchment, they can try to: 1) control it, setting up staff development and recruitment which encourage conformity with the expectations of managed care and other funding. This promises to cut down on the emount of conflict by cutting down on diversity. Or they can: 2) resist change, setting up staffing and policies which accord more with the demands of grass-roots community leadership. However, if the agency's purpose is to provide therapy and not community-organization, its administrator will need to attend to the credentialing requirements for payment/funding, if the agency is to stay in business. Often, the choice for administrators feels like "being caught between a rock and a hard place", as if one must choose between maintaining diversity and community connections while going out of business or playing by the rules of funding sources while sacrificing diversity.

Administrators who have polarized their choices in this way have not just been rigid individuals, but have understood the institutional difficulties of promoting diverse programming in the 1990's. In revising the final chapters of this book, the author came upon a book which was an "aha experience" in terms of these administrative dilemmas, although not directly about them: Santiago Colas' *Postmodernity in Latin America: the Argentine Paradigm*. This is not a book at all about therapy or agencies. Rather, it analyses three Argentinian novels, relating ways in which the organization of these novels parallels political changes in Argentina. While it might beg the reader's patience a bit too much, a digression into the connections made by Colas in Argentina casts some light on agency programs in the United States.

Colas (1994) compares three novels: *Rayuela*, by Julio Cortazar; *El Beso de la Mujer Arana*("The Kiss of the Spider Woman") by Manuel Puig; and*Respiracion Artificial* ("Artificial Respiration") by Ricardo Piglia. In *Rayuela*, the main character is committed to finding a "happy ending"for himself, but finds, along the way, ordinary relationships, which he decides to leap into, whether or not they are only a detour; the novel is concerned about the value in making this leap *per se*, whatever the consequences. Colas parallels this with the Latin American search for Utopia as a product of its encounter with Europe, a search which blinded people to the shortcomings in the present and paralyzed their ability to deal with those shortcomings. Rather than to continue to reify Utopia, Cortazar espouses a "leap" into social change, exernplified by the Cuban revolution's seeming ability in the 1960s in Latin America to provide a way to cast off the paralysis since European colonization, a way in which there were no gray areas, and the need for conflictual politicking could be replaced by a sudden break from history. In *El Beso...*, Manuel Puig identifies an inherent problem in any totalizing Utopia, whether the "old" or the "new" replacement for the old. He sees hope in the laborious critical procedure of deconstructing and then reconstructing history, not in leaving the past behind but in envisioning Utopia as continually in crisis. He wrote from exile in the mid-1970s in the period in Argentina in which Peron's repressive "totalizing Utopia" was not yet in full flower, and when resistance could be expressed indirectly; and when the Cuban revolution could be seen to be a Utopia in crisis. Ricardo Piglia wrote *Respiracion Artificial*, however, inside Argentina during the first savage years of Peron's regime. He saw that the regime foreclosed the possibility of an oppositional historical representation by fragmenting social life and filling it with such authoritarian logic that the public sphere became privatized. In order to shape the movement of history, connections between the public and the private spheres of life would need to be reestablished. And so Piglia wrote about a man who was disappeared, just as the regime did not openly kill, but disappeared, thousands of Argentinian youth. Importantly, those who are the best witnesses to the movement of history are swept aside into marginal locations where they have the least access to the discourses through which history is narrated. Piglia's novel is concerned with building a bridge from fragmented personal experience to public expression and change.

The author's "aha" came in seeing a similar purpose for this book. The agency is a place where such bridging can happen. Of course, it is not explicitly concerned with social change and is funded mostly for individual symptom relief of clients, divorced from social context. This role alone gives staff plenty of responsibility. Many administrators keep this role very carefully delineated, but promote diversity by seeking out and maintaining other supports in the community, in its grass-roots organizations and spiritual and political leaders, as in Chapter Seven; or they share authority with department heads who will make these community connections and then inform the executive, as in Chapter Five; or they *participate with other agencies in the same geographical area in a common project which combines and coordinates resources.* This kind of coordination, especially when it involves *natural* leadership in the community, makes the geographic community the organizer for services. It enables personal experiences of those in the community to directly influence policies of the agencies which serve them, and so creates a bridge from the personal to the public levels of experience. It takes some inordinately weighty responsibility off the shoulders of agency administrators, and helps them to feel more connected to client contexts and less alienated from their needs. *Agencies can help therapists to relate more personally to their clients by having membership in clients' communities, and by setting up experiments out of this common community membership.* Administrators who do this know that they need other sources of information and support beyond managerial and financial. Community linkages enable service visions to be maintained, during hard times, which are based more on the actual lived realities of clients than on the assumptions of those far removed from these realities.

CHAPTER NINE:
BUFFALO FAMILY SYSTEMS TRAINING,
IN RETROSPECT

"Intuition can erode the barrier between science and art. Much of the knowledge practitioners seek resides in the action, rather than preceding the action. Intelligence resides within the act of using one's body and mind together to meet some changing aspect of the environment. People come to know their world through full immersion, participation, and identification with it. Eros or "soul" is essential to knowing. In practice, if we want people to feel understood, it is necessary to become a person who does understand."

--Elizabeth A. Gowdy
"From Technical Rationality to Participating
Consciousness", *Social Work*

******

With   Carmen delValle, Christine Douds, Carolyn Lee, Anne
Marie Smith, Margo Villagomez, and Lillie Washington

Our Design and Our Goals

Buffalo Family Systems Training (BFST) was an incorporated family therapy training institute begun by four women who brought together credentialled family therapy supervision and extensive life/work experience and knowledge of the Lower West Side community in Buffalo, where we established a storefront facility in 1983. Our goal was to train people from our community, or working in it, using *their experience* as the basis for the work. Trainees contracted with us for 1-3 years of work, meeting over ten months of the year in 4-hour weekly practicum training groups of 4-5 trainees each. Since the work was hands-on practicum training, it involved the use of a one-way mirror, with the training team and supervisors observing one of the trainees working with a family, and offering suggestions and help to the trainee and family in many different ways. Each team had two supervisors: Carmen delValle and Margo Villagomez were direct supervisors in different groups, and Jane Piazza worked with all the groups as a consultant to the direct supervisors. Since Spanish is a primary language with families in the community, it was spoken primarily or often in all groups, with translations available, then, for those who spoke only English. A prerequisite for training was that applicants had to have significant experience in the Lower West Side community and its cultures and/or plan to use training to enhance further work in the community.

Trainees needed to have a minimum of a high school diploma as a prerequisite, but did not need advanced clinical training. Since our training was *experientially* based in their history in the community and then in *practicum* work, we thought that we could design a training experience which would be comfortable for many different levels of education, and that *the mix would encourage everyone's growth*. However, many of our trainees were professionals, and some were very advanced professionals. We assigned readings and papers for trainees to do, as we got to know them and could get a sense of their particular interests, needs, and talents; and as the teams each evolved their own identities. Readings and academic work were secondary, and meant to amplify learning experiences we were having with particular families (which was a challenge for the consultant to keep a huge file of journal articles and keep connected to a wide range of material, so that she could match an article to the immediate need of the group).

In addition to academic augmenting of the practicum experience, various community leaders came in to give lectures about other resources and work going on with families in the community, and about relevant cultural and historical influences on family life. Often trainees needed to make an emergency contact or home visit between training sessions, or various members of the team worked together with a family, so that one trainee might attach himself to an acting-out teen and another to a depressed mother, often in the position of a benevolent "auntie" or mentor, adding to the intensity of the overall family work. At times we used the team as a temporary extended family for overwhelmed families who might have lost important leadership due to immigration, addiction, or death. We encouraged our trainees and our families to link with the community's political and social organizations and churches, just as we also participated in them.

We frequently invited into sessions with families their religious advisors, other counselors, child protection, foster care, and probation officers, often trying to get this whole helping network to support each other in new ways. We focused usually on helping severely acting-out family members get more powerful support in order to make the desired changes; and we detoured or defused conflicts between *natural* extended family and healing systems and the *formal service system.* In teams,*we tried to match the intensity of the divisions and stresses experienced by our families, so that interventions could have enough power to effect change in seriously symptomatic persons.* We tended to get referrals both from agencies and by word of mouth from one family to another. Many families had known of our work in the community individually, most often the work of Carmen or Margo; and knowing who we were personally was very important, assuring clients that they would be understood and treated confidentially, and that they would be able to express the *full range of problems and feelings they were experiencing*, rather than to have to restrict themselves only to cognitive and reductive ("one problem at a time") modes of presentation. Due to this pattern of referral,we often worked with more traditional Hispanic families who felt comfortable coming to our small place, but avoided agencies. Agencies tended to refer more difficult cases which they felt could use the support of our consultation and training. So we were filling a gap in the service network.

Counseling was without a fee, but all families were encouraged to donate whatever they could into our general fund, which was used to keep up our supply of coffee and snacks. A few families offered donations in terms of home-made food or skills repairing our video equipment or plumbing. We accepted these rare in-kind donations, but did not have any kind of formal barter system. Trainees paid tuitions on a sliding scale. Over the course of the four years of our operation, we wrote twenty-nine proposals to obtain grant funding from federal, state, and local government and private foundation sources, but were only successful in obtaining a small grant from New York State. Lack of adequate funding was a constant problem. At times we gave lectures or workshops or provided consultation to agencies to bring in income but, for the most part, we were only able to pay operating expenses and not salaries. This meant that the three of us (our fourth partner, Elizabeth Bishop, had died unexpectedly shortly before we opened our office) supervised groups two evenings a week and on Saturday mornings, while working other full-time jobs during the day and raising teenaged children. Financial stresses eventually closed the institute in 1987.

However, the absence of stable funding enabled us to design the program the way we wanted it. We could do what was clinically indicated, without accounting to funding sources. We could set up an atmosphere in which there was always a pot of coffee in the waiting room, and generally some crackers or cookies, for people who might be hungry or cold; we thought it rude to expect poor and hungry people to focus on the work of sessions without helping them to take the edge off their hunger. We could set up a schedule with flexibility enough to handle families dropping in "on our way to the store this afternoon" at times. We required that trainees be responsible only for a record with accurate intake sheet information and a log of contacts made in behalf of/with each family, so that paperwork accounted for very little of their time. Carmen could design,with other community leaders, a candlelight ceremony to help families grieve the loss of loved ones in the 1986 mud slide in Puerto Rico; and we could have our trainees participate in this, along with their client families. We could accompany a Native American family to the reservation to bury their son again according to longhouse traditions and unite the family and help them grieve larger family and cultural losses, in order to stop a rash of suicide attempts in that family.

Four of us founded BFST out of convictions that poor people and people of color needed to identify strongly with the therapy process in order for it to have any power, just as with middle-class or white people; that poor people and people of color suffered the usual stresses of those with more privilege in this society, intensified by the difficulties of surviving in poverty and in a culture in which one was on the outside (not "majority") constantly; and that therapy needed to use expansive enough interventions to impact these difficulties. We felt that general counseling/social work training provided a good base for necessary work, but that *advanced* training should be available to teach therapists interventions befitting the needs in our community. The power of majority culture and institutionalized agency practices made it difficult for therapists often to even realize that they were not joining families well enough to effect change. When the therapist could not see his/her own part in the failure of the therapy, it looked as though families were "hard-to-reach", "multiproblem", "crisis-oriented", "resistant", or "abnormal" in some way, and left families with all the responsibility of failed therapy, even though they had many fewer resources. We located problems in treatment systems as well as the clients served, so believed that change also needed to occur in treatment systems. We tried to design interventions which would enable *change for the whole system(client and therapist), and more shared responsibility and communication between those giving and those receiving services.* We had observed a lack of fit between services and families on the Lower West Side when the strengths of families were not acknowledged, from which one could then build successful, positive, up-beat change in a relatively short time. In the community, we had had so many experiences of people moving on out of poverty, being extremely wise elders or teachers, or building good connections to their extended families, churches, and neighbors that we wanted to teach therapists how to be aware of strengths like this and use them directly in clinical work. We wanted to expand the range of interventions for therapists who served this community in many different settings.

Influences Which Set the Stage for Our Work

Before we talk about BFST, we have to talk about the organization which spurred our growth. Three of the four founders of BFST came of age as social workers, and then family therapists, at Child and Family Services of Erie County , a family service agency well-respected in Buffalo for many years. It was the result of a merger in the 1970's of two private agencies, Family Services Association and the Society for the Prevention of Cruelty to Children. The main downtown office for the merged agency came to be the building which had housed the latter of the two agencies, located quite close geographically to the Lower West Side, but quite far away culturally. Families identified the building as "that place where they took your children away", and were afraid to go there. Class issues played into this discomfort, with the building being well-appointed and on a main avenue which projected a sedate middle-class atmosphere. The agency's board had no representation from the community, and the agency did not belong to any of the community's organizations. It had no bilingual bicultural staff.

However, in the 1970's, administrators came on board after the merger who were determined to examine some policies relative to minority communities. The agency had established a Reach-Out Program in the black community and a West Side Services outreach office, and was beginning tobe sensitized by some of the tensions between the mainstream organization and its grass-roots "wing". The agency offered tuition assistance to Carmen delValle to complete study for her MSW degree, and then supervisors Carolyn Docrat and Bob Nelson listened to her recommendations for some changes in service which involved reaching out to the community at board, administrative,and line service levels. Carmen's work in the downtown office exemplified a policy shift: 1) she was a trained professional, so that her bilingual bi-cultural work was considered therapy,and was not given the *lesser* connotation of other bicultural work done in Reach-Out by those without MSW degrees; and 2) she did work similar to that done in Reach-Out as a therapist, leaving the office a lot for home visits, advocacy for clients, and large-system work to help groups of client families to better meet their needs.

The mid-1970's was an exciting era for Child and Family Services, and a fortunate time in which to work there. Administrators encouraged supervisors Alice Kennedy and Carolyn Docrat to work with their staffs in innovative ways, and there evolved a great team spirit and sharing in the downtown office among therapists. Weekly staff meetings centered on case presentations, but also were think-tank meetings of a kind none of us has experienced in agencies since then. Administrators were focused   on bringing diverse staffs together after the merger, so that effective expression and resolution of differences was worked at on a weekly basis and in frequent parties and a yearly staff retreat weekend for play and brainstorming together. Jane Piazza and Carmen delValle became friends while working together in the downtown office during this time, and were given models of supervision which made a lasting impression. The kind of respectful focus on group process and the real interest and encouragement given to individual therapists nurtured their professional development, and that of many other staff members. It was truly a wonderful place to work, and leaving after thirteen years was difficult for both Carmen and Jane.

One project the agency encouraged was a training program in family therapy, partially paying for Jane to attend two training programs at Philadelphia Child Guidance Clinic in 1980, with plans to train two teams which would bring together three Reach-Out and three downtown staff for one year for 2½ days/week per team. This was a tremendous allotment of staff time for training, and would be unheard of now! Our grant proposal was funded, which enabled us to do the training without taking any monies out of regular program monies, and we set up headquarters in the basement with family and observation rooms separated by a one-way mirror, and with another large program room.

We inherited some structural difficulties: the director of Reach-Out had not been involved in the conceptualization of the project or the writing of the grant proposal, so that he was asked, *after* parameters had already been established, to relinquish three staff for many hours each week for training in therapy. There had been some positive bridges built between the staffs of Reach-out and downtown, but the fact that the salaries for "counseling" done by black "paraprofessionals" was so much less than that paid for "therapy" done by white professionals downtown,and that teaching in the agency went more in the direction from downtown to Reach-Out than the reverse promoted tension between the two offices. Then, introducing our training in this way did not give it much support from Reach-Out, so that initially our Family Therapy Training Program was a lightening rod for the tension and unresolved racial and class tension in the agency. Our separation into a part of the building not often visited by other staff persons tended to isolate us from the flow in the downtown office,and our schedule did not often allow us to attend regular unit meetings, although the training was a part of the downtown unit. We found ourselves often straddling two worlds, without strong connection to structural administrative supports.

However, the work itself was stimulating and rewarding, as we were referred very difficult family situations and experienced meaningful positive shifts with our families. We spent a lot of time out of the office as well as behind the mirror, and we went together to many out-of-town family therapy conferences. We invited in well-known family therapists to consult with us, notably Peter Urquhart and Barbara Bryant-Forbes from Philadelphia Child Guidance Clinic. The work was exhausting, but fun. As the participating staff members returned to their regular offices again full-time after the program, Jane continued to consult with them for 2 hours/week for another year, helping them to implement what they had learned.

Getting Started

Toward the end of the program at Child and Family Services, we were contacted by several clinicians outside the agency who wanted to participate in the training, so we put their names on a list for referral and explained that we were only operating a specific small training program for our staff. Then one of these persons suggested that we do another training group, so we approached the executive director to get permission to use the facilities for a training group on Saturday mornings, when the agency was closed. We began this group in 1983, informally calling ourselves "Buffalo Family Systems Training". As others requested training, we rented space for the community storefront which would continue to be our home until we closed in 1987, and we incorporated under the same name.

We recruited a board from our associations in the community. It was composed primarily of community leaders and educators who were often *much more involved with us than is usual for board members*: 1) board members came in to lecture on the history of the community; 2) they helped us design interventions for families which would involve the whole community; 3) they served as "elders" who could advise, in a very structured way, those families who had lost their elders in immigrating to Buffalo, and who were out of control, with symptoms such as repeated physical of sexual abuse (Piazza and delValle 1992); 4) they helped us to twice replace video equipment when it was stolen; and 5) leaders provided legal and accounting work for us free of charge or low-cost, and helped us with the business aspects of things.

In addition to being connected to the community through our board members, *trainers at BFST regularly attended meeting of several community organizations, and participated in numerous fund-raisers, campaigns, and community functions. This took a lot of time outside our normal training hours, but it informed our clinical work, giving us ideas for large-system interventions which would be appropriate to what was going on in the community.* In this work, we would often encounter client family members. This did not present us with a threat to confidentiality, since we all knew that data from BFST would never leave BFST; rather, it gave us a context in which trainers/therapists and clients were peers. *When training flowed from the institutions in the community in which both clients and therapists were nurtured, the power differential in therapy could shift to more of an equal partnership in the process of therapy.* We found that our work with families could happen more as a collaboration when we had this common ground in the community.

Over the four years of our operation, we trained about forty counselors, most of them for a one-year period, about ten of them for two years, and five completing three years. Trainees were selected primarily from the community, and were interested in continuing to work for the benefit of the community. They were counselors in schools, mental health and health clinics, alcoholism/drug facilities, and private agencies. They were "para"professionals and professionals. Ethnically, trainees tended to reflect the composition of the community, being primarily Hispanic, with also a number of African-American and Native American trainees, and only one European American.

Reflections of Some Trainees

A few of us who participated in the training at BFST have come together to talk about what that experience was like for us. Mostly, it was fun, it was stimulating, and there was a lot going on. We can still use what we learned there in work with clients,and we were encouraged, by the certificates we earned at BFST, to do advanced levels of work after that. It's been interesting that the master's level of work some of us have done after BFST has been much less demanding of us and informative of our process that that at BFST; however, the certificates earned at BFST could not give us much clout for professional advancement without a master's degree gotten elsewhere, even though Jane was an AAMFT-approved family therapy supervisor. While we knew this up-front, of course, it's still an example of the difficulty in finding education which applies to the community and the realities here, and then getting credit for it. To try to do real work here,and get paid, you have to do *both*: another example of the adage that if you're minority you have to work twice as hard. But most of us are in more bureaucratic settings now,and not in community-based settings. We can try to make those settings a bit more aware of the communities served,but that's a big task.

There always was a big gap between our work experience, when we were in training, and the experience at BFST. Then, family work was not as acceptable in my own drug treatment setting as it is now, so that it was not possible to get time off for training or any help with tuition. Often, when supervisors knew you were taking extensive training in a modality they did not understand, they got an attitude, which made it extra hard on you. We did wish that Margo, Jane, and Carmen could have worked with supervisory and administrative staff in our agencies to help them understand the frameworks somewhat,and to help them plan how to use our skills.When this was done with two of our agencies, it was much easier for us. We had talked about this somewhat, but there just wasn't time then.

We did feel that we got a lot of support in training, and that we became closer to the team and more knowledgeable about resources. We were surprised at how easy it could be to actually get families and networks together, and how much in sync that was for our own family- and community-oriented cultures and values.that part made the training easier, being able to work more according to our own values. It was good to see changes in families and in ourselves. We liked formulating ideas or a plan on the spur of the moment, and comparing cultural interpretations. When some of us on the same team were from South America, some from Cuba, some from Puerto Rico, and some from Mexico, it was easy to see how superficial the word "Hispanic" was: so many different meanings to the same Spanish words, so many ways to perceive behaviors!

We were glad for the live supervision. In educational experiences and conferences since then we have learned, but not in ways which really help to really jump in there and work with the family. We worked often with very large families at BFST, and so that stopped intimidating us and helped us to understand "family" beyond just "household". Most of our colleagues now say they work with families,but what they really mean is usually the child's mother. It's hard to keep remembering that one individual *has* a family when you're in an agency which defines the individual as the client, and when the insurance is geared to the individual...hard for us, even, who grew up encouraged to value extended family and community.

The system of two levels of supervision at BFST was really helpful. Jane moved fast and jumped to an intervention with a family fast, often doing things which were unpredictable. It was good to watch her, but hard to follow her thinking. Carmen or Margo would often slow her down to our pace or get her to explain to us why she did certain things. They often interpreted to us why the intervention made sense to them without really asking her, or called in to interrupt it if they disagreed, or we all went in to talk about it with the family. Carmen and Margo were closer to us and the actual supervisors, while Jane was further out there, sort of suggesting things you never would have thought about and didn't have to commit to. Without Carmen or Margo she would have been intimidating, but with both levels you were encouraged to try new things. While certain skills like reframing have become part of our usual practice, we don't seem to have learned one *method* to apply in our work. We often remember back to the variety of solutions tried at BFST and they really were individual, for those specific families. We can't just apply them to totally different situations. However, we are in the habit of looking for strengths. We do work from the community base and share knowledge with our clients, and they with us, about how to keep body and soul together nowadays. We can often imagine ways to handle a problem now by thinking what the team at BFST would have done with it. We do remember the good results with families, and think that that is still possible in our work, even though that work is now in totally different contexts.

We wish we could have had more time in the training groups to get to know each other. In Carmen's groups, she often started by having the group talk together for a number of times at first about their growing up in the community, with its special values and history, in a personal way. This gave those trainees a real way to get to know each other and see each other as expert, based on their community membership, right up front. We think trainers should have done that in all the groups, so that we could work from the community relationships which were our strength and the basis for the family therapy. Without that grounding, it was often too pressured and rushed,and we wished that we would have more "no-shows" so that we could talk more. We liked having community leaders come in,and liked going out to the community and participating in the grieving rituals, but this took a lot of energy, especially when the weather was terrible. Alone, without the group support we had then, it is hard to imagine doing those kinds of interventions.

The Significance of BFST for Family Therapy

The operation of BFST took shape from the ongoing relationships of its three founders and trainers, Carmen, Margo and Jane, to the community, to other educational institutions and mainstream agencies, and to each other. With so little time and money available, we "administered" BFST in regular short dinners with each other or on the way to meetings elsewhere. We clearly wish we had not been so rushed, and that we had had more time to develop connections to administrators and supervisory staff which employed our trainees at the time. But our use of time was prioritized in order to allow us to talk out stressful things with each other and get support from each other. Without this priority, our wires could easily have gotten crossed, and trainees would have been triangulated between conflicting expectations of supervisors. The dual level of supervision depended on our trust of each other.

In our past family therapy training or experience giving training in a university setting, we had been encouraged to set clear boundaries between trainees and trainers, as between therapists and client families. We were encouraged to take firm control of the process behind the mirror, directing the team to see some patterns in sessions which they would tend to overlook. Generally, we had been taught that, with experience, we would be able to see behavioral sequences and intervene in them quicker. While we agreed with this, our experience in both CFS and BFST training programs led us to soften and share supervisory control more than we had been taught to do. Members of our training teams talked quite a bit to each other behind the mirror, often in very fast Spanish, and often with a great deal of disagreement as to what various behaviors meant (often representing a wide mix of cultures). Spanish was spoken in all groups, and was often the first language used. The decision to speak Spanish, then, in spite of Jane's poor Spanish, was important. It reinforced our intention that the levels of training not be hierarchial ones, with Jane automatically viewed as the one at the "top", since she was Anglo and had more formal family therapy training. We needed Jane's skills, but no more so than we needed Carmen's and Margo's. Generally, we found that it was more appropriate culturally , and appropriate to our styles as women, for us to intervene more slowly and to tolerate more ambiguity and contradictory impressions from the team as to how to intervene. We often shared our confusion with families, and had them help us to sort it out, sometimes in the Pick-a-Dali Circus Model (Landau-Stanton 1983), but often just more straightforwardly with family members. It seemed that *our choice of language, our multiculturality, our community base, and our styles as women all necessitated some differences in the authority and structure of training.* Sacks expresses well our experience:

> The activity of leadership as network building draws on familial, communal, and life-cycle events to express its logic. Leadership, in this view, becomes a practice for establishing networks that sustain connections among members of a political group and augment formal ties by means of rituals that stress family and life-cycle events and make use of a familylike set of symbols that cross racial and class lines (Sacks 1989, 119).

DiStefano (1990) makes sense of this sort of network-building style of authority as "postrationalism", a transcending of the Enlightenment linear discourse with its belief in "objective" truth. Rather, postrational discourse recognizes all experience and truth as subjective and partial, limited to one's experiences. Constructionist family therapists have certainly deconstructed linear hierarchial thinking in this way in recent years (for example, White and Epston 1990). However, during the time of our work at BFST, we relied on our multicultural and community-based context to teach us roughly the same non-hierarchial lessons. Our work seems a bit similar to the "Just Therapy" work done in local community development projects through The Family Centre in Lower Hutt, New Zealand (Waldegrave 1990). A small group of therapists banded together there originally with the intention to address race, class, and gender imbalances in their own work; and to discover how to work together by unearthing and using knowledges which had been "minority" or disqualified. As we tried to do, they moved away from the international and intercultural models, and found psychology explanations of family problems insufficient to address the social nature of those problems:

> Denying the lack of access to survival resources for 20% and often 30% of people in Western societies is to deny the influence of these factors on the problems presented in therapy. Such an approach ensures ongoing self-deprecation and dependency(*Ibid.*, 25).

These therapists positively connoted family members' behaviors in the context of the powerful social and political problems of discrimination and lack of resources faced. They openly discussed with staff and clients the effects of racism, sexism, and classism on all of their behaviors. Similarly, Paolo Freire, a noted Brazilian educator, developed collegial methods of education which would promote social change; and developed a set of questions which could be used to focus student and teacher (or client and therapist) on the systemic power dynamics inherent in their relationship, opening up these "sacred cows" for examination and change. These questions arose out of the non-hierarchial experience of community between teacher and student (Freire 1990). Freire's work reminds us of the work trainers at BFST did in the community, side by side with clients and trainees, and the effects this had on the nature of our therapeutic communication, with clients more actively engaged as peers. *Community mediates between the larger society and individuals; and when therapists connect to community, their interventions become more socially aware, more just, and less scapegoating to individuals in therapy*(See Chapter Two for Korin's discussion of Freire).

Issues of power are not new in systems therapies. Feminist family therapists such as Goldner (1985) and Goodrich, Rampage, Ellman , and Hallstead (1988) remind us of the danger of diagnosing too narrowly, through a lens which only encompasses the nuclear family and not the effect on family functioning from power imbalances in the larger society.

Community leaders and community organizers are constantly aware of these power imbalances and, when we work with them, our vision gets larger. At BFST, we tried to make clinical work fit community concerns, such as the ritual to help families grieve after the 1986 mud slide in Puerto Rico. This is akin to family therapy's attention to culturally sensitive work, when the trainer educates herself as to the culture and ways of working of the trainee/client, and then designs training/therapy to fit this culture (Schwartz 1988), rather than lecturing or imposing a "new" framework and expecting it to be put on eagerly, like a new coat. Celia Falikov explores effective ways in which to introduce cultural perspectives into family therapy training, offering that culture should not be taught as a separate course apart from the meaningful context of training, but that it should be integrated into the family's ecosystemic ways of conceptualizing problems and into the relationship issues between therapist and client (Falicov 1988). Often in education, we introduce training topics in abstract ways, out of context (topics such as culture, grief/loss issues, or communication). *Our educational system is biased toward this kind of process in which we move from general theory to specific examples of it. Family therapy, with its focus on live supervision and tape review, helps us to draw our ideas more from specific data. Community-based work, likewise, helps us to draw our ideas about systems from our actual participation in community*. At this level of participation, it is easier to see that destructive patterns in families are maintained by policies in larger systems, as well as patterns within those families.

Training is a political process, conferring expertise on some more than others, and offering "appropriate " clinical frameworks. When trainers make their expertise second to that of the small grass-roots community, they are helping to reverse the process of fragmentation and alienation in education and in therapy. The community is the healing force for clients, trainees, and trainers. It provides mid-range structures which can mediate the effects of societal deprivation and advocate for more of society's resources for resident families. By working in the community to strengthen its organizations and small institutions,and working *with* our clients, we realize the appropriate limits of any therapeutic models, alleviating burnout. Concrete material needs are not separate from psychic and interpersonal needs, nor are "environmental" functions given to a specialist such as a case manager, while "psychic" functions are given to a specialist such as a therapist. Interventions must be down-to-earth and practical,the antithesis of family therapy training being marketed now at international levels, due to the lack of funding for training in this country.

At BFST we often experienced our work to be *distinct from* the family therapy training which had been helpful to us and to our communities, but which had not been close enough to it. In part, of course, we were suffering from our own "first stage" of learning in which one notices *differences from* the previous mode, and so makes a linear stab at arriving at something which is *more* useful, rather than adding on to the old repertoire and not needing to make the old mode outmoded. Western education invites polarities of *either-or*, when new knowledge must be *either* dispensed with *or* be a replacement for the old. However, the fact that our trainees and trainers reflected various non-Western cultures made *either-or* ways of thinking just not very interesting or helpful. Contradictions were accepted as "that's life" or "go with the flow". With this kind of atmosphere, we could feel comfortable about departing from the styles of those who had trained us, while not "throwing out the baby with the bath water". We wanted to *use* various family therapy frameworks in our training, but without teaching one model, keeping the community's ways of handling differences and hierarchy in training, and this differed in ways earlier explained in this chapter.

We continued to teach a lot of structural family therapy. We liked its concreteness and its attention to power dynamics in families(Aponte 1976, Minuchin and Fishman 1981). We had gone on for more training at University of Rochester Family Therapy Training Program, and had incorporated also some of the strategic focus on communication and brief transitional work with extended families taught there (Landau-Stanton 1981). These fit the immigration experiences of those we worked with and fit more with the positive ways we had of viewing our families. We tended to identify with families due to our community base and so found it difficult to achieve the distance necessary to see them as "dysfunctional". As we worked together longer we got better at keeping the focus on our families and community connections more than on one model or another, taking pieces of this or that model as it fit and discarding others. We also liked the Brief Therapy Solution-Focused model of Steve deShazer and Insoo Berg in Milwaukee (de Shazer 1985; and expressed later by Berg 1994) because it was concrete like structural work but more attuned to client strengths than deficits.

We learned that training only according to one model or another promoted more hierarchy and distance between trainers and trainees. It stepped up our pace and made us focus on getting a certain amount of material learned rather than making the material fit where the trainees were coming from. We used a way of working in which Carmen and Margo were primary trainers and set the pacing of the work according to the needs of individual trainees and client families. Jane consulted with them and took a faster pace with more distance, offering alternative interventions from various models which would then be re-shaped by the primary trainers to fit the appropriate style and timing for the group.

We encouraged, first and foremost, a *lot* of sharing in groups from the trainees' own life and work experiences, validating that experience constantly as a basis for interventions and ideas: how would you handle this problem in your own family? in Colombia...Peru...Puerto Rico? in your agency? We wanted to envision solutions with our clients which would *be close to* and *fit* their life and community experiences, rahter than putting them in the uncomfortable position of respecting the expert therapist and trying to understand advice which "must be important and something I should do" even when it did not fit, at a time when they were already vulnerable.

We focused the therapy team generally behind the mirror and the family team in front of it on finding a common theme which would help us all to understand the family's current dilemma. This "theme" would usually include: a) a positive reframe, a way of understanding what appeared to be negative behaviors in terms of their useful functions for the family; b) historical and social contexts for symptoms, then suggesting future possible outcomes if choices were made to discontinue the symptoms; and c) the need for economic, political, and family supports, if the choice was not to continue the symptoms, giving examples as to how the support system would have to expend in order for change to occur. We respected the difficulty of change, and the really serious grief and loss issues in our families, often complicated by poverty and lack of resources as well as addiction, domestic and street violence. In order for us to maintain a hopeful stance and faith that we could help families effect meaningful changes in their lives, we had to believe in their inherent ability to take control when significantly more support was available to them. We had to be ready to deliver such support,and to help their natural supports and agency supports to shift a bit so as to be able to work together more smoothly toward a specific goal.

We followed the same basic process with trainees as with families, in order for them to learn new ways to work (change). We often talked about the difficulties they would face in implementing family systems frameworks in their agencies when the culture of the agency was focused more on diagnosing pathology and keeping more distance from the client. Our trainees were encouraged to make their professional work evolve more from their own cultural and community norms at BFST; and we expanded their supports by helping them to use the community directly in clinical work, just as we expanded our families' supports. This helped trainees to be more in control and confident in their work, with clinical expression of familiar values. However, it also presented them with difficulty in bridging the worlds of the new practice learned and the interventions expected in their agencies. Some agencies had sent steff members to training, partially paid their tuitions, or continued to work at supervisory levels with a BFST consultant to implement training in ways *suitable* for a particular agency. When this happened, trainees could accomplish a lot and continue to advance their skills. However, this was rare.

In retrospect, if we were establishing BFST now, we would have a contractual relationship at the outset, not only with the individual trainee, but with his/her agency, planning opportunities for mutual sharing of agency needs and systems community-based clinical frameworks during training-- perhaps, in periodic workshops. We were then so focused on helping trainees learn to use natural family and community helping systems in their work that we did not gear this to their organizational systems as well as we could have. We were focused on bringing into clinical *thinking* the cultural values of clients and trainees, and bringing into systemic *practice* their own natural systems. It was rewarding to see beginning clinicians help families with very difficult symptoms and histories to step out of defeating patterns, but it was not enough. *We needed to have the full consent, cooperation, and imprint on our training of all the agencies employing our trainees.* Without this, we were missing a powerful link which would help the training take root and grow. We were not training people to operate in private practice, but to do work in our community in the agencies serving it. With our limited time and resources, we coulkd strengthen ourselves as a clinical "minority", but we could not address well the needs of the majority organizations which set practice parameters. This was a bit like working with a family without involving in sessions those who were primary authorities in the family, and it was a bit defeating.

However, given that we all do whatever our bit is to improve the whole situation in our fields and communities, BFST took an important first step not generally taken in training and, specifically, in family therapy training. We took a step away from our own isolation as professionals. We created a place where we coulkd evolve practice out of our own experiences, instead of denying the validity of these experiences; and where we could use support in our work from those who were our own natural leaders. When we could support ourselves in this way, we could better help families with their own issues of isolation, grief, and unresolved losses. First, we had to learn how to *be* a "cuddle group" in our structure, according to our community norms, before we could help our families to increase their supports. We knew that our families were facing very difficult tasks of raising children in poverty; unable to find employment and encountering institutional racism, classism, and sexism constantly; and trying often to recover from addictions. We were familiar with these problems from our own personal experience. We knew that the first step in the solution of problems for *both* our clients *and* ourselves was to *come together*, out of the isolation of being "the" Hispanic therapist in the agency to being part of a community in our work.

Effects of community membership on the therapist-client relationship

Paradoxically (in spite of our stresses and limited resources) we did not feel responsible for our clients in the way we had in agencies. At BFST we did not have to *be* the community for our clients as we had felt we had to be in agencies which were not grounded in the community. Without such grounding, there was too much of a gap between family members' experience of a crisis, the various resources which could ameliorate it, and the therapist's understanding of it. Interventions there were not powerful enough to match the series of crises families faced. Often, white middle-class clinicians compensated for their social distance from the client's crisis by developing a sense of over-responsibility for their clients. This drained staff and sapped their energy and creativity; and it promoted dependency with clients who could have better been helped to use their own natural supports. But we understood it. We had been in the position of being separated from our communities in our work, finding it difficult to know about the real supports available there. We had been encouraged in our training to think of "therapy" as a long-term, verbal encounter in which the psyche was explored, but this psyche was separate from the physical needs and crises of clients (see Chapter Six),the Western mind-body split.

In other training contexts we had been admonished to keep a certain distance from clients, and not fall into the trap of over-identifying with "them" and rescuing "them". In the mainstream clinical world, taking care of your clients and taking a nurturing, caretaking stance with them had generally been referred to as a kind of "rescuing" which promoted the pseudo-strength of the therapist more than the independence of the client. Generally, the task of therapy was to move clients from a more to less dependent position, assuming that they were stuck developmentally at levels precluding sufficient individuation. We had accepted this conceptualization in our social work and family therapy training and had found it helpful to recognize "enmeshment". But we also thought that this was not a complete picture. *We could see a cycle, of sorts, in which distance from the experiential world of the client promoted an over-compensation, which then needed to be remedied by getting one's distance as a therapist, then, restarting the cycle again.*

But, while we were therapists and trainers, we also had other roles in the community. We worked beside our clients in organizations, and used their help and advice in these contexts about many things. We saw each other often socially. We all heard the same lines of gossip or "bochinche". Our trainees and clients would have experienced our detachment as insincere or inappropriate to their definitions of help and healing. Generally, from the African and indigenous bases of our cultures, healers were *of* the people, and gained their ability to heal from years of experience *in* the culture and the community, rather than from brief training in a certain specialty outside the community. *The expertise resided in the community, not the individual healer; that person showed his/her prowess by making a concrete concern better immediately; and this healing expressed the community's beliefs/spirituality.*

Thus, the client would expect his/her therapist (not a case manager or case aide) to have spiritual and community mandates, and to prove his/her connections to greater power by, for example, getting the heat turned on, or helping the family to get financial assistance, if these were the main worries. We felt that trust was developed best by our advocating and helping the client with certain tasks. The community's primarily Puerto Rican culture provided models for this kind of active concrete help and concrete precedents in our community of organizations and clubs which had constantly extended help to new arrivals in crisis. In extending ourselves as professionals, we were behaving according to community norms. This extension of ourselves, since it took place in the community's cultural context, was not only a personal but a general expectation, beyond dyadic closeness or enmeshment. So, for us, our membership in common with clients in the same community (which might seem to some to increase closeness and enmeshment) had the effect of *decreasing* the blurring of boundaries and dependency which many think accompanies such closeness to clients. Our clients, our trainees, and ourselves had many ways to get our needs for dependence and help met, "the more, the merrier". This was particularly true for Carmen and her families and trainees. She brought many in from the community to teach, had trainees themselves teach, and designed communitywide rituals in which we were all involved. We found that, when services and training were contextualized this way, all of us--clients, trainees, and trainers--felt more grounded.

An Example of Community-Based Work: The Case of A.

Since we are talking in this chapter about BFST *after* its closing, the author presents a case example of work which flowed from both the thinking and the community membership at BFST, but work which occurred 1-2 years after its closing.

Although only 59 years of age, A. lived in a small town in a supervised adult residence for mentally ill senior citizens. She attended a day treatment program at our facility three days a week, and worked in a sheltered workshop the other two days. Her time was pretty regimented, and her routines set. She expressed to me that she would like a little more opportunity to work on her art independently and that she would like a little more individual choice as to whether or not she would attend program, hating "to be treated like a number all the time". The recreational director arranged for special supplies and a private area for A. to work in, but we could not allow her too much time out of program. State regulations demanded a certain level of involvement from clients.

A. was used to these routines after thirty years of repetitive hospitalizations, but, periodically. she would start to "decompensate", muttering to herself, having auditory hallucinations, and then pacing frantically around the big program room until the psychiatrist increased her medication. Usually the increase would not calm her, and A. would leave the program for another 6-12 month stay in the hospital.

Shortly after I began to work in the program, A. began to pace and staff remarked that she was "heading for the hospital again" I asked permission to try something different before the psychiatrist would increase her medication. Then, for the next few weeks, A. and I paced outside the program room and took long extended walks around the small town at breakneck speed for almost the whole period after lunch in which she seemed to be most tense I asked frequently whether A. wanted to continue this or have her medication increased, as she was obviously suffering and refused my attempts to talk to her. "What's the matter, you tired?" she smiled, as she refused.

One day I asked her how she felt being the only Native American and only one of two rninorities in the program and, it seemed, the whole town. She got quite angry and told me in no uncertain terms that she was "as white" as I was. I apologized,but then she continued to talk about the fact that I probably would not even know an Indian if I met one. I countered by telling her honestly about the Native people, I had met in my recent work at BFST in Buffalo. She was not impressed. But when we walked she began to tell me about the voice she heard sometimes which she called "the black cloud". It was telling her that she had sinned and was not a good enough Christian--consistently the same message, which would bring tears to her eyes. She asked if I was Christian, and I told her I didn't go to church much, but had been raised Catholic. "Well, then, if you're not religious! you won't understand my problem" she said. "True", I agreed, "we know that you're having a spiritual problem and not a mental health problem. Since I'm only a counselor, you probably need your family to be praying for you".

"Well, you know what would happen if I gave you my sister's number", she said. "She would give you the number of all my other sisters and they would all pray for me, and they'd want to come here and see me". I was astounded! The record had not indicated that A. even had any family! However, she gave me her sister L.'s phone number, and the rest happened pretty much as she had said.

Her Other Self

I learned that it was really not that unusual for her sisters to come and visit. Not only had she stayed in close touch with them and their families over the years but, in between hospitalizations, A. had had six children and had seen them and their father regularly. We had a series of about five family meetings at her sister's home and at the homes of her oldest daughter and her younger son. The purpose of these meetings was to get advice from the family on how to keep A. from decornpensating and going back into the hospital. But all were mystified: "I'll pay somebody to find the key as to how to keep her out!" her husband said. "What happens is the tension just mounts up and she has to get away from the regular world." Nevertheless, her children had done pretty well, and A. was proud of their nice families and her two grandchildren.

What was unusual in these meetings, her sisters told me, was that A. had never talked to "any of you people" about her family, figuring that those who thought she was crazy could just stay away from the part of her "that was not crazy". I thanked them for letting me see the love which had helped A. to bear such a painful life.

A. and her family and I constructed a genogram of the family over three generations (like a"family tree"), which helped us to see family relationships graphically over time. A story unfolded which put things much more in place for me, as follows:

A. was the oldest of four daughters born on the reservation. When she was ten years old, her father left and never did return, his whereabouts a mystery. When she was thirteen years old, her mother died. An aunt took care of the children, then, but A. understood it to be her responsibility, as the eldest, to take care of her younger sisters. However, shortly after her mother's death, A. was sent to a Christian boarding school nearby, where she lived for seven years, "to get all the Indian out of me and learn to wear white gloves". When A.was finally discharged home from that school, her sisters were just reaching adolescence and were being sent to the school. This meant that she did not see her sisters, except for very brief visits, for almost fourteen years. Not only was she totally alone without her family and trained to deny her culture, but she felt a tremendous burden of guilt from "having deserted my sisters, and not keeping them from having to go to that horrible place, too". Her aunts and the older people in her family had moved into the city or died by the time A. was in her early twenties, and it seemed that no one could release her from this burden of guilt. The family all laughed and said that they knew no counselor could do it, and I agreed.

Insofar as we could understand things together, though, we understood that A. seemed to flip-flop back and forth between two loyalties: the one toward her family, and then the one she wished she didn't have toward the Christian boarding school and the oppressive majority culture. When she got "too" close to her family, she began to hear "the black cloud" tell her that she had sinned and was not a good enough Christian, That hallucination would land her back in the hospital, which was akin to the boarding school in her mind.

The Community Connection

When I had previously worked at Buffalo Family Systems Training, I had met many Native Americans from A.'s reservation and others nearby. Through them I had met a very respected faithkeeper named Fleeta. I asked a colleague if she thought Fleeta would remember me, and if she thought it inappropriate to ask Fleeta for a consultation on this case. I had seen A. work her way out of what had looked like another trip to the hospital, and the recreational director in our program had taken a special interest in A. Her art work was beautiful, and the director was helping her to market some greeting cards to sell on consignment to local stores. A. had a new spirit, but the family urged me not to get too optimistic. They had seen all the previous cycles, even if they admitted that this was the best that she had been. In fact, they thought that she was so good that she would have to have a really big crash to balance out the loyalties, and I agreed.

I called Fleeta. She remembered me. She came out to talk with me the next day, and then made a plan to come and visit A. several times. "You did the right thing to call me", Fleeta said. "in order for her to be at peace she needs to talk to an elder, someone above her who knows much more. Since her aunts died, there has been no one available to her at that level."

I had to get A 's agreement to meet with Fleeta, and feared that she might think I was too intrusive to have already consulted with Fleeta confidentially. But she agreed to see Fleeta rather easily. They met in private four times, and never told me what transpired. However, about a week after Fleeta's last visit, A. told me that she never had been "crazy", but just "going through the same identity problems all Indians go through". She thought "The black cloud" was gone for good.

When I left the program and moved out of town, she gave me three of her hand-painted cards for a going-away gift. She had been in program, then, for a year without any further decornpensation. The cards, she said, were for me to send to her after I moved and knew my address, so that she could stay in touch. About a year later, I was in town again visiting, and saw A., who wanted to show me her new apartment. She had her own independent apartment in a beautiful building for well senior citizens who needed some physical assistance. She was budgeting her money well, and putting her family up when they came to visit. She was still in program and still selling her cards on consignment. We sent cards back and forth at Christmas until we lost touch two years ago. However, in the four years of our corresponding, A. had never returned to the hospital.

It took a lot of teamwork to help her get to a place where she could stay out. While she is a woman of tremendous courage, she needed to bridge the huge gulf between the aspects of her identity which she had kept isolated from each other, a split maintained by oppressive patterns in this society. The mental health system, like Thomas Indian School, could never provide necessary guidance for A. because it required her to deny her culture and spirituality. Three inches of record accumulated over a thirty-year period had never gotten data on her family or culture, as if assuming that she had been born a patient! I could ask questions about her family and culture because of my training as a family therapist, but also because of my slight knowledge of Iroquois history due to the education I had received in the community in Buffalo. Her family was a tremendous help, but they knew they were not enough.We needed an elder to provide the guidance for A. from her culture which she had never been able to get after her mother died. Counseling can never substitute for natural spiritual/community leadership, and does not have enough power to address complex situations without help from these leaders. When therapists are themselves members of a community, that connection enables them to use natural leaders as "co-therapists". In this case, we can see that these connections maintain for years, even though the therapist may leave the community.

CHAPTER TEN:
THE "FAMILIES-IN-CRISIS"
CONFERENCE IN DELAWARE

"We find that the energies and talents of people can be focused to provide essential supports, satisfactions, and controls for one another, and that these potentials are present in the social network of family, neighbors, friends, and associates of the person or family in distress "

Carolyn Attneave,
Family Networks

******

With Margaret Anderson, Leta Cooper, Cheyenne Luzader, Helen McCool, Elizabeth Metzler, and Beverly Roupp

The State of Delaware, while part of the very small Delmar Peninsula between Chesapeake Bay and the Atlantic Ocean, still is a state of many contrasting identifications and lifestyles. From northern urban Wilmington to Delmar in the more rural Sussex County is only a three hour drive. However, the trip is seldom made by residents of either locale. Wilmingtonians, while they may come south to the beaches in the summer, generally identify with the problems and interests of nearby Philadelphia, where many work. Sussex County residents, in the past decade, have seen family farms taken over by corporate interests in the soybean and chicken industry, or land sold to developers for summer homes of urban "tourists" intending to be part-time residents. Families who want to hold on to a slower-paced lifestyle have become more isolated with these changes. Many families are poor, and there is a high incidence of alcoholism, drug addiction,and sexual and physical abuse. There is a growing Hispanic population, primarily Guatemalan and Mexican migrant laborers settled near the chicken factories where they work in Georgetown. About twenty-two percent of the population is African-American, and six percent Native

American.

Whether poor or middle-class, families rely on the church for social support in Sussex County. Social services and mental health/counseling services are underfunded and fragmented. Psychiatric treatment facilities are in the northern part of this small state, and foster home, group home, and other specialized placement resources are scarce. Rural families may not voluntarily seek counseling for problems but then find themselves referred involuntarily to services which may be "the only act in town", or funded for only one kind of problem, or not connected in any way to the usual supports in their lives. Counseling is an alien process because of funding limitations and the way services are structured from the more urban part of the state, even when client values espouse counseling, and even when the counselor may be someone from the area who is trusted. Worse, when the client is referred out of the area and must travel upstate for substance abuse or psychiatric treatment, it is clear that services have not been designed to serve client needs. The travel time and lack of public transportation is prohibitive, and is especially painful when children are placed in psychiatric treatment facilities near Wilmington and their families cannot afford to visit or participate in treatment. Often such treatment confuses people and separates family members from each other. More readily available jail facilities are over-used.

The annual "Families-in-Crisis" Conference has been held each May for the past twelve years, at Delaware Technical and Community College in Georgetown, the county seat of Sussex County. It addresses the fragmentation of services by bringing together professionals from a great variety of agencies and services in the county and state; and brings them together around some aspect of the above crisis situations faced by families and those who serve families. The format of the conference is one full day, with a guest keynote speaker and then several small workshops throughout the day. Hallways are a "Marketplace" for twenty-five agencies to exhibit and publicize programs and services. A large low-cost lunch is provided in the cafeteria. There is a lot of talking in the hallways and in the small workshops, since most of those attending know each other or have some kind of common connection. The atmosphere is open and friendly.

The conference is planned by a committee of representatives from various agencies. This chapter is the work of several of the current committee members, who have assembled to discuss the history, goals, and process in putting the conference together. We hope that our discussion can exemplify the ways in which human service professionals can be educated from the inside out, such that theory follows from action and experience in the community. We think that community-based education can provide a kind of synthesis of action, reflection, and experience sorely lacking in mainstream education today. Without this kind of synthesis which makes sense of our life experiences and puts them to use for others, theory becomes abstraction which is too thin to support social services and planning.

Our History

The conference began with the intention of getting together social workers from different agencies over lunch to present their ideas and see what people in Sussex County or Lower Delaware were doing. We never thought of becoming a large conference, but wanted to come up with local ideas to solve local problems. There were many fewer of us then and funds weren't so tight. Agency administrators had the time to attend, and so came as committee members to monthly meetings; this meant that, when we talked about doing things to support our ideas, administrators could commit their agencies to the plan right there on the spot. Now agency administrators don't have time to attend, although they want to; and so they send lower level personnel, which tends to slow our process by a month or two when decisions need to be made.

We also wanted to include people who weren't professionals, volunteers who are very important in providing services throughout the County. We wanted to get a whole picture of what was going on regarding current resources and services for families, and to network and update each other as to what was going on. We were frustrated with published brochures and lists of services which were outdated as soon as they came out. We also wanted to have some face-to-face contact and share ideas in an ongoing way. Many of us had been used to going away to professional conferences for our own development, but those were not related to needs in Sussex County. When various social workers, volunteers and others in the community such as judges and nurses met to discuss what we needed, the format of the annual conference evolved, with eight to ten small workshops focused on the most pressing needs discussed by the conference committee. Each time we met we would take minutes and then see that they were distributed throughout our agencies, so that the ideas which came up for workshops were then reflective of the interests of a larger group of people who did not attend monthly committee meetings but communicated with their representative.

It was not our intention to grow or to make money. We just wanted a way to come together to network and support each other. We got a lot of the community involved, outside the system of service providers, as we got donations of flowers, food, and services. The more the community was involved and knew about the conference the more non-professionals attended. At first, we wanted to limit it to professionals, but we wanted to allow students in various disciplines to come, and then we really couldn't tell any more who was who. We have figured that all these people have expertise because they know the area and its needs, and know the people. This is what "community-based" means, you might say. In fact, it follows the community college concept of developing skills from within the community, providing exposure for local persons, and a way for them to compare ideas with others. Our goal was some kind of new knowledge in the community, not to get a large audience, but to have a small audience get what they wanted and needed to serve families better.

Of those on the committee now, about two of the twelve of us have been involved from the beginning There are some routine things now in the planning that we know have to be taken care of in a certain order; and we know that some of us are just good at certain of these things, others with other tasks. So we just leave certain things to certain people Otherwise, our organization is pretty informal, and this parallels how things get done in the community. No hierarchy, no Roberts Rules of Order. Whoever shows up at the monthly committee meetings makes the decisions. It isn't because those people are the bosses or have more status; it's just that the work has to get done, so, if you want to get it done your way, you'd better show up to have a voice. Generally, it's the same few people who show up regularly due to busy schedules. This is a problem in all organizations, but we try to make it less so by sending out minutes to everyone and then getting feedback.

We go over the evaluations of the workshops filled out by those who attended, and we really pay close attention to the comments in the planning for the following year. We poll those on the committee regarding their knowledge of a certain kind of expertise on a requested topic, and give feedback to all the presenters about comments received regarding their presentations. We often pair up presenters with a similar interest, or a senior presenter with someone who has never done it before, or people from the same area who could then be encouraged to collaborate further. In general, we see the conference as a springboard for ongoing collaboration of people who are in the same community and can get to know each other better and have the opportunity to continue to come together to refine their ideas over time--not just a one-shot dose of "brilliance" by one presenter.

We have a keynote or guest speaker each year to provide stimulation. Three times in the past twelve years the guest speaker has been from outside Delaware, when we wanted to provide an outside perspective or wanted the person to be able to speak on a sensitive subject, and then exit. We had a woman from Baltimore as a guest speaker on race relations a few years ago, at a time when people were saying there were no race problems in Sussex County, and were shocked at our choice of a topic. She was able to be well-received, and to keep the subject more "objective" than she would have been able to do if from the area. Then, in subsequent years, once the ice had been broken on the sensitive subject, other local people came in to do work on ethnic and cultural issues.

We set up workshops with the idea that learning is not always strictly theory or practice, but that *people learn things on an emotional level, from hearing the experiences of others they know, and disagreeing on issues which will affect then personally.* This year, in formulating ideas for a workshop on the prison system in Delaware, it became expanded into two workshops: the morning, in which various officials, judges, guards, etc. explained the system from their vantage points; and then the afternoon, which brought together some community residents who talked about the experience of having a family member in jail. In the afternoon workshop, many people in the audience had come because they wanted to hear this talked about. They too had family members incarcerated, but had never talked to anyone about it. Out of this workshop came a plan for an ongoing support group for families of prisoners, directly meeting an unmet need in the community.

We also have a somewhat standard format for some of the workshop content each year. We always include a workshop on work with the elderly because our conference is the only one budgeted for staffs serving the elderly in lower Delaware. We always include something for nurses, and we always include religious perspectives. People in Sussex County have a strong religious base and look to their ministers for support. The ministers are very active and so they participate in the conference quite a lot. *We tie religion into social services in our presentations, which would not be done in Wilmington as much or in other professional conferences. We gear our Conference to the community's values, as we think services should also be geared. Indeed, the secular nature of professional conferences often sets a barrier between services and the people being served in smaller communities.*

Relevant Education for Our Community

We are a group of social service providers representing court, educational, and mental health systems in Sussex County. We are not coming together here because individually we have expertise as teachers *per se*, nor because we think that that individual expertise would then qualify us to plan what continues to be the major conference and training resource in our area. *What qualifies us to plan this conference is our membership in this community, our knowledge of the people and their needs, and our roles in its institutions.* We can plan meaningful experiences for others educationally because we represent the others who we report back to, and they tell us what they want directly by responding to the minutes or by their evaluations. We simply follow their wishes, and, from our knowledge of who is in the community with what kinds of expertise, we then link the expressed wishes of others with the expertise we know is locally available. We act like links or bridges for people to come together to share problems and solutions with each other.

This assumes that expertise is in "common" people and that we do not have to go outside our area to get it. Often this kind of belief in ourselves and our local resources in small communities is seen as insular, outdated, and not very progressive. Yes, many in urban areas should tend to see such cohesiveness as a not very interesting characteristic of small communities. Urban professionals get used to conferences where experts with a big name give them content. We didn't want someone giving us something, although we have all had that type of education and like it when we are overworked and overtired and don't want to participate. In fact, if we are professionals, we have probably gone away to school, belonged to national professional associations, and updated our learning at conferences in Washington, Baltimore, Philadelphia, or New York. In these conferences, materials and lectures have certainly not reflected the reality of our daily life here. If, indeed, we were *only* to be educated in the above mainstream ways, we would hardly be aware of the needs of this county at all.

Our conference offers people a balance in their education, an alternative to the mainstream, *so that services can be designed out of their relationship to each other--i.e., training with a focus on process rather than content.* While both process and content are important, our tradition in the conference is to make process more important. By this way of thinking, skills are not something which are written down somewhere out there and a given bag of tricks we can just tap into. Skills must come out of ourselves, our values, and our relationships with others. So a conference needs to enable that joining of peoples ' internal selves, and expression of their skills and values.

However, we realize that it takes a long time to be aware of this, and that formulas are often useful in the learning process. We struggle constantly in our committee with requests to bring someone in from outside the area to present a particular topic "in depth"--i.e., specialized knowledge in a smaller area reflecting some peoples' work specialties . We have done this several times, and will be bringing in a guest speaker this year with some specialized practice skills. We want to continue to hash out struggles involved when people want different things, and we don't have to rigidly choose one set of values over another.

Our conference, like our community, has a tradition and a certain purpose. It does not have to be for everyone and does not have to satisfy everyone. We are not a business having to make a certain margin of profit. We are not sponsored by only one or two institutions with a certain viewpoint to sell . We are not affiliated with a certain university or service controlling our policies. We are independent, with a multipurpose community base. These economic and political realities make it possible for us to just keep offering alternatives which fit our communities.

However. our communities are changing, and have a much bigger mix of cultures now. People will be asking different things of us, and we will need to respond, maybe by changing or adjusting our goals a bit. As long as our attendance stays between 250 and 500, we seem to be striking a chord of need. As long as our local agencies and institutions continue to support us, and the volunteers keep coming and running things, and the donations of goods comes from private individuals and businesses, well, then, we keep on going. However, as agencies grow beyond a certain point, the intimacy and sense of family and community changes. This is probably due to increased pressure to obtain funding in agencies, but it changes things. It steps up the pace, and everyone has less time for anything which isn't putting money in their pocket. We sense it here in the committee. It used to be more fun and easier to participate together. Now we are just more pressured.

But then we look at the families we work with, those "families in crisis" for whom the conference is named. In Sussex County clusters of families have been taught not to share with other clusters of families. We constantly work to come up with effective ways to break through that resistance, but it is difficult when you are not yourself in their cluster, let alone when you are from out of the county or state. We know that, to help them, we have to

keep refining our knowledge of each other here. The conference is a big
boost to help us do that.

****

Networking and Community Organization Themes

Spiritual Traditions and Leadership

When people move into lower Delaware from more urban areas, it takes
them a awhile to learn that the way to meet people in different communities
is through the churches there. When we are used to separation of church and
state in government, and church contact being limited to Sunday services,
it is surprising to find that the church is the social hub. Churches pass
information about employment, job training, food, clothing, shelter,
babysitting, youth groups, and just about everything. They keep you
informed about local gossip and politics affecting your area. If you have a
marital problem or problems with your children, you will seek advice from
your pastor or a member of his/her staff. That advice is likely to be taken
because you already trust the authority of the advisor. You have probably
known his/her family at least by word of mouth. When agencies move into
an area, they often rent beginning space from a church in order to legitimize
their services. Politicians curry favor with church leaders, respecting the
fact that they can assemble a crowd quickly around a relevant issue.

While rural areas have lost population rapidly during the last
generation and many churches have lost their congregations, it is still true
that rural churches have less of a specialized "preaching on Sundays"
function than in larger cities. Historically, farmers made worship the center
of family life out of a recognition of dependence on the land and
uncontrollable weather. With small towns having been less industrial,
people did not gather together in their work and did not gather in great
enough numbers to make specialization feasible. Less specialization has
probably promoted less hierarchy and more wholistic thinking and
"crossover skills" in which, as the stereotype goes, the guy who runs the
general store is also the postmaster and real estate broker.

However, as in most areas of rural America, this hub of community life
is changing in Delaware. The suburbs of larger cities such as Wilmington

and Dover have grown and become interspersed with farms, particularly since few zoning restrictions exist in Delaware to protect the integrity of different areas. As one travels Rte. 3 South, it is common to see developments springing up in the midst of farms, with these new "bedroom cornmunity" residents commuting to jobs in larger cities and focusing their energy there. Certainly, churches are centers of community activity in big cities, also, but these churches tend to define spiritual needs more narrowly, in terms of religious practices, and not the whole context of one's life. Certainly, class and cultural differences divide the suburbanites from the long-timers, but this basic wholistic vs. specialist difference is a big one. The Amish community is migrating from the area as they find it harder to live traditionally with the influx of more urban people.

While these kinds of population changes inevitably demand more specialized kinds of education, projects such as this yearly conference enable a bit of a more gradual transition, and enable service providers to realize that services cannot just fit with other bureaucratic services, but have to be delivered with a view to the whole ecology of the area.

Community Organization

In Delaware, as in most parts of the country, whether urban or rural, *the services themselves* need help as much as the person in need. When services are inadequately funded, are designed by those outside the area and with little understanding of local needs, and are not connected to informal structures in the community which have been providing help there for years it is a wonder that any real connection ever happens. One could say, then, that the "Families-in-Crisis" Conference needs to be one which addresses the crisis in services as much as family needs. The problem, though, is that, if one wanted to design such a conference, how would s/he do it? Almost every conference brochure sent out for the past decade contains lectures or workshops on various client crises, and some call attention to the crises we all experience in our society. But, *if we wanted to not only call attention to a service crisis in our area, but then propose some positive solutions for the crises, how would we do it?*

This conference is an example as to how we could do it. We don't need to overwhelm each other by a constant laundry list of deficits, or "sophisticated" analyses of how the problems got so bad, or even more sophisticated and abstract diagnoses of the problem. Most conferences intended to draw large audiences from "everywhere" already do that. When we want to propose solutions, we have to: 1) assemble those involved in the particular area service network; 2) involve those in the area who provide support outside the formal service network, churches and fraternal organizations; 3) involve those outside those supportive services who can give something valuable and need to understand what you are doing, such as restaurants which are local "hang-outs"; 4) give all of these people something to do which will contribute to solutions; 5) give all of these people some structured and unstructured ways to interact with each other; and 6) explain what has been done to try to solve the problems before, and ask them to design something new which many others will support and work on together.

A conference can be a way to organize a community, and can provide the spark which helps people to design services appropriate to their needs and culture. It is more the democratic political process in action than the delivery of content by experts. As with most real process, a lot of it is spontaneous. Planners cannot set a structure which will run smoothly fron beginning to end because they do not know how the process will develop ahead of time. Here, the planners set some parameters in terms of workshop times, and then allow for people to disrupt their scheule and get together around a certain issue for the afternoon, as we did with the prisoners' families and the service providers.

In this way, the conference itself is the service, while it remains an adjunct to the regular service delivery done in agencies throughout the year. To the author, this is similar to the use of the *network* as an adjunct to ongoing clinical work with a family.

Network Intervention

Isolation, of course, is a major problem we all have in this society, as we travel to find work and as the national economy becomes global. In rural areas with traditionally strong family and community values, the young people are rapidly leaving and corporate agribusiness has replaced the family farm. In Delaware many rural areas seem quite crowded when farms are interspersed with "suburban" housing developments. In the midst of these changes, we struggle to keep alive consistent nurturing relationships, and to encourage them to take new forms which still fit the demands of society. This is no easy task. Families in the midst of these changes find themselves in shock when they suffer deaths or separations from those they were close to, without having enough supports or rituals left to help them grieve loss and get on with their lives.

And so people get depressed, drink more, lose their tempers more. They may express their feelings of isolation from all traditional authority and connection by sexually abusing their own children. Children act out more, and turn to drug and peer substitutes for adult support. Counseling enters the picture as a "cure" for the symptomatic behaviors of disturbed individuals. If it can only propose individual remedies, counseling will encourage further isolation, as individuals seek professional support instead of family and community supports.

Therapists have often avoided this outcome by assembling a network of family, friends, and acquaintances. These people are not only immediate family and intimate friends, but not-so-close friends, also. Non-intimates are very important in that, as families become more isolated, they typically try to preserve the intimate relationships, but do not also nurture acquaintance levels like the man at the corner store, the "super" in one's apartment building, one's children's scout leaders, coaches, teachers. Most of us have social networks of 40-50 people, when we include acquaintances such as these. More isolated people tend to have networks of only 10-20 people, and try to handle change independently and privately. Crises, however, signal that this is not working. Crises are usually occurring at the time one requests help from a counselor, and one or more members are acting in ways to bring attention to the family's private business. The counselor can then use the crisis as an opportunity to offer the family some alternatives to isolation.

Generally, therapists who respect the complexity of the family's issues can normalize the acting-out in one family member or another ("Junior is doing a good job of getting help for the family, but we want him to see that there is enough support in the family so that he can go on being a kid. and not keep exercising his leadership in this way"). The therapist may plan with the family to see Junior individually at times and all of them together at times until they are comfortable with new alternatives. But it will be difficult for the therapist to stem the flow of the crisis at the beginning when she does not know the family well; or when there is not enough trust of agencies or counseling, in general; or when she has a high caseload and cannot work a 24-hour day to tend to threatening behaviors on the spot, as family members would.

Generally, the elders in a family or community still know best how crises should be handled. Their help can be enlisted to get others to come on board and help out for a brief period of approximately two weeks to help the available, he will state to the family his need to involve others for a brief period to get past the crisis. The goal might be to help Junior avoid rehospitalization, detention, or foster care, or to help him get drug treatment, or go to school regularly. When the network has used its resources to help the family achieve this goal, counseling can then proceed in routine ways to reinforce new behaviors and communication with family members.

The actual assembling and operation of the network is modeled after town meeting, Native American, and African American kin and spiritual support patterns. Social work literature is replete with studies of the informal support systems of black families, and treatment strategies which emulated these structures or used them in co-therapy (see references for MacAdoo; Hayes; Martineau; Neighbors and Jackson; Billingsley; Stack; Miller and Dreger; Aschenbrenner; Hill, King, Dixon, and Nobles; Foley; Hall and Bourne; Hall and Eying; Hall; Taber; Myers; and Jones). Knowledge of the spiritual support of the Black Church has infused the work of African American Colleagues who have assembled networks as they were taught to use the support of the church(e.g., Lincoln and Mamiya) in bringing people together, generation after generation, to get resources to deal with the extreme oppression of slavery and institutional racism. In Delaware, the work of European Americans in rural areas showed the same influence of the Church, so that here, one would also want to use the expertise of church leaders in networks, when at all possible.

The network should be assembled primarily from the family's list of its natural supports, since it functions to strengthen that natural system in the process of resolving the family member's crisis. However, at times, it is also a good idea to involve professional supports. We have done so when staff persons are also from the community and can serve as natural links themselves; and when an agency has placed a team or intensive case manager in the home to spend a lot of time there, and we then want the "natural" and "professional" teams to dovetail their efforts rather than triangulate the family. This helps a family through a crisis and helps the therapist to use the crisis resolution to inform the ongoing therapy process; or can be used to help an addict through various stages of resistance/relapse (Galanter).

Models of Large-Scale System Change in Delaware

Delaware is an interesting example of the state-wide application of a family-based services model to children's services. The Delaware Family

Preservation Project studied the fragmented array of services to children throughout the state in 1986, and, with grants from a foundation and from state and federal human services administrations, designed a system of home-based alternatives to placement and family-focused training to all staff working in children's services throughout the state. This ambitious design made the family the basic unit of intervention, rather than the child, and coordinated all services around the state to make this conceptual leap (McCarthy). By 1992, awareness and participation among agencies around the state had been achieved, and staffs had begun to network together, and to train at beginning and at more advanced levels in family systems clinical frameworks.

Even given the small size of the state, this was a very progressive accomplishment. In the early 1970's, children had gotten lost in placement systems and Permanency Planning was the goal, whereby, if parents did not benefit from treatment, their rights were terminated and an adoptive home was sought for the child. It had been difficult for parents to benefit from treatment when so many systems tried to reform the family from different perspectives: educational views were that parents lacked knowledge; legal views emphasized that parents be given consequences for their behavior; the mental health system focused on pathology; and the child welfare system tried to get more resources to the family. The unifying philosophy amongst all these systems was that the family *lacked* something, and was to be the target of help from systems which were *not the problem*. When the goal had not been to work with the family together to prevent placement, terminations of parental rights increased.

Then, nationally, Home-Based Services offered solutions which facilitated more contact between families and services, and more cooperative than blaming orientations. The focus was on what families were doing right, and on keeping parents in leadership roles in their own families, with assistance from various services. Many workable "Homebuilder" or Home-Based Services models developed initially in the states of Washington and Iowa became known to national policymakers (Shaw).

Work in Delaware combined these models and structural family systems approaches; consolidated children's services into a unified department; and structures training opportunities for staffs of various agencies around the state to come together and network. This approach focused change not only on client families, but on service delivery systems, as well. It built more exchange and mutuality between families and service providers, and collapsed the various provider hierarchies into a system of more lateral sharing. By 1992, fewer children were languishing in detention, and the foster care rate had stayed the same, while rates inother states were increasing. In only five years since the study of state services began, these changes had been implemented and had gotten good results (McCarthy).

However, this system originated in Wilmington and used trainers from Philadelphia who had been given the job of making models fit service needs in Delaware,at least in the initial inception/design. Without the perspective of time or membership in the state to inform their work,they did not tend to have the *informal* connections necessary to build bridges for families in the more rural southern part of the state where formal services were sparse. In rural areas, families sought help from the church, recreational, and fraternal organizations which provided indigenous leadership for their communities. *When agency experts do not plan based on the advice of indigenous leaders in rural areas, programs will tend to separate the formal service system from the informal one; and to set up competition for leadership between "professional experts" and "indigenous leaders".* In this way, professionals, even those who may use community-based models, inadvertently serve to reduce that unity in communities which is based on a firm allegiance to informal leadership. Moreover, since experts are paid to produce some result in a specified period of time, they do not have the luxury of slowly getting to know others and building the relationships which are the basis for word-of-mouth informal resources.

The "Families-in-Crisis" Conference serves to bridge this gap. It can involve those professionals in the area who have been involved in the state training, but it does so in a way which connects them to informal resources,and *makes their knowledge fit local structures.* The assumption in the conference, as in national family support programs, is that uniform interventions cannot be applied across programs and communities. Variations must evolve according to the needs of each individual community (Jacobs). It is helpful to have a way, such as the conference, in which you can regularly bring local service providers together to formulate ideas.

Issues in Community-Based Education

This conversation in Delaware has many similarities and differences from that with trainers and trainees who had been together at BFST in Buffalo. Both that institute and this annual conference work to discover how to share that knowledge which comes out of peoples' daily routines and rituals. This is similar to Paula Gunn Allen's explanation, in *Spider*

Woman's Granddaughters (1989), of some of the major differences between Western canons of literature and the Indian ethos: in the Western canon, the classic short story has one hero and one theme, occurring in one geographic location over a brief time-frame, and it becomes a novel when themes and settings are more complex; in Indian literature, the presence of an individualistic hero and a conflict-centered plot do not define fiction as such, but the coherence of common understanding derived from the ritual tradition that members of a tribal unit share.

Both of these training efforts are independent ventures not linked to mainstream sources of funding, organizations, or universities. However, both *are* linked to the community structurally. Committee members who plan the conference come from local community agencies.Trainers at BFST belonged to the community's grass-roots organizations, and got funding through community leadership and residents. Both of these training efforts also maintained themselves on very low funding and volunteer efforts.

We can hardly think of these smaller, more experimental, and less secure training efforts as competition for much larger and more tightly organized programs. Rather, their strength lies in their ability to bring options and alternatives to bureaucratic educational structures, and to bridge the gap between larger educational systems and small indigenous communities.

CHAPTER ELEVEN:
CLINICAL TRAINING
BY AND FOR COMMUNITIES

'For every complex problem there is a simple solution"
—H. L. Mencken

******

This quote bears a little bit of a pause. The author borrowed it due to its tongue-in-cheek application to the use of training models for problems taken out of social context. On second reading, another meaning emerges: when we think of "solutions" to the vast social problems which can maintain individual problems, they will *have* to be simple, effective only when enabling or linked to other action.

The Business of Training

The assumption of Europeans "discovering" America was false, and it was then followed by a one-way system of education which did not "assimilate" to indigenous cultures but sought to convert them to the "mainstream." The idea of a mainstream, or one rightfully dominant group or culture more knowledgeable than another, has dominated the American system of education. A demanding education, then, has usually been one which stressed European "classics," deportment, individual achievement, and competition. Individuals who have done well in this system have been rewarded by class/race/gender privilege. Colonized groups have done well when they have enhanced the power of the dominant group. However, those without the wherewithal to enhance existing power are outside it, and therefore, inadvertently, threatening it. Perceived threat from "the masses" encourages education to adopt business free-market hierarchy and competition, so that "might is right" and "other" ideas are secondary or inferior. Unfortunately, this protects education from diversity. Our youth can master it without much doubt or personal expansion and growth.

However, on the surface, free-market competition seems to encourage sophistication and diversity. We have many publishing houses, many more channels on TV each year, etc., although they seem to follow the same formats and formulas or basic themes. The more technology seems to offer us "newer" and "better" alternatives and choices, the more we become aware that it offers more ways to say the same thing, evidencing control by fewer and larger corporations. We cannot, for example, look at who controls TV without examining who controls a wide range of information-as-power: control of the vast network of magazines, news, cable, TV networks, telephone and wireless communication systems, newspapers, insurance companies, nuclear power plant and waste disposal plants, transportation services, books, publishers, etc. by only *four* conglomerates: General Electric, Time-Warner, Disney/CAP Cities, and Westinghouse (Miller 1996).

In one month's issue of *The Family Therapy Networker* (May/June, 1966), the author could find advertisements for the following "different" schools of therapy/training; Thought Field Therapy (TFT); Talk Power; Mediation Training; Psychosynthesis; Conflict-Focused Treatment; Eye Movement Desensitization and Reprocessing; the Sexual Crucible Approach; Parent-Child Relationship Inventory; Narrative Therapy Training; Solution-Focused Training; Brief Therapy for Managed Care; Family Mediation Training; Divorce Mediation Training; Contextual Therapy Training; 12-Hour Therapy with Children; Ericksonian Approaches to Hypnosis and Brief Therapy; Heart-Centered Hypnotherapy; Strategic Brief Therapy; and Satir System Training. Most of these are very well-established approaches. These approaches may be reflective of very serious expertise, but this advertising process itself guarantees their similarity. While the advertisements promise new and unique specialty skills, they are not skills appropriate for a particular region or population but, apparently, for everyone. While they may target a particular problem (e.g., phobias), they do not specify it in relation to any other context. If a course might incorporate an awareness of the differences in treatment related to class, culture, or gender, cerainly the advertisements do not imply this. Ads are pitched to appeal to a wide audience, and so, must make invisible these specifics. *The need for larger markets and profits affects the presentation of content.* Once students have signed on out of interest in content in which specific contexts have been omitted, their interest is kept in a process which does not specify the urban white middle-class biases of trainers.

Of course, it is valid to teach urban white middle-class perspectives. However, the need to omit or even be conscious of this specificity in good business advertising is the real problem. We smile at even the suggestion that one might advertise the partiality of training offered, and our smile divulges our understanding of the ways in which *institutionalized* racism, classism, and sexism deny the existence of those not "mainstream." Admitting the *partiality* of our training perspectives and the limited life experiences upon which training is based would help us to be aware of the existence of rural, poor and lower-class perspectives, and those of people of color, often outside the experience base of training models. But the business of *marketing* professional education maintains control by one set of values over others.

Clinical training is hierarchial, with a few prestigious universities and institutes at the top setting parameters for credentialing; and depending on many consumers at the bottom who need the credentials of "higher" education and good training in order to practice. Postmodern theorists such as Foucault and many in various therapy fields have addressed the need to deconstruct expressed "universal" approaches—i.e., put them into their specific historical contexts. Awareness of historical specificity could, then, open the way for inclusion of cultural information which could offer new life to our training and education. However, for this kind of change to really happen, it needs to be accompanied by some kind of political pressure from outside the educational hierarchy which profits from the current system. *Action from those communities not represented well in the educational system needs to be taken to empower postmodern awareness,* as in the 1960's when community action demanded American Studies departments in many universities.

As a family therapy trainer, the author was taught to believe that beginners would best learn family therapy by initial introduction to one *model* or another—e.g., structural, strategic, Satir, contextual, etc. After rigorous training in the model of one's choice, which would generally entail about three years of postgraduate individual and group supervision, one would then have integrated the model well enough into one's own style, practice setting, and previous clinical field to consider oneself a practicing family therapist. With this grounding in one model of family therapy, one would then continue to refine one's work and include parts of other models as need be. When the author was being trained in family therapy sixteen years ago, there were always a lot of debates about the merits of one model over another: was one model more relevant for one ethnic or socioeconomic group than another? for one kind of problem more than another? for one kind of family or another? These debates were very thought provoking, more so when the groups having the discussions were reflective of diverse cultures and communities. They invited us to "deconstruct" the models used.

But these debates occurred during the days when agencies in poor communities were paying occasionally for in-depth family therapy training for some staff members, and when training groups were more often race and class mixtures than now. As time went on and funding no longer paid for those who could not afford to pay themselves, the market needed to grab *more* middle-and upper-class practitioners and so the competition increased. Advertising was pitched to those far outside the local areas of the recognized institutes who could attend and then be accorded special expertise in their local communities after training, based on the reputation of the model or training center. Since managed care has reduced the incomes of practitioners in private practice, as well as those in the public sector, training institutes have advertised to even wider *international* markets. While many family therapists value postmodern constructionism, they seem not to relate it to postmodern business and political realities in the field, nor to connect it to the specific grounding available in local communities which is needed to translate abstract philosophy into clinical practice (e.g., Hoffman 1993; and White and Epston, 1990).

The increasingly global focus of family therapy can encourage sharing and communication between different countries and cultures, obviously. In practice, however, the motivation for sharing is generally a business need for a wider market, paralleling our global economy. This does not make it a bad thing *per se*, but makes it fail to declare the specificity of class/culture/gender experience which it reflects, the very opposite of deconstruction. Power remains with those *paid* to "share" a model, without the mutuality of true sharing which would educate as to the specific expertise available in many various communities and would pay these experts equally (as in the more horizontal definition of expertise exemplified in Chapter Ten). Diversity is discouraged.

But we do not have to reject models, out of hand. They can be introduced as important information which is *secondary* to local expertise ("thinking locally"). We can then encourage trainees to *come together to use their common experience in the community as the basis from which to critique various models,* using aspects of models which fit their experience and discarding other aspects which do not fit ("acting globally"), making this critiquing process *consciously* the work of training. This is the essence of community-based clinical training, and can be seen in examples in the two preceding chapters.

Our dilemma is a difficult one without easy answers. When we live in a world in which it takes a lot of money and power to simply stay afloat, then one takes risks bordering on foolishness in not following the rules which enable that power. By the same token, if the goal is to promote any priorities other than profits, one also takes risks bordering on foolishness in not following rules which enable those priorities. The postmodern dilemma is that we need very large amounts of *both* money and *diverse* expertise to get the job done, but *when we follow business methods of acquiring broad-based knowledge we end up with that which does not threaten the business interests of those in power.* Our "broad-based" knowledge has no depth, and "Generation X" doesn't seem to be buying it. Can a society survive when some of us go along with the program, but none of us much believe it anymore? What is a democracy when less than half the population of voting age votes, and when a president can get into office with only 23% of the votes, having spent a fortune to get them?

Speeding To a Halt

As social services have been privatized or transferred from government to corporate resources, business/profit-making standards have scaled down a welfare state supposedly in need of being scaled-down, even though less than three percent of the federal budget is spent on financial assistance and family support services, and *even with* the changes in the economy from industrial to postindustrial--i.e., computerization of many services, with less manpower needed, while the working-age population continues to increase.

A study done in Massachusetts from September, 1991, to May, 1992 (Motenko, Allen, Angelos, Block, DeVito, Duffy, Holton, Lambert, Parker, Ryan, Schraft, and Swindell 1995) documented social workers and client impressions of changes in agency policy and service delivery with privatization. After an increase in the 1980s in the centralization of departments and the size of catchment areas, more costly clinical services were replaced by emergency services, case management, day treatment, and residential services. Without very sophisticated clinical services, hospitalizations of mentally ill people were needed while the number of inpatient beds decreased. Social workers reported higher levels of stress and burnout, with increased demands that they document their work and increase the efficient use of time, thus having less time for staff meetings and communication (also noted at Morrisania in Chapter Six). In many agencies, clients no longer received advocacy, mediation, and brokering for support services; and the focus was on rapid termination/discharge of clients to meet stringent reimbursement guidelines—*and on continually redesigning programs to look "unique" and to prove that no one else could do it better, in order to keep private contracts.*

The imposition of frequent changes and upgrading is consistent with a business mentality concerned more with "product" than with "process." In therapy, though, *how* one gets there is often the product, and *relationship* is central. We have been used to government bureaucracy and paperwork which interrupts the therapy process in certain ways, but business emphasis on fast-profit/product efficiency interrupts the timing of interventions and the pacing of change with the client. Computer programs *can* be designed to help us do *quicker* treatment plans, with software packages containing a large database of *prewritten* statements about problems, diagnoses, and cures. The therapist could plug a program into her computer and have a prefabricated treatment plan without having to enter a lot of her own data, saving time and also the *reflection* which has been one of the actual merits of record-keeping and treatment planning (MacFarquhar 1996). Moreover, programs tend to be precise and measurable, so that treatment which recognizes ambiguity, complexity, and contradictions in clients' lives and therapists' thinking is out of tune. We know that learning and creativity occur when contradictions bump into one another and generate confusion, so that clinical training and therapy should not aim for this kind of oversimplification.

However, simplistic thinking can be quite welcome when we are overwhelmed. We cannot expect the overstressed agency clinician to sort out the contradictions in ever newer universal clinical treatment models, nor clients to siphon what is relevant from ever more fragmented services. In the previous two chapters, the object of training was to make models fit the community so that those from community agencies would have less of a gap between the models used and their life experience. At Buffalo Family Systems Training, trainers learned from trainees the importance of including agency supervisors and administrators in some way in the training process which their staff was getting, to also keep the new clinical methods in tune with agency requirements, often extremely difficult in times of rapid change. *When clinical training can help to ground agency staff and clients in their shared community experience, overwhelmed feelings will be lessened so that simplistic thinking need not be welcomed to relieve stress.* While we are offered numerous literature teaching individual methods of stress relief, we are seldom reminded of the power of simply coming together and sharing our strengths. When we expect therapists to be sensitive and able to relate to others, we must provide an atmosphere which respects complexity and communication.

Consumer Reports surveyed its predominantly white, middle-class subscribers (a bias not noted in the report) in 1995, and found that longer-term therapy over six months was more successful than that under six months; and that most subscribers felt that the psychotherapy *per se,* whether accompanied by drugs or not, was helpful (*Consumer Reports* 1995). Were subscribers reporting on the effects of a powerful relationship with a therapist? How will this be changed when therapists relate primarily to the insurer, as exemplified in Poynter's *The Preferred Provider's Handbook: Building a Successful Private Therapy Practice in the Managed Care Marketplace,* which recommends concurrent contracts with *eighteen* (!) managed care companies to ensure a steady flow of referrals. (In Cornell 1996). This strong a relationship with managed care triangulates the therapist-client relationship, making treatment secondary to business management.

Often, what makes for efficient management is not conducive to treatment. Recently, a hospital in Buffalo built a new clinic in a poor community very close to the street to allow for a bigger parking lot for staff. One day some neighborhood residents at the clinic were discussing the difficulty this entailed for them when they were walking in the Buffalo snow and wind with several children and a stroller, being afraid that, when they opened the door to the clinic, their children might be knocked into the busy street. One woman laughed and commented that the building was very efficient, though: "If they just put a window on the side, you could walk by and stick your arm in for a shot...or your Medicaid card, the main item."

Community-based training slows us down to: 1) consider how programs operate in depth in our *particular* service settings and in our *particular* neighborhoods; 2) make available to trainees the strong cultural traditions which can guide clinical work; and 3) understand the kinds of agency teamwork with *natural* community leaders and support networks which are needed to maintain services in a given area. *Preservation of the relationship core of clinical work cannot be accomplished without the balance of community supports.* Postmodern dilemmas demand that agency administrators and direct line staff address complex problems with a complex system of supports beyond those which are strictly monetary. *Trainers can be the link to these resources, when they are members of the client's community and understand the resources it offers.*

Inherent Limitations in Professional Training

When a therapist thinks that a problem is maintained primarily by an individual client who "has" the symptoms, s/he can work with that person according to many combinations of cognitive, experiential/emotive, or behavioral methods. When this therapist is a student in training, both student and supervisor are familiar with a particular method used, and the student therapist can use it with a client in a session, then reporting the client's responses from the session to the supervisor in terms of their common frame of reference. The student's sessions are often video- or audio-taped, or written down in summary form, so that the supervisor can understand how the student is applying the framework. Or the supervisor can observe the session from behind a two-way mirror.

This kind of supervision follows certain basic premises: 1) that the student must *first* learn a model to work from, 2) that work with clients then comes as an internship *after* the "basic" coursework is completed, 3) that work with clients can be considered good or effective insofar as it is *measured against* an initial method gleaned from readings and research and then refined in the supervisor-student relationship and interpretations, 4) the client is not represented in the formulation or assessment of the method, and 5) the student therapist and supervisor participate in the same context of university/agency, while the *client's context is not mentioned or taken into account.*

Most of these premises of usual clinical supervision seem to work well when the therapist and supervisor are from similar cultures as the client(s), although the process does tend to make the client a passive agent. However, when the therapist and the client are from radically different cultures, it is easier to see how the clinical training process maintains control within educational/agency systems, and does not really "start where the client is," even though this may be a favored adage. When we undertake a task as personal and empathetic as therapy, concerns as to the ways in which some values become accepted procedures and others do not are crucial to ethical practice and to the ability of our clients to make use of what we offer them. When trainees or clients cannot *identify* with what is being taught or presented in terms of their own life experience, they tend to simply detach from it a bit and not really participate. Therapeutic change cannot happen without emotional commitment and involvement, but the community can engage us in the world of our clients which has often been absent from our professional training, so that our clients do not have to do all the work of joining us in relationship at a time when they are vulnerable and need empathy.

It is important to note that the experiential gap between professional training and clients served is *not* maintained at will, by persons with little concern or sensitivity to others. Rather, the point to be made is that it is a by-product of certain *institutionalized* power relationships, according to which some training practices seem "clearly" logical, such as the description of clinical supervision noted previously here. Our own culture and values always seem to be logical and right, and clinicians cannot be expected to be any different from other human beings in terms of their responsiveness to their own cultural imperatives, no matter how much we care about our clients. When we are in relationship to others with less political and economic power than we have, our values dominate and define the nature of our interactions; and this is just as true in social services as in areas of employment and housing. Civil rights demands in the 1960s were for more community control of services, understanding that the client's frame of reference would be better understood when it was reinforced by the community's political and economic power.

It has not worked for us to train according to our own frames of reference, and then to offer a course or two on cultural competence or multicultural perspectives because these courses miss, and then cover up for, the basic institutionalized imbalances. Rather, *the cultures of our clients need to be represented in the planning of our generalized curricula*, and not added as an after-thought, after the "basic" principles have been learned. *When advanced training is based in the particular communities of our clients and done by those who are also members of the community and who are guided by its natural leadership, there is a better chance of this happening.* This may seem unrealistically idealistic, given the current business climate. To not take steps in this direction, however, is to miss the desperate need to do so in this society. Unfortunately, we have gone so far in the direction of capitalist fragmentation that we need to be able to make our pieces of effectiveness fit *into* a whole community.

Even so, we will still be engaged in a constant uphill battle. In a racist, classist, sexist society, leaders in all communities *must* be aware of and support the practices and values of the dominant groups, as well as those in their own communities; while leaders in majority communities can afford to ignore frames of reference outside their own. It is the responsibility of education to question the universality and logic of our culturally limited operating assumptions. But it is not likely that this will happen in institutions of higher education, any more than it is likely that our history will reflect the contributions of "minorities," until those having decision-making power are also "minorities."

Training Therapists to Treat Social Problems

When funding pays for treatment of the mentally ill, why should we "treat" social problems? Before budget cuts we were funded for social action and advocacy programs, but now we must "treat" individuals in ways which can be reimbursed as direct service by insurances. If we think, indeed, that there is a connection between individual symptoms and societal dysfunction, we must find a way to "treat" *both* in order not to scapegoat individuals for the larger dysfunction which they are not powerful enough to maintain. So then the concern emerges as to how we will train therapists who will be able to treat both individual and systemic dysfunction.

It would seem that one way to preserve *social* as well as mental health focuses in therapy would be to train therapists in a broad range of interventions which would encompass both Western individualistic, scientific, and linear kinds of solutions and the more inclusive, expansive, political and spiritual remedies offered more by people of color. Social work has always done this to a great degree, offering casework, group work, and community organization curricula; and designing interventions which would address the concrete living circumstances and social supports of the client as well as his/her individual feelings and behavior. Another way we have tried to encompass both social and individual realities was in mental health treatment teams consisting of psychiatry, psychology, and social work specialties, bringing together their various specialty areas after having first separated them according to the "separate aspects" of the whole person of the client. In these teams, the three specialty areas did not come together as equals, but with the psychiatrist generally at the head, giving more weight to individual pathology in treatment.

Family therapy entered this scene about thirty-five years ago as a response to the fragmentation involved in the process of first separating knowledge into individual and social categories and then knitting the categories back together again. It was also a response to the Civil Rights Movement of the 1950s and 1960s which pressured the government for community control of social services. As poor communities began to take control of their own services, definitions of therapy shifted more toward the strengthening of client supports, and toward interventions which could effect changes in larger systems as well as individual clients. *Family therapy is in the fortunate position of owing its evolution to both Civil Rights/community development and to mental health expansion, and has developed some interventions targeted at extended families and communities as well as individuals.* If we think that an individual's problems are maintained within certain *family, cultural* and *societal* patterns, family therapy has added to the existing abilities of psychology, psychiatry, and social work to build tools for therapists which will bridge these spans of experience. *When problems of racism, classism, and sexism are severe in society, therapists need tools to address larger dysfunctions in their work with troubled individuals, including the dysfunctions in our training and treatment systems.*

A major contribution of family therapy to the development of systemic tools has been in the use of practicum training. When early family therapists realized that they needed to effect change in the nuclear family as well as the individual, they knew they could not rely on supervisee's verbal reports of family sessions or tape recorded sessions, because the supervisor had to get a sense of many simultaneous interactions in the room which the supervisee would not be aware of, many of them non-verbal. And so, the idea of an observing team, including the supervisor/trainer watching the session from an adjoining room with a one-way mirror intersecting came into wide use in family therapy. This method of observation gave the supervisor more control and active input into the therapy process, and so more power to affect learning. As with any increase in power, there were some unfortunate side effects, as mentioned above in terms of the development of "gurus" or masters who could at times market charisma more than content.

However, practicum training in systems work was/is also a tool which can weaken supervisor control in the training process, and open the supervisor-student relationship to an observing group. In groups in which there is a strong "master" there tends to be less discussion among those observing the same family therapy session together. In those groups, trainees usually talk only when the master steps out to go to the bathroom, or when they are in the hallways, or at lunch, etc. They learn that the rules of the practicum training are to be the same as those in classroom lectures in which the teacher talks and the masses take notes. But in family therapy training, trainees are already professionals, have experience and a base of knowledge, and tend to be older than those in graduate schools. So the "hallway discussions" or the discussions behind the mirror involving less dominant trainers tend to be among equals, and tend to be very informative, especially when the group is a mix of gender, race, and class.

The trainees at BFST in Chapter Nine reflected the mix of cultures in the community. Trainees were recruited according to some knowledge of the community and intended to continue to work there; knowing they would have continuing connection to each other in the community *after* the training, their discussions *in* the training tended to be much less hierarchial. Respect was accorded to trainers, but the basis for expertise was not only family therapy training but experience in the community and cultural understanding. This meant that a good deal more listening to trainees' viewpoints happened than in traditional family therapy training institutes. It meant that interventions tended to be much less according to a particular model, but according to what fit the agreed-upon interpretations from the group as to what was needed. The opportunity to come together and think and talk together around commonly observed family interactions enhanced the group's social solidarity, diverse options, and collective self-management (process goals of institutions which promote community development, noted in Albert et al 1986). Moreover, in the community-based training in Chapter Nine, trainers could not rely solely on practicum training: large natural systems such as families, work settings, and communities did not come together to assemble before the one-way mirror, any more than they could come into an office for a session. Quite often, the trainees and supervisor would have to "go to the mountain," and would then be caught up in many levels of interaction, often in languages not understood. *They would have to participate in community rituals, organization, and institutions "after hours" so that training would become membership*, a kind of commitment beyond the usual expectations of training.

This kind of emphasis on membership reduces the gap in expertise between trainer and trainees, and allows for many kinds of expertise to interact in the group. There is a lot of valid knowledge from group members who may have less of the European formal education but follow older community traditions in which knowledge originates in a *certain context* and continues to enrich *that* context. This kind of knowledge is *obviously* limited and partial, and does not pretend to be otherwise. Each small community will have its own kinds of cultures, rituals, and knowledge bases, so that there will be *many varieties* of local wisdom. One becomes more knowledgeable, then, by participation in the life of the community. Experience in primary face-to-face connections is the basis for expertise which takes a long time to acquire, so that the elders are valued. It takes a good deal longer than three years to make a competent family therapist with this kind of thinking. When those with more formal education come together with those with community expertise in an atmosphere which promotes the clinical blending of skills, what results is a kind of group composite expertise, one located *in the connections, more than in the individuals.* When the community can foster ways to maintain these connections, clinical skills will strengthen the community as well as individual clients.

Community Membership: Accumulating Continuing Education Credits

When training is defined as an effort to strengthen small communities in rural and urban areas, it tends to teach diversity and innovative strategies across disciplines. It teaches clinical work which does not choose between individuals and their family and community contexts: since the community context is primary, individual interventions within it will also be appropriate for the community.

Previous chapters Nine and Ten exemplify different ways to train in which the community guides the training and then benefits from it. These are not unique efforts, but spring from social work and family therapy networking traditions, as noted in the readings cited in those chapters. Therapy/training based upon membership, belonging, and inclusion rather than the development of individual status and expertise is a different emotional experience for clients, therapists, and supervisors/trainers alike. An energy is detectable in the halls of the "Families in Crisis Conference," a friendly buzz of a lot of people talking informally and then meandering into different rooms to talk together around topics which concern them immediately. It's the same buzz in the hallways between clients and therapists in community-based settings such as those noted in the chapters in this book. The trainers in Chapter Six knew it and actively facilitated interpersonal relationships within the staff and closeness as a part of the training process. Perhaps this is one of the ways in which clients can decide whether or not they can feel safe to tell therapists in agencies their personal business: can staff relate *with affect,* as caring people who have some connection to each other?

Those of us who have felt the tremendous high of helping to organize community-based training projects will probably keep working to have our burdens lifted in that way, even though our efforts may be short-lived, experimental demonstration projects. This high is the opposite of burn-out, and it provides a lot of support beyond that of a high paycheck or a moonlighting job. It is a spiritual high, a feeling of being connected in meaningful work, of being only one small being in the larger order of the cosmos. *Clinical training, like therapy, is a European invention, often a very good one. When it acknowledges its partiality and it joins with non-European traditions, it has tremendous power.* Indeed, it generally lessens the need for both pharmaceuticals and jails, as well as foster homes and mental hospitals. It encourages the strength of extended families, good schools, active churches of many denominations, and recreational opportunities for all. In understanding the social contexts of individual problems and symptoms, good therapy normalizes crisis and uses it to promote change at many levels, which will include change in the therapist and in our training and service institutions. In times as hard as those we are in, we especially need to promote vibrant support for our students, institutions, and clients, by using the generations of expertise available in our communities.

CHAPTER TWELVE:
THE CLIENT, THE THERAPIST, AND THE COMMUNITY:
NOT SEPARATE CATEGORIES

"People and their cultures perish in isolation, but they are born or reborn in contact with other men and women, with men and women of another culture, another creed, another race. If we do not recognize our humanity in others, we shall not recognize it in ourselves."
— Carlos Fuentes,
"The Mirror of the Other"
The Nation, March 30, 1992

******

Ashes

The changes all of us face now seem to be occurring at breakneck speed. In 1980, $2.1 billion was spent on prison building/maintenance in the U.S. but, in 1994, this escalated to $31.2 billion—even though the homicide rate has decreased in the last 25 years, and 84% of imprisonment has been for victimless crimes (Danziger 1995). If we gather our news from TV or newspapers and even if we watch fictional drama on TV, it seems that crime is rampant. Yet our actual expenditures on prisons are not well publicized. Media encourage us to think that more prisons are needed and to support this contention with tax dollars. Corporations controlling the majority of contracts for new prisons (Correctional Development Corporation, American Detention, Spacemasters, and Wachenhut) have profit ratios of 500%, making crime and punishment a growth industry in this country second only to pharmaceuticals (*Ibid.*). Historically, our prisons reconstituted the plantation system after slavery, and helped to maintain the *status quo* of race and class imbalance. Now, 75% of prison admissions are African-American and Latin-American.

As social services have been privatized or transferred from government to private or corporate resources, business/profit-making standards have scaled-down a welfare state supposedly in need of being scaled-down, even though less than 3% of the federal budget is spent on financial assistance and family support services, and *while* the economy has changed from industrial to postindustrial (i.e., the computerization of many services, with less manpower needed while the working-age population continues to increase). Companies can demand a higher level of education for existing positions; and, since governmental tuition assistance programs have been cancelled or sharply reduced, jobs are filled more from the ranks of those who can pay for higher education. This system of institutionalized racism/classism discriminates against those with less power in this society, and pits them against each other for even fewer jobs when corporations "downsize" to protect or increase profit margins.

The Child Welfare League of America found that forty-one of the 49 child welfare services administrations they surveyed in 1995 were planning to apply managed care principles to the financing and delivery of child welfare services. Some states who are already contracting to do this plan to use family-preservation and family-support services to decrease reliance on foster care; and to develop community-based therapeutic models as alternatives to placement (Landers 1996). *While these models may work, their effectiveness depends on proper training and support for staff used to non-systemic models, and on a context of community support and preservation.* Otherwise, program models which have produced good results in some communities get borrowed without consideration of the particular community relationships and structures which made the original models successful in the first place. Without being grounded in or supported by the community and suited to its traditions (i.e., "process," or *how* things are done), new models (i.e., "products," remedies, techniques) do not have enough power to work well. Indeed, a recent article reported about the cost-saving benefits of family preservation treatment over foster care *per se* in the 1980s being challenged in the 1990s after horror stories of children returned to abusive parents and then being further abused or murdered (Cooper 1996). The concerns about program effectiveness and continuing funding for them seem to assume that models *can* exist out-of-context, and that concern need not be paid to creating a context in which they will be effective. Surely, treatment models reified like this promise much more than they can deliver—and then, when they fail to *always* deliver, can be discontinued in favor of a newer, quicker fix.

In the case of the current family preservation "controversy," investigations, by virtue of casting doubt on that reified in the first place, then set the stage for the further downsizing of potentially and actually good programming. When they plant the seed of doubt and expose the partiality of success, a nation programmed to expect quick and universal "cures" for complex problems will be encouraged to remove its enthusiasm and its funding to a newer and more "complete" remedy, guaranteeing no costly lawsuits. Does this mean that we can expect the pendulum, in this example, to then swing back to financing foster care, and more expensive conventional treatment? When the focus is on saving money, this is unlikely. If we put the current "downsizing" within the pattern of colonization of less powerful people which has been an integral part of our economic development here, we might expect that the next move toward helping the population accept downgrading of services to children will be suggested small moves toward *institutionalization* of children, an idea already seeded by Congressman Newt Gingrich.

Five years ago when this book was begun, the white middle-class author would not have thought of making the comparison between the decimation of community-based social programs, privatization of funding, and increase in spending for institutionalization and imprisonment as belonging within the context of colonization. Perhaps the author unconsciously identified with the colonizers/oppressors, and did not really admit into consciousness the likelihood that she would no longer be "protected" by their control. Surely, the policeman is a friendly helper, and an entire social service system cannot be decimated! But now, of course, we see that it can, that our paychecks are not sacred, and our services will not be a necessary part of the "new order."

Phoenix

It seems obvious that the individual therapist cannot reform this system. These days, many people have gotten out of counseling fields, seeing the "handwriting on the wall." But those who are committed to this work, and who enjoy being part of positive, creative solutions to problems are certainly not packing up and going away. These chapters are examples of *current* effective therapy in *usual* agency settings. The examples do not follow one model, but are quite diverse from each other. Yet they are not diverse in the sense of being unique or unrepeatable in different communities and settings. We know that there are many other such programs which readers will recognize in their own areas. How can there be such a kind of recognizable-ness in these programs which were not designed according to any particular model?

We are a country of diverse cultures. While there is a trend here to be threatened by that diversity which is non-European, and so to control it by hierarchy which places it at the bottom, our institutions cannot continue to excessively depend on European values for sustenance.

In this book, we have tried to credit and explain briefly some of the non-

European traditions which have molded all of the work in these chapters *through the community structures which clinicians have participated in.* Therapists and their administrators in the public sector do not need to be super-human to try new ways to deal effectively with the current crisis. It is not a time for individual heroes, but for *relationship, sharing, and coordination.*

To preserve the core value of *relationship* in therapy, we must try to see ourselves as *part of the phenomenon we are observing, part of the client's problem and part of the client's solution,* and not only as detached observers and diagnosticians. Molly Layton gives a beautiful account of her work with a "borderline" client which moved beyond a focus only on the client's rage or depression to *relationship,* believing that the client needed to experience connection and trust before she would be ready to deal reliably with risk and separation; and then locating the roots of the borderline functioning in a history of trauma. When this happened, change occurred in the perceptions of the therapist as well as the client, shifting from a focus on character to one of character-in-context (Layton 1995). With this kind of a shift, the client becomes *one of us,* less objectified, more *related to.* When we understand the client in terms of contexts outside her/himself which have maintained certain behavioral responses, we are brought closer together, sharing the same social fields, even if not exactly in the same way. This book has emphasized knowledge of the social fields of our clients through knowledge of their cultural histories and communities when institutional race/class/gender gaps block our ability to appreciate the experience of our clients. To appreciate common social fields with our clients (which helps us to experience more relationship to them, as Layton explains), we need the help the community can provide to bridge the barriers to relationship unintentionally inherent in our service organizations and policies long before managed care, and the widening race, class, and gender gaps in our society.

A recent article reports on an innovative treatment program for domestic violence which treats the whole family in which domestic violence has occurred *by providing them with the experience of community* (Wylie 1995; also referenced in Chapter One). The family is embraced by a network of sponsors of fellow community residents which makes their private family violence a community issue, lessens their isolation, and changes the community and political climate maintaining violent behaviors at the same time that it changes behavior within the family. Individual/family therapy is secondary to the family's involvement in community process, and the relationship between therapist and client is then mediated intentionally by community, one relationship among many healing relationships. This program is a good example of the *sharing* we need to build into our programming in times of crisis, sharing between formal agency systems and natural family and community networks. When we share like this, the role of the therapist is akin to the role of the Native healer, faithkeeper, or shaman in which the healer or "therapist" has an honored role, but the role *emerges from* ongoing participation in the life of the community, and is supported by that context. This kind of sharing is a great stress-reliever, even when the stresses are monumental; and readers might be reminded here of the experience of community-based family therapy trainers in Chapter Nine, without salaries or nearly enough time, but still feeling supported and nurtured much of the time.

Betty Carter, a distinguished family therapist who has long related private marital and family issues to larger political and social struggles about gender, recently discussed her work with a white middle-class couple (Carter 1995). She came to realize that their family values re: male-female roles and the work ethic were allowing them nuclear family time, but no *community lives*. Listening to the context for their problems helped this therapist to understand that the couple was missing that level of human interaction which could bridge the gap between the private personal family and the great impersonal public sphere. This left them isolated and without spiritual support and meaning, even though they could only identify the pain at the level of their relationship. Through participation in the client's community, therapists can help clients to rebuild these lost connections necessary for relationship at all levels...and necessary for therapists in their settings, too.

These are just a few examples in the recent literature across several counseling fields which focus attention on the need to integrate work at the community level into work at individual and family levels. They remind us that such integration is as important for white, middle-class clients as for those poor people and people of color who have relied more on community for survival. We have often assumed that only poor people needed to be organized, while those with more privilege could rely on money and status for social support. But the middle-class is easily unstabilized and the ability of our environment to sustain us depends on cooperative efforts.

The longing for community is not just sentimental or nostalgic. Community provides grounding for family relationships and individual identity, *and* for political and economic power. None of us, whether clients or therapists, can afford to let state or corporate interests provide for us without relating to each other. When national and global structures act in ways which perpetuate themselves, we must act in ways which support us adequately or else suffer a kind of state of shock and lack of control over our lives. Calling this human crisis "PTSD" (Post-Traumatic Stress Disorder) or "Adult ADD" (Adult Attention Deficit Disorder, distinct from childhood Attention Deficit Disorder, named first) diverts attention from the political and economic contexts maintaining it and from the increasing frequency of these "diseases" among normal overstressed people.

At this point in our history, it is imperative for those who have gotten out of touch with the meaning and maintenance of community to learn from traditions other than white middle-class cultures which have so easily accepted corporate and bureaucratic fragmentation. Postmodern America, in the vast variety of its Western and non-Western traditions, contains the seeds for its own healing. So, in this book, we have reported on the non-Western underpinnings to the examples of community-based work cited in various chapters.

Work which ties symptoms of mental health to the *actual trauma* suffered in the client's history (e.g., Layton, above) deconstructs mental illness and helps us to see it as a reaction to something real, an attempt to communicate. Many therapists would have a hard time working this way because they have been trained to think primarily of illness as a chronic condition rather than a transitional break in the continuity from one state to another. In this book, Chapter Six shows us the effects of a shift from the community focus, which encouraged normalization, to the medical focus, which respects primarily the difficulty of chronic illness. The community focus tends to be grounded in hope for significant and permanent change of symptoms because it sees these symptoms as having to do with one's history, and sees community connection in the present as capable of supporting a change in that history. This same kind of work is exemplified in Chapter Five, in the work at Cumberland when ex-addicts are helped to recover by getting involved in social action in their community. When medical explanations for symptoms stop at the level of the individual, they must, of necessity, be pessimistic in their expectations for positive change. Targeting only individual behaviors without attending to the complex social and political network maintaining them tends to guarantee weak interventions needing hospitalization or drugs to shore them up. Therapists can use cultural and community contexts to empower individual interventions and reduce the need for costly hospitalization and drug use (e.g., the example cited above by Almeida and staff's work with domestic violence in New Jersey (Wylie 1996), and the kind of interventions taught in Chapters Nine and Ten here). These social system interventions do not so easily separate individual and social problems, and are designed to "cut both ways," increasing the solutions available in the therapist-client relationship.

Complexities and Contradictions in Community-Based Work

Therapy always occurs in a social context. Changes introduced by managed care make us aware that in private practice the therapist-client relationship is mediated by the medical insurance which sets certain parameters. The relationship, then, is not as "private" as it was traditionally imagined to be, but is influenced by external economic and political factors, just as the "public sector" has more obviously been buffeted by shifts in political power and economic resources. We used to say that our public institutions related to citizens' needs through regular programs of health, education, etc.; and that agencies were called upon to serve the community when the "regular" mix of programs failed to meet the special or temporary needs of some citizens. Thus, therapy and social services have always responded to changes in the functioning of societal institutions, and have often been rigidly determined by their failures. In the 1980s, for example, treatment of homeless clients usually consisted of helping those who had gotten out of the habit of relating to regular structure to relearn and reconnect, assuming that suitable housing would soon be found for them. When this assumption has not been borne out, treatment fails when it continues to do business as usual and does not acknowledge that housing policies seem to be creating a permanent homeless population. Our clients' problems are systemic, and we are all in the stew together.

Generally, however, when power imbalances in society create social problems, solutions need to be political ones, with people *organizing* to seed redress of the imbalance. When people come together and vote in one way or cooperate together in a certain course of action, they have power, even though they may not have the power of personal status or high income. In the 1960s, as in many other periods of American history, people organized in their local communities to secure improved civil rights for people of color here. Then the federal "War on Poverty" pumped money into minority communities, but organized residents demanded more control of these programs designed to serve their communities. Residents wanted geographic boundaries of areas served spelled out and the agency site located within that area; they wanted those providing services to be *from* the community, and wanted board members to be *from* the community. Some agencies interpreted the "*from*" to mean of the same ethnic group, and so might bring in an African-American or Chicano staff member from outside the area with the desired educational prerequisites. They were surprised to find that these persons were often rejected by residents because residents meant community *membership* by "from," not solely ethnicity. Community residents needed someone to represent their interests who knew them and was accountable to them, and who would have been participating in all the informal organizations, activities, and rituals which were the glue of the community. *These persons, then, would have been educated by their own participation in the community.* If they were also educated in universities by agency standards, all well and good; but they had to have been educated by the community.

These *two* bases for education in public agencies in poor communities during the era of community-control caused a lot of confusion in agencies. Those educated in universities tended to be aware only of the university as *the* basis for clinical knowledge, and a whole system of credentialing structures had grown up around this belief. Grants were given to agencies based on staff having such training, and insurances paid for licensed service based on degrees more than experience. Prompted by local pressure, agencies did come to value community experience as a basis for work with clients, but even then only at the level of the "case aide" assisting the "real" work of the degreed therapist. The agency could then meet the community's demands in ways which did not change the essential power arrangement between the communities of poor people of color and those of whites from outside who would go into the community armed with degrees which provided them with externally-based solutions. Such co-optation echoes colonization and the missionary assurance that foreign solutions for local problems were "better."

Many in the 1960s polarized this situation, defining the choice as *either* the relevance of traditional university education *or* knowledge of the community. However, the author's experience in graduate school and agencies during that time was of an extremely thought-provoking and emotionally-charged climate *perfect* for growth and institutional change. If one was involved in service provision in the public sector then one *could not polarize*: the agency needed to have *both* the community *and* the university bases of knowledge, if it wanted federal grants. Clinical education had to prepare students to operate in this climate where *both* were valued. In my graduate experience at the University of Wisconsin-Milwaukee School of Social Welfare, all casework majors desiring to "do therapy" were *also* required to take a minimum of three community organization courses. Casework majors complained at first, but 40% of the student body was African-American and understood the requirement better than European-American students and professors. Minority student recruitment and assistance and federal funding for community-controlled programs challenged the assumptions of white, middle-class privilege in this graduate program and countless others. So we were trained to do a kind of therapy in which clients would be enabled to find connections and group resolution of individual problems. Moreover, we were trained to think together and do projects together, rather than to develop individual "star" ideas. University professors were preparing us for membership, and for respecting community expertise, at a time when *community-based work in agencies was paying professionals to join rather than to lead.*

Even though the funding for this kind of creativity was withdrawn, agencies are still affected by models set then. Most boards are still somewhat more reflective of poor communities than they had been. Most agencies have branch offices in poor communities staffed by residents who have strong voices in determining the character of services offered.

However, "therapy," for the most part, tends to be offered more outside the community, and clients are referred to "therapy" by mainstream resources who seek only the degree credentials of therapists and not their knowledge and experience base in the community. When there is recognition that the balance has been skewed and that therapists do not know enough about the real life contexts of their clients to be effective, brief courses in "cultural competence" or "cultural diversity" are offered. While these courses may provide good information about the content of different cultures, they confuse "community" and "culture" and miss the point of the need for connection to actual community structures and rituals. While promoting information, they deny the need for *membership*. Without this, clinicians will assume much more understanding than they can ever get from a brief course, and will tend to approach poor people of color even more simplistically and from a distance. Just as good therapy makes often brief and effective interventions in the context of personal and political *relationships*, it can help to remedy race/class/gender biases in the context of its *membership to community*.

Class, race, and gender gaps are maintained by institutional structures which are separate or which operate primarily by one set of values *over* others. When agencies serve poor people and people of color and those with a variety of gender role expectations, their policies and staff perceptions must be wide enough to encompass many values. This makes agencies very interesting places in which to do therapy. Conflict and contradictions *will* be part of the work, and administrators can deal with it in many ways. An agency is not overtly concerned with social change and is funded often only for individual symptom relief, divorced from any connection to social context. This is enough of a role and enough responsibility for any staff. Many administrators keep the role very clearly delineated, but understand that it can, at the same time, promote diversity and social change. When an administrator patches together many funding streams, s/he cuts down on the inordinate power of only one or two. However, this method of encouraging diverse programming is limited in that it demands a great deal of support staff and administrative time in monitoring and accounting to many funding sources. Often diverse agencies merge into one to maximize their ability to attract multiple funding sources (e.g., Hispanics United of Buffalo, Inc. in Chapter Three); but merger can actually cut down on diversity and the building of *many strong institutions* in a community (as at Ibero Community Action League in Chapter Three).

Many administrators are trying to combat the desperation and fragmentation of our times, not by merging and consolidation, but by cooperatively participating with other agencies in the same geographical area in a common project which combines and coordinates resources (e.g., Bailey and Koney 1996). This kind of *coordination,* especially when it involves natural leadership in the community, *makes the geographic community the organizer for services* and keeps the focus more on the needs of residents in a certain area than on competition for those residents' health care dollars.

This kind of "third way" solution demands highly skilled administrators who will network with a wide variety of other agencies and community organizations, and who will look for staff able to design programs or experimental projects from their knowledge of the community as well as their ideas about therapy learned in professional education. The reality of fewer resources directs us to cooperate ways to *share* them, realizing that competition and advertising *our* services as continually *better than* others can only work when we do not depend on each other for survival. In actual communities, the effectiveness of one service depends on the effectiveness of many.

In order to help clients make bridges back from alienation, we must come closer to them and be on the bridge ourselves. They will not traverse the distance alone, according to European-American values of extreme individualism and detachment of the therapist. *Agencies can help therapists to relate more personally to their clients by encouraging their membership in clients' communities, and by setting up program experiments which help this to happen.* Administrators are the conduits for this kind of expansion and diversity.

The chapters in this book are real stories told by a group that defined itself by membership **both** *in the agency or organization* **and** *the community.* In agencies that do not reject the credentials of university-based clinical training, but base services in the community and use community connections to inform and expand thinking, administrators and staff get more support and clients get better connected. Social action may not be a specific mandate within the agency but the community's power and ability to influence larger structures is increased indirectly by this kind of agency process. Therapists, then, need not omit social context from their work with individuals couples, and families, even when the political and economic climate make it difficult.

Case Vignettes

"**M**" begins to work with me in a mental health setting, referred by Family

Court for not attending school for most of the last three years. She is 14 years old, European-American, the second of four children. Her 18-year-old sister is close to her emotionally, but they do not see each other often, since the sister lives in a small town an hour away near the father, and public transportation between here and there is poor. "M" and her sister had lived with the father for a year when "M" was 12-years-old, but this had not worked out well. Father lived a rather free-wheeling lifestyle enhanced by the regular use of recreational drugs. While he could be nurturing, he had identified his primary responsibility as his job and left the management of two teenage girls to his girlfriend, with predictable conflicts then unsuing. While "M" had gone to school when previously living with her mother, at dad's she rebelled against the girlfriend by refusing to go and hanging out with older friends who drank a lot, like her sister. While "M" says she never remembers feeling good in her life but always was depressed, as she is now, she did feel good about everything when she drank. She quit drinking when she returned to live with her mother a little over a year ago, except for when she visits her father and sister every 2-4 weeks for the weekend.

Now, at mother's, there is more structure going on around her than at dad's. Mom works full-time and is raising 4-year-old and 6-year-old siblings from a second marriage of twelve years which recently ended in divorce after "M" returned home. Mom works hard to provide for the three children and keep their small apartment clean and orderly. "M" seems to be visiting, sleeping on the couch, not knowing many people, and not going to school as mom constantly urges her to do. While mom has standards and is critical when they are not followed, "M" knows that she will not enforce her standards, and that her husband, more the enforcer, is gone.

"M" is close to her mom, in spite of their conflict. The mother was raised by her father after her own mother had left the family when she was three years old, but when mom became an adolescent, father sought foster care placement for all the children so that he would not be too overwhelmed and lose his job, maintaining regular visiting. The mother had acted out in her adolescence, without serious drugs or crime, and had been placed in nine foster homes and two institutions. Now she does not want "M" to be placed and wants to be able to be firmer with her at home, but she also feels overwhelmed and will not allow herself to get to the point where she loses her job or jeopardizes the younger children.

Mom had gotten a PINS (Person in Need of Supervision) Petition in Family Court before coming to see me, to have the court's authority enhance her own and, hopefully, tip the balance so "M" would go to school, but she has not gone. In the beginning of our work together, I had arranged to drop her off at school for two weeks if she missed the school bus, to get her into the habit of some regularity and to get to know her better. Generally, "M" sleeps and watches TV all day, isolated and depressed. For the two weeks in which I picked her up for school, it was hard for her to get moving, but she did. She was happier when participating in the structure of school, although feigning boredom. On the few days in which I could not drive her, she stayed in bed.

After missing these days, Family Court has notified the mother that they are returning the case to court to place her unless we can show that she has gone to school on her own recognizance before the court appearance in 3-4 weeks. In the work thus far, "M" has taken initiative to come to appointments on her own, and has engaged well in the process. The mother has moved away from her earlier "double messages" to "M"(I want you home; I'm overwhelmed and only prepared to welcome you as a visitor) to now deciding that she wants to keep her at home and work through her fears of being overwhelmed with me.

For only seven weeks of therapy, we are moving pretty fast. However, I feel pressured. In order to be able to keep "M" working, I need to be able to get them bonded to me very fast; while working with the Family Court system to allow them to keep her with me even though her symptom cannot be completely stopped in seven weeks. There has not been enough structure and support to keep the children at home in this family for two generations, and the court cannot provide enough support to keep her in the home, but threatens removal. We all answer to her probation officer, and the law says that missed days of school are a probation violation. *If* I can be allowed enough time by the court to get to know the family and give it emotional support, then I can use the court's authority as a motivator to get "M" going. However, I am entering the system after almost three years of poor to no attendance, no previous therapy, and no real family supports. There is much more pulling her toward placement than toward stabilizing her at home. It is quite difficult for out-patient therapy to have the power of the family's history and the court's mandates.

My work environment does not help. It is the rule of thumb that therapists here sit in their offices and wait for clients to come in. It is certainly not accepted practice to go out and pick kids up and take them to school, and might be regarded as the case manager's job or the parent's job. Neither this activity, not my collateral contacts often to the probation department, are billable, not being covered by the family's medical insurance. If I want to work as I have chosen to, it will have to be outside the office's norms and the insurance's coverage. I'll have to be "dedicated" to do it, while maintaining adequate *billable* activity to keep my direct -service statistics on par with what is expected. My setting also is not designed for crisis work, so that this adds to my pressures.

"**S**" is a 15-year-old African-American boy who also doesn't like school, but generally goes, giving teachers a hard time once he is there. While he is bright and can get high grades even when he sporadically takes tests or does homework, he is defiant and frequently is sent to the principal's office or suspended. He has gone to five schools in the past four years and has "gotten all of them to want me out of there", seeing himself as powerful and able to get rejected in racist schools.

"S" lives with his mother, stepfather, and 10-year-old brother in a nice apartment above the maternal grandmother, in a crime-ridden neighborhood. Both adults work full-time, and the younger brother is on the honor role in school. "S"s dynamics complement his mother's. She and the step-father are ex-addicts, but mother has not used cocaine for seven years. Step-father has been off alcohol for two years, but recently began to drink again, starting a rush of marital arguments and "making me act up again" in school, "S" says. In family sessions, everyone fears losing all that they have built up. Mother and step-father agree to separate while he goes into out-patient treatment again. After he leaves, mother unexpectedly tries to kill herself with pills. It is not a real serious attempt, but has the effect of getting order and getting "S" to behave in school for a while, at a time when the step-father cannot be enlisted to back up the mother's authority. We meet and discover that "S"s acting-out often has served to keep mom diverted from her depression, needing to get after "S" and go to many school meetings; and her acting -out occasionally with suicidal threats gets "S" serious and worried that "she'll go back to drugs" if he doesn't shape up. We decide to work on helping both of them to *focus* more on their *own* daily goals, while I take the role of the helper temporarily which they had been taking with each other. This puts a little more distance between mother and son, but cannot substitute very long for the more substantial supports needed by this family.

Mother decides to take a referral from me to learn to read. While also very bright, she was raised in an alcoholic home in which she was physically and sexually abused and her needs were ignored. She is a fighter and has learned to translate her anger into positive action, with drugs giving her a vacation in the past from the weight of all the solitary responsibility. She has seldom shared the weight with other people. She goes to "S"s school with me and we spend 2 hours meeting with his teachers, an unusual opportunity, since the school has had to cut staff and classes are large and more unruly. We discover that they have not been standing up to his antics at low levels and been as firm as mom is at home, where he behaves well and helps a lot. We make a plan for the school to use mom's authority to help "S" learn that he cannot intimidate teachers. "S" wants to move on to another school again as he has in the past, but we get the school to work with us to keep him there. The next day, he tries to steal a car and is arrested.

Now we are in the middle of court appearances, but "S" is being tried as an adult and has spent two days in the adult jail before going home. He has a little extra swing to his gait now and tells me he is "free of all that", as he has indeed used the system to overpower his mother and I. As we could predict, the school transferred him to an alternative school for delinquent and "problem" children, where structure and academic standards are much lower. Now he also gets "counseling" from probation and another social worker assigned by the court when I was out of town, even though I sent the court information on our continuing work. The strengths of the family bonds are weaker in comparison to the pull of the streets,and the fragmentation of the court system.

Both of these cases are examples of acting-out youth *in a system which does not support their strengths or the strengths of their families.* The court and counseling systems operate in ways that encourage distance, fragmentation, and weak interventions. Children quickly assess that involvement in counseling and/or court will not enhance parental functioning, but separate children from it. These are vignettes about problem *systems* in which children certainly can be responsive to in-depth crisis treatment when counselors know how to do it, are paid to do it, and can be given a window of opportunity in which to do it. But with reductions in training, most therapists can only operate at the level of trying to motivate individual children, apart from their contexts. This is about all that funding allows. Neither the criminal justice system nor youth really expect counseling to work to support their families, so that, when they are angry at families or want adult status prematurely, the system reinforces them getting away from conflicts instead of resolving them. Detention/punishment is enlisted quickly, forgetting that this can be only a stop-gap measure which does not *resolve dynamics within* families. Over-reliance on medication and incarceration *prevents resolution* of family problems and fragments those with weak support systems even more.

Fifteen years ago, I would have had more time to work with these students. With my experience in family, adolescent, and addiction dynamics, these cases would not have been particularly difficult. I then worked in a family counseling setting which was neither mental health nor delinquent/criminal. Funding was for alleviation of "family problems", and I got credit for out-of-office collateral sessions, as well as in-office strictly verbal therapy. These would tend to be easier cases because both of these children and their family members involve themselves easily with treatment, and show the ability to change behaviors when extra support can enhance the family's own weak organization.

But in the 1990s we are not paid to increase the normal strengths of families to meet crises. We must define problems as *pathology in* the family in order to get paid. For poor and minority persons, the scapegoating quickly changes from emotional pathology to criminality. In our community, some CBOs, schools, agencies and social work educators are coming together to design a project to address some of these gaps. We are not planning another "new" program to send more people into the homes when there is a crisis, but want to aim our efforts at shoring up the natural community support and the support to therapists *already working* in programs serving families. We want to help therapists buy time in the system to work more effectively, maximizing the skills they have already and enabling families to paritcipate more in the regular life of the community.

The cases in these vignettes are not "M" and "S". They are "M" and "S" *and* all of us: us when we do not tap into family and community strengths, and us when we put our heads together to do so.

Pride in the Role of Therapy

Communities are places where people of diverse backgrounds try to get along together and promote improvements in their lives. The richness in community participation, as in family life and other serious commitments, lies in the conflictual and often contradictory *process* of participation.

Of course, communities are not motherhood and apple pie. Often community leaders oppress residents and imitate ways in which they themselves have been oppressed. Often lack of resources does not lead to sharing but to sell-outs, private gain, hoarding, and mistrust. The drug industry and promotion of addiction discourages the best of us. Moreover, one cannot just walk into a community and get to know it and understand its dynamics overnight. Professionals are often put off by the slowness of this process, and the very personal time-consuming attention which must be paid to relationship-building. It goes in exactly the opposite direction from that taken by a computer- and technology-oriented society, and may *seem* to be going nowhere. Education and status outside the community may often make one suspect inside it, so that s/he will have to be tested if s/he is not from the community, whatever his/her ethnicity.

The first reason to bother with it all is for one's own good, with the knowledge that personal growth and change are necessary, but they do not happen alone, without a supportive context. Secondly, the reason to bother is because one has come to take his/her work very seriously and *loves* doing it. When one's work is grounded in community networking, beyond only the network of agencies, fresh alternatives, projects, and interventions constantly emerge. The work, however difficult, offers renewal and joy which suggest the beginnings of a social movement—even though the therapy has not been directly concerned with political content. There is a unity and wholeness in the dialogue with clients which is reparative of the separation encouraged by advertising (Lears 1995) in this society, the separation of humans from the material world, and human subjectivity from the world of experience. Participation in the client's community makes the relationship with the client part of a larger world and allows us to be more personal and real with each other—without the excesses and abuses of power which would need to be guarded against if the relationship were isolated from community context.

Participation in the community makes one more aware, in the author's experience, of his/her own multiple identifications and partial belongings in this world. Sometimes that can feel broadening, and sometimes painful and incomplete. One's associations with some people carry a certain kind of gossip, and preclude associations with other persons for a time. One's color, accent, speech patterns, dress, etc. all put him/her in a certain category of race, class, etc. As one changes over the years and becomes part of new communities, one can never quite go back to the old self and associations completely. We do not assimilate, but grow constantly changing identities, needing constantly to deal with issues of change and loss.

The multicultural United States offers these bittersweet growth options more than any other. Therefore, doing therapy in the public sector with many cultures needs to be based on experience in community process. Since well-defined communities are disproportionately poor and minority, the process will necessarily focus on getting *changes* in social policies which have been set *outside* the community and which place unfair restrictions on residents. Our interventions as therapists, then, will work with families to change their communities—and, thus, sociopolitical contexts (Elkaim 1979).

Many therapists consider themselves apolitical, and therapy a neutral, non-political protected space in which the individual can reflect, away from context. This volume contends that neither the therapist nor the client can step into the office and leave the real world behind. As they talk about intimate conflicts and feelings, each of them has perspectives complicated by their race, class, and gender memberships. Often there are impasses which must be acknowledged and worked through, and the difficulty of working through relationship issues in real communities helps therapists to engage in difficult process with clients, rather than avoid it. Clinical education which links therapists to community and to consideration of race, class, and gender issues in therapy empowers and encourages hope, rather than abstracting away from biases. A frequent theme in this book is that our ability to relate to our clients is closely related to our *membership* in their communities. Academic traditions have really not recognized or understood well the importance of community membership for therapists, so this volume has tried to emphasize and explain it.

Therapists and their clients and their agency settings need to get support from the community of their clients in order to make possible the dialogue which can create alternatives. Administrators need to take responsibility to link their agencies to natural supports available in grass-roots communities, just as they link them to funding streams. From the writings of Ignacio Martin-Baro: when what is of value in psychology is not put to work in the service of a people's quest for *collective growth and freedom*, it only scapegoats and catalogs individual weakness, and should be dismantled as an alienating endeavor which only increases peoples' oppression (Aron and Corne 1994). Brazilian educator Paulo Freire has influenced the thinking of many who contributed to this volume, and his central thesis is that change at one "level" always involves change at another "level" (Freire 1990). Interventions will always be used which effect change at multiple levels, *with the community educating therapists as to the appropriateness of interventions, and helping agencies to have other bases of power besides those who fund services.*

More specifically, therapists can use networking interventions (Chapters 3, 9, and 10) in situations with clients in which symptoms are maintained by too much isolation or unresolved grief in adult family members. We see this constantly in practice when clients have not participated in their support networks for a long time due to substance abuse (Chapter 5); or when they are severely depressed or suicidal (Chapter 6); or when they withdraw from family life and neglect or abuse their children (Chapter 7). At these times, adults need more support than the therapist can give them for one hour a week...or even for three hours a day in an in-home program. Adults and nuclear families need the support of extended family, friends, and community, just as children need the support of their parents. This web of relationships provides social security in time of trauma or stressful life transitions. Therapy is an adjunct, a temporary service which can help to bridge the way to more consistent support for clients *when it is connected* to the client's natural support systems and culture in the community. Then, the therapist can use brief, concrete, time-limited models of therapy with the client or the family, and not have to feel that s/he is ignoring the serious needs for more than that support in the client's life.

Professional training can be given in the community which will enable it to make linkages there toward social action and institutional change, helping to assure that therapy will not be used as a scapegoating tool to frame *social* problems as *individual or family* dysfunction. But the main point is that, in community-based therapies, *the community itself supplies models for interventions.* Community-based work takes therapy out of the office and into the world of our clients, enabling us to expand our solutions to those which are most effective in that world and most able to affect it and make it work in the client's behalf. Therapy is straightforwardly a political, as well as a personal, process. When this is understood, the client has resources, is less dysfunctional, and has less long-term need for therapy. The therapist has a more clearly defined and smaller job, and can more easily avoid burn-out while working with poor and disenfranchised (and more middle-class majority, as well) populations.

The Final Word

In the Central to Western New York area, there is an annual conference which I attend, given by the Native American Council on Alcoholism and Substance Abuse, Inc. (NACASA). It is organized by a Native conference committee predominately from the Iroquois Confederacy (Anne Marie Smith, President; also a contributor to this volume in Chapter Nine) and is attended by a great number of Native and other persons concerned with the health of the Native Nation here. As I am finishing final revisions for this book, I have just attended another NACASA conference, and again have come back full of a much clearer idea of community and sense of who I am than before I went. I wish I could reproduce that conference here for readers, the whole atmosphere of honesty, respect, warmth, and good humor. But the book is finished now, and I hope that readers will continue to find more examples of community-based therapy, such as the NACASA conference, in their own areas. I would just like to end here with some of the words I took with me, which seem to be so close to the themes in these chapters:

"We are not disconnected; we are part of a bigger process, a family, clan, and nation. Since the creation of reservations and urbanization, the nation is now called "community." We need to go from multigenerational grief to rebuilding a good life, dressing one another in good feelings. We need to reclaim the responsibilities we've given over. Spirituality is that responsibility inside yourself which can't be transferred to anyone else. It demands that you take risks, and experience balance and peace. It takes a severe state of emergency to get in touch with the spirituality way inside yourself.

Technology does not facilitate spiritual growth very well. English is a technical language which reduces everything, but misses the point: a 3-hour speech about The Great Law in our Native language was reduced to twenty minutes in the English translation...all the context gone. In a fragmented society, therapy needs to focus on connections, and on focusing that energy which reconstitutes life. If certain things happen in your communities, then certain bad consequences will flow from that for all the people. So we cannot let certain things happen. We need to draw from the older healing societies the discipline of how to heal; and break from negative inheritance so that we can use our positive inheritance.

"All heads are the same height." There are no professionals; we all have talents. In community, we hold each other up. We need satisfying lives and loving relationships to cure social breakdown and to rebuild our beliefs. We are thankful every day and we sing songs and celebrate, recognizing all the gifts we have received.

BIBLIOGRAPHY

Agosin, M., ed. 1993. *Surviving beyond fear: women, children, and human rights in Latin America.* Fredonia, NY: White Pine Press.

Albert, M., L. Cagan, N. Chomsky, R. Hahnel, M. King, I. Sargent, and H. Sklar. 1986. *Liberating theory.* Boston, MA: South End Press.

Alcoholics Anonymous World Services, Inc. 1957. *Alcoholics Anonymous comes of age: a brief history of A.A.* New York: Alcoholics Anonymous Publishing, Inc.

Alford, R. R. 1972. The political economy of health care dynamics without change. *Politics and society* (winter): 127-154.

Alvarez, J. 1994. *In the time of butterflies.* Chapel Hill, N. C.: Algonquin Books.

Anderson, H. and H. Goolishian 1988. Human systems as linguistic systems. *Family process.* 27:371-393.

Aponte, H. J. 1976. The family-school interview: an eco-structural approach. *Family process.* 15(3):303-311.

——. 1976. Underorganization in the poor family. In *Family therapy: theory and practice,* ed. P. J. Guerin. New York: Gardner Press.

Aponte, H. J., J. J. Zarski, C. Bixenstine, and P. Cibik. 1991. Home/community-based services: a two-tier approach. *American journal of orthopsychiatry.* 61(3):403-408.

Aponte, H. and J. VanDeusen. 1981. Structural family therapy. In *Handbook of family therapy,* eds. A. S. Gurman and D. P. Kniskern. New York: Brunner Mazel.

Arendt, H. 1958. *The human condition.* Chicago: University of Chicago Press.

Aron, A. and S. Corne, eds. 1994. *Writing for a liberation psychology: Ignatio Martin-Baro.* Cambridge, MA: Harvard University Press.

Arredondo, P., E. Orjuela, and L. Moore. 1989. Family therapy with Central American war refugee families. *Journal of strategic and systemic therapies.* 8:28-35.

Asante, M. K. 1988. *Afrocentricity.* Trenton, New Jersey: Africa World Press, Inc.

Aschenbrenner, J. 1975. *Lifelines: black families in Chicago.* New York: Holt, Rhinehart, and Winston.

Attneave, C. L. 1969. Therapy in tribal settings and urban intervention. *Family process.* 8(2):192-210.

——. 1976. Social networks as the unit of intervention. In *Family therapy: theory and practice,* ed. P. Guerin. New York: Gardner Press.

218

———. 1990. Core network intervention: an emerging paradigm. *Journal of strategic and systemic therapies.* 9(1) 3-10.

Auerswald. E. H. 1982. Thinking about thinking about health and mental health. In *American handbook of psychiatry.* Vol. 2, ed. S. Arieti. 316-338.

———. 1983. The Gouverneur Health Services Program: an experiment in ecosystemic community health care delivery. *Family systems medicine.* 1(3):5-24.

———. 1990. Toward epistemological transformation in the education and training of family therapists. In *The social and political contexts of family therapy,* ed. M. Pravder Mirkin. 19-50.

———. 1995. Sustaining the life of movements. *American family therapy academy newsletter.* 60 (summer): 19-23.

Bailey, D. and K. McNally Koney. 1996. Interorganizational community-based collaboratives: a strategic response to shape the social work agenda. *Social work.* 41(6): 602-611.

Baker Miller, J. (1976). *Toward a new psychology of women.* Boston: Beacon Press.

Barreiro, J. 1993. *The Indian chronicles.* Houston, Texas: Arte Publico Press.

Barry, T. 1987. *Roots of rebellion: land and hunger in Central America.* Boston: South End Press.

Bellah, R. N., R. Madsen, W. M. Sullivan, A. Swidler, and S. M. Tipton. 1985. *Habits of the heart: individualism and commitment in American life.* New York: Harper and Row.

Bepko, C. and J. Crestan. 1985. *The responsibility trap: a blueprint for treating the alcoholic family.* New York: The Free Press.

Berenson D. 1987. Alcoholics Anonymous: from surrender to transformation. *The family therapy networker.* 11(4): 24-31.

———. 1990. A systemic view of spirituality: God and twelve step programs as resources in family therapy. *Journal of strategic and systemic therapies.* 9(1):59-70.

Berg, I. K. 1994. *Family-based services: a solution-focused approach.* New York: W. W. Norton and Company, Inc.

Billingsley, A. 1968. *Black families in white America.* New York: Prentice-Hall.

———. 1992. *Climbing Jacob's ladder: the enduring legacy of African-American families.* New York: Simon and Schuster.

Birkert, S. 1994. *The Gutenberg elegies: the fate of reading in an electronic age.* New York: Ballantine Books.

Blau, P. 1987. *Bureaucracy in modern society.* New York: Random House.

Bower, E. M. 1987. Prevent219ion: a word whose time has come. *American journal of orthopsychiatry.* 57(1): 5.

Boyd-Franklin, N. 1987. Group therapy for black women: a therapeutic support model. *American journal of orthopsychiatry.* 57(3): 394-401.

Bratter, T. E., E. A. Collabolletta, A. J. Fossbender, M. C. Pennacchia, and J. R. Rubel. 1985. The American self-help residential therapeutic community: a pragmatic treatment approach for addicted character-disordered individuals. In *Alcoholism and substance abuse: strategies for clinical intervention,* eds., T. E. Bratter and G. G. Forrest. 461-507. New York: The Free Press.

Brieland, D. 1990. The Hull House tradition and the contemporary social worker: was Jane Addams really a social worker? *Social work.* 35(2): 134-138.

Brown, D. B. and M. Parnell. 1990. Mental health services for the urban poor: a systems approach. In *The social and political contexts of family therapy,* ed. M. Pravder Mirkin. Needham Heights, Mass.: Allyn and Bacon: 215-235.

Carlson, E. B. and R. Rosser-Hogan. 1993. Mental health status of Cambodian refugees ten years after leaving their homes. *American journal of orthopsychiatry.* 63(2): 223-231.

Carr, R. 1984. *Puerto Rico: a colonial experiment.* New York: Random House.

Cavanagh, J. and R. Broad. 1996. Global reach: workers fight the multinationals. *The Nation.* March 18: 21-22.

Carter, B. 1995. Focusing your wide-angle lens. *The family therapy networker.* 19(6):31-35. Silver Spring, MD: The family therapy network.

Chambon, A. 1989. Refugee families' experiences: three family themes: family disruption, violent trauma, and acculturation. *Journal of strategic and systemic therapies.* 3:13.

Clark, T. R. 1975. *Puerto Rico and the United States, 1917-1933.* Pittsburgh, PA: University of Pittsburgh Press.

Colas, S. 1994. *Postmodernity in Latin America: the Argentine paradigm.* Durham, N.C.: Duke University Press.

Collins, P. H. 1991. *Black feminist thought: knowledge, consciousness, and the politics of empowerment.* New York: Routledge.

Comas-Diaz, L. and Padilla, A. M. 1990. Countertransference in working with victims of political repression. *American journal of orthopsychiatry.* 60(1):125-134.

Consumer Reports. 1995. Mental health: does therapy help? November, 734-739.

Coontz, S. 1992. *The way we never were: American families and the nostalgia trip.* New York: Harper Collins Publishers.

Cornell, W. F. 1996. Capitalism in the consultation room. *Readings.* 11(1):12-17. New York: American Orthopsychiatric Association.

Danziger, S., ed. 1995. *The real war on crime.* New York: Harper Collins.

Deloria V., Jr. 1994. *God is red: a native view of religion.* Golden, Colorado: Fulcrum Publishing.

deSamper, O. 1988. Ibero American Action League, Inc.: historical background--yesterday and today. Unpublished.

deShazer. 1985. *Keys to solution in brief therapy.* New York: W. W. Norton and Company, Inc.

DeSoto, H. 1989. *The other path: the invisible revolution in the Third World.* New York: Harper and Row.

DiStefano, C. 1990. Dilemmas of difference: feminism, modernity, and postmodernism. In *Feminism/Postmodernism,* ed. L. J. Nicholson. New York: Routledge.

Domokos-Cheng Ham, M. A. 1989. Empathetic understanding: a skill for joining with immigrant families. *Journal of strategic and systemic therapies.* 8:36-40.

Dumont, M. P. 1992. *Treating the poor: a personal sojourn through the rise and fall of community mental health.* Belmont, Mass: Dymphna Press.

Dumont R. 1970. *Cuba: socialism and development.* New York: Grove Press, Inc.

Elkaim, M. 1979. Broadening the scope of family therapy: from the family approach to the sociopolitical approach. *Psychologic and Gesellschafskritik.* 9-10:82-101.

Elkin, M. 1984. *Families under the influence: changing alcoholic patterns.* New York: W. W. Norton and Company, Inc.

Falicov, C. J. 1988. Learning to think culturally. In *Handbook of family therapy training and supervision.* New York: Guilford Press.

Feiner, J. and Brown, D. B. 1984. Psychiatric care of the urban poor: an ecological systems approach. *Einstein quarterly journal of biological medicine.* 2:126-135.

Fisch, R. 1986. The brief treatment of alcoholism. *Journal of strategic and systemic therapies.* 5(3):40-58.

Fisher, D. 1980. *The third woman: minority women writers of the United States.* Boston: Houghton Mifflin Company.

Flores-Ortiz, Y. and Bernal, G. 1990. Contextual family therapy of addiction with Latinos. In *Minorities and family therapy*, eds., G. W. Saba, B. M. Karrer, and K.V. Hardy. New York: Haworth Press.

Foley, V. D. 1982. Family therapy with black disadvantaged families. In *Questions and answers in family therapy*, vol. 2, ed. A. S. Gurman, 255-257. New York: Brunner Mazel.

Foster, D. 1994. The disease is adolescence. *Utne Reader*. July/ Aug: 50-56.

Foucault, M. 1980. *Power/knowledge: selected interviews and other writings*. New York: Pantheon Books.

Franklin, R. M. 1990. *Liberating visions: human fulfillment and social justice in African-American thought*. Minneapolis: Fortress Press.

Freire, P. 1973. *Education for critical consciousness*. New York: Continuum.

———. 1990. *Pedagogy of the oppressed*. New York: Continuum.

Garrett I. 1994. *The coming plague: newly emerging diseases in a world out of balance*. New York: Farrar, Straus, and Giroux.

Genijovitch, E. 1992. Once an immigrant, always an immigrant. Audiotape from the 15th Annual Family Therapy Network Symposium. *The resource link*. 1-800- 241-7785.

Gilligan, C. 1982. *In a different voice*. Cambridge, MA: Harvard University Press.

Goldner, V. 1985. Feminism and family therapy. *Family process*. 24: 31-47.

———. 1988. Generation and gender: normative and covert hierarchies. *Family process*. 27:17-31.

Goldstein, S. 1936. Bye bye Brady bunch: a poor family discovers its competence. *Family therapy networker*. 10(1).

———. 1990. Urban poverty and unavailable family members. *Journal of strategic and systemic therapies*. 9(3):35-48.

Goldstein, S. J. and L. Dyche. 1983. Family therapy of the schizophrenic poor. In *Family therapy in schizophrenia*, ed W. R. MacFarlane. New York: Guilford Press. 289-307.

Gonsalves, C. J. 1990. The psychological effects of political repression on Chilean exiles in the U. S. *American journal of orthopsychiatry*. 60(1):143-153.

Goodrich, T. J., C. Rampage, B. Ellman, and K. Hallstead. 1988. *Feminist family therapy: a casebook*. New York: W. W. Norton and Company, Inc.

Gowdy, E. A. 1994. From technical rationality to participating consciousness. *Social work*. 39(4):362- 370.

Greene, G. J., C. Jensen, and D. H. Jones. 1996. A constructionist perspective on clinical social work practice with ethnically diverse clients. *Social work.* 41(2):172-180.

Grinde, D.A. 1992. Iroquois political theory and the roots of American democracy. In *Exiled in the land of the free: democracy, Indian nations, and the U. S. Constitution,* eds. J. C. Mohawk, and O. R. Lyons, 227-280. Santa Fe: Clear Light Publishers.

Guinan, J. F. 1990. Extending the system for the treatment of chemical dependencies. *Journal of strategic and systemic therapies.* 9(1):11-20 .

Gunn Allen, P. 1986. *The sacred hoop: recovering the feminine in American Indian traditions.* Boston, MA: Beacon Press.

———. 1989. *Spider woman's granddaughters.* New York: Fawcett Columbine.

Haight, D. 1989. Self-help: a Black tradition. *The Nation.* July 24/31 (Scapegoating the black family: black women speak): 136-138.

Haley, A. and Malcolm X. 1964. *The autobiography of Malcolm X.* New York: Ballantine Books.

Haley, J. 1976. *Problem solving therapy.* San Francisco: Jossey-Bass.

———. 1981.Why a mental health clinic should avoid family therapy. *Reflections on therapy and other essays.* 174-189. Chevy Chase, Md. The Family Therapy Institute of Washington, D.C.

Hall, E. H. and G. C. King. 1982. Working with the strength of black families. *Child Welfare.* 61:536-544.

Hall, G. W. 1932. The influence of significant others on the continuation of low-income black clients in treatment. *Dissertation Abstracts International.* 46(6-A):2104.

Halleck, S.L. 1971. *The politics of therapy.* New York: Science House, Inc

Hardy-Fanta, C. 1993. *Latina politics, Latino politics.* Philadelphia: Temple University Press.

Hare, N. and J. Hare. 1984. *The endangered black family: coping with the unisexualization and coming extinction of the black race.* San Francisco: Black Think Tank.

Hayes, W. and C. Mindel. 1973. Extended kinship relations in black and white families. *Journal of marriage and the family.* 35:51-57.

Hernandez, M. 1996. Case studies: a Rose by any other name? *The family therapy networker.* March/April: 69-75.

Hill, R. B. 1971. *The strengths of black families.* New York: Emerson Hall.

Hoffman, L. 1991. A reflexive stance for family therapy. *Journal of strategic and systemic therapies.* 10(3 and 4): 4-29.

——. 1993. *Exchanging voices. a collaborative approach to family therapy.* London: Karnac Books.

Hong, G. K. 1989. Application of cultural and environmental issues in family therapy with immigrant Chinese Americans. *Journal of strategic and systemic therapies.* 8:14-21.

Imber-Black, E. 1986. Families, larger systems and the wider social context. *Journal of strategic and systemic therapies.* 5(4):29-35.

——. 1988. *Families and larger systems: a family therapist's guide through the labyrinth.* New York: Guilford.

Inclan, J. 1985. Variations in value orientations in mental health work with Puerto Ricans. *Psychotherapy.* 22(2):324.

Jacobs, F. H. 1988. The five-tiered approach to evaluation: context and implementation. In *Evaluating family programs,* eds. H. B. Weiss and F. H. Jacobs. 37-68. New York: Aldine DeGruyter.

Jacobs, P., S. Landau, and E. Pell. 1971. *To serve the devil,* vol. 2: *colonials and sojourners.* New York: Random House.

Jerrell, J. M. and J. K. Larsen. 1986. Community mental health services in transition: who is benefitting? *American journal of orthopsychiatry.* 56(1):78-88.

Jimenez deWagenheim, O. 1993. *Puerto Rico's revolt for independence: El Grito de Lares.* New York: Marcus Weiner Publishing.

Jones, K. B. 1993. *Compassionate authority: democracy and the representation of women.* New York: Routledge.

Jones, R. L. 1980. *Black psychology.* New York: Harper and Row.

Kaminer, W. 1992. *I'm dysfunctional, you're dysfunctional: the recovery movement and other self-help fashions.* New York: Addison-Wesley Publishing Company.

Kenyatta, J. 1965. *Facing Mt. Kenya.* New York: Vintage Books.

King, L. M., V. J. Dixon, and W. W. Nobles. 1976. *African philosophy: assumptions and paradigms for research on black persons.* Los Angeles: Fanon Research and Development Center.

King, M. 1981. *Chain of change.* Boston: South End Press.

Kirschner, D. and S. Kirschner. 1986. *Comprehensive family therapy: an integration of systemic and psychodynamic treatment models.* New York: Brunner Mazel.

Korin, E. 1994. Social inequalities and therapeutic relationships: applying Freire's ideas to clinical practice. In *Expansions of feminist family theory through diversity,* ed. R. Almeida. New York: Haworth Press.

Kyung-Hee, N. 1993. Perceived problems and service delivery for Korean immigrants. *Social work.* 38(3):289-296.

Landau, J. 1981. Link therapy as a family therapy technique for transitional extended families. *Psychotherapeia.* 7(4):382.

Landau-Stanton, J. and M. D. Stanton. 1985. Treating suicidal adolescents and their families. In *Handbook of adolescents and family therapy,* eds. M. Pravder Mirkin and S. Koman. New York: Gardner Press.

Landau-Stanton, J. 1986. Competence, impermanence, and transitional mapping: a model for systems consultation. In *Systems consultation: a new perspective for family therapy,* eds. L. C. Wynne, S. H. McDaniel, and T. T. Weber. New York: Guilford Press.

Landers, S. 1996. Child welfare: under new management. *NASW News,* June 3. Washington, D.C.: National Association of Social Workers.

Lasch, C. 1979. *Culture of narcissism: American life in an age of diminishing expectations.* New York: W. W. Norton.

Layton, M. 1995. Emerging from the shadows. *The family therapy networker.* 19(3):35-41. Silver Spring, MD: The Family Therapy Network.

Lears, J. 1995. *Fables of abundance: a cultural history of advertising in America.* New York: Basic Books.

Lekachman, R. and B. VanLoon. 1981. Capitalism for beginners. New York: Random House.

Lin, T. 1984. A global view of mental health. *American Journal of orthopsychiatry.* 54(3):369-374.

Lincoln, C. E. and L. H. Mamiya. 1990. *The black church in the African-American experience.* Durham, N. C.: Duke University Press.

Lindblad-Goldberg, M. and J. L. Dukes. 1985. Social support in black, low-income, single-parent families: normative and dysfunctional patterns. *American journal of orthopsychiatry.* 55(1):42-58.

Lopez, M. M. 1995. Postwork society and postmodern subjectivities. In *The postmodernism debate in Latin America,* eds. J. Beverley, M. Aronna, and J. Oviedo. 165-191. Durham, N. C.: Duke University Press.

Lyons, O. 1992. The American Indian in the past. In *Exiled in the land of the free: democracy, Indian nations, and the U. S. Constitution,* eds. J. C. Mohawk and O. R. Lyons, 13-43. Santa Fe: Clear Light Publishers.

MacFarquhar, L. 1996. Point and click. *The new republic.* April 8:14-16.

MacKinnon, L. K. and D. Miller. 1987. The new epistemology and the Milan approach: feminist and sociopolitical considerations. *Journal of marital and family therapy.* 13(2).

Madanes, C. 1980. The prevention of rehospitalization of adolescents and young adults. *Family process.* 19:179-191.

Madsen, W. 1996. Integrating a "client voice" in clinical training. *American family therapy academy newsletter.* 64. Washington, D.C.: American Family Therapy Academy, Inc.

Marmor, J. 1988. Psychiatry in a troubled world: the relation of clinical practice and social reality. *American journal of orthopsychiatry.* 58(4): 484-491.

Martin, J. 1991. The mental health professional and social action. *American journal of orthopsychiatry.* 61(4):484-488.

Martin, J. M. and E. P. Martin. 1985. *The helping tradition in the black family and community.* Silver Spring, Md.: National Association of Social Workers.

Martineau, W. 1977. Informal social ties among urban black Americans. *Journal of black studies.* 8:83-104.

McAdoo, H. 1977. Family therapy in the black community. *American journal of orthopsychiatry.* 47(1):75-79.

———. 1978. The impact of upward mobility on kin-help patterns and reciprocal obligation in black families. *Journal of marriage and the family.* 4(4):761-776.

McCarthy, p. 1992. *The Delaware family preservation project: implementing planned organizational change.* Division of Program support, Delaware Department of Services for Children, Youth, and their Families. Unpublished paper.

McFarlane, W. R. 1993. Multiple family therapy in schizophrenia. In *Family therapy in schizophrenia,* ed. W. R. McFarlane. 141-172. New York: Guilford Press.

Menand, L. 1994. A critic at large: behind the culture of violence, the war of all against all. *The New Yorker.* March 14:74-84.

Menchu, R. 1984. *I, Rigoberta Menchu: an Indian woman in Guatemala.* New York: Verso Press.

Miller, D. 1983. Outlaws and invaders: the adaptive function of alcohol abuse in the family-helper supra system. *Journal of strategic and systemic therapies.* 2(3).

Miller, K. and R. Dreger. 1973. *Comparative studies of blacks and whites in the United States.* New York: Seminar Press.

Miller, M. C. 1996. Free the media. *The nation.* 262(22):June 3. New York: The Nation Company.

Minuchin, S. 1994. Literal fostering: joining family forces to create a quality kinship system. *Mental health news.* VI(3). Albany, NY: New York State Office of Mental Health.

Minuchin, S. and H. C. Fishman. 1981. *Family therapy techniques.* Cambridge, Mass: Harvard University Press.

Mohawk, J. 1992. Indians and democracy: no one ever told us. In *Exiled in the land of the free: democracy, Indian nations, and the U. S. constitution,* eds. J. C. Mohawk and O. R. Lyons. 43-73. Santa Fe: Clear Light Publishers.

Montalvo, B. and M. Gutierrez. 1984. The mask of culture. *The family therapy networker.* July/August: 42-46.

Montalvo, B. 1986. Lessons from the past: what have we learned about serving poor families? (An interview with Braulio Montalvo). *The family therapy networker.* 10(1):37-44.

Mosher, L. R. and L. Burti. 1989. *Community mental health:principles and practice.* New York: W. W. Norton and Company.

Motenko, A. K. and E. A. Allen, P. Angelos, L. Block, J. deVito, A. Duffy, L. Holton, K. Lambert, C. Parker, J. Ryan, D. Schraft, and J. Swindell. 1995. Privatization and cutbacks: social work and client impressions of service delivery in Massachusetts. *Social work.* 40(4):456-462.

Myers, L. W. 1974. Mothers from families of orientation as role models for black women. *Northeast journal of African and Black American studies. 2(1):7-9.*

Neighbors, H. W. and J. S. Jackson. 1984. The use of formal and informal help: four patterns of illness behavior in the black community. *American journal of community psychology.* 12(6):629-644.

Nichols, M. 1987. *The self in the system: expanding the limits of family therapy.* New York: Brunner Mazel.

Nobles, W. and L. Goddard. 1985. Black family life: a theoretical and policy implication literature review. In *The black family: an Afrocentric perspective*, ed. A. R. Harvey. 21-89. New York: United Church of Christ Commission for Racial Justice.

Nkrumah, K. 1964. *Consciencism: philosophy and ideology for decolonization and development with reference to the African revolution.* London: Heinemann.

O'Hara, M. 1966. Divided we stand. *The family therapy networker.* 20(5):46-53.

Paster, V. S. 1986. A social action model of intervention for difficult to reach populations. *American journal of orthopsychiatry.* 56(4):625-629.

Petras, J. 1970. *Politics and social structure in Latin America.* New York: Monthly Review Press.

Piazza, J. and C. M. delValle. 1992. Community-based family therapy training: an example of work with poor and minority families. *Journal of strategic and sytemic therapies.* 11(2):53-69.

Pinderhughes, E. 1989. *Understanding race, ethnicity and power: the key to efficacy in clinical practice.* New York: The Free Press.

Perry, W. G. 1981. Cognitive and ethical growth: the making of meaning. In *The modern American college,* ed. A. Chickering. New York: Jossey-Bass.

Poerksen, U. 1995. *Plastic words: the tyranny of a modular language.* State College, PA: Pennsylvania State College Press.

Price, R. H., E. L. Cowen, R. P. Lorion, and J. Ramos-McKay. 1989. The search for effective prevention programs: what we learned along the way. *American journal of orthopsychiatry.* 59(1):49-58.

Proctor, E. K., N. R. Vosler, and E. A. Sirles. 1993. The social environmental context of child clients: an empirical exploration. *Social work.* 38(3):256-262.

Reich, R. B. 1991. Secession of the successful. *The New York times magazine.* January 20:27-31.

Rifkin, J. 1989. *Time wars.* New York: Simon and Schuster.

———. 1996. Civil society in the information age. *The nation.* February 26:11-16.

Ritterman, M. K. 1987. Torture: the counter-therapy of the state. *The family therapy networker.* 11(1):43.

———. 1991. *Hope under siege: terror and family support in Chile.*

Norwood, New Jersey: Ablex Publishing Corporation.

Rodriquez, M. M. 1983. *Voices from El Salvador.* San Francisco: Solidarity Publications.

Sacks, K. 1989. In *Women and the politics of empowerment,* eds. A. Bookman and S. Morgan. Philadelphia: Temple University Press.

Saegert, S. 1989. Unlikely leaders, extreme circumstances: older black women building community households. *American journal of community psychology.* 18(3):295-316.

Sawatzky, D. D. and J. E. Lawrence. 1989. Dealing with dualisms: working with counselors in the treatment of substance abusers. *Journal of strategic and systemic therapies.* 8(1):24-35.

Scharff, D. and J. Scharff. 1987. *Object relations in family therapy.* New York: Jason Aronson.

Schor, J. 1993. The overworked American. New York: Harper.

Schorr, E. and D. Schorr. 1988. *Within our reach: breaking the cycle of disadvantage and despair.* New York: Anchor Books.

Schumacher, E. F. 1973. *Small is beautiful: economics as if people mattered.* New York: Harper Row.

Schwartz, R. C. 1988. The trainer-trainee relationship in family therapy training. In *Handbook of family therapy training and supervision.* New York: Guilford Press.

Schwartzman, J. 1985. *Families and other systems.* New York: Guilford Press.

Speck, J. L. and R. V. Speck. 1985. Social network intervention with adolescents. In *Handbook of adolescents and family therapy,* eds. M. Pravder Mirkin and S. Koman. New York: Gardner Press.

Speck, R. V. and U. Rueveni. 1969. Network therapy: a developing concept. *Family process.* 8(2):182-191.

Stack, C. 1974. *All our kin: strategies for survival in a black community.* New York: Harper and Row.

Stanton, M. D. 1985. The family and drug abuse: concepts and rationale. In alcoholism and substance abuse: strategies for clinical intervention, eds. T. E. Bratter and G. G. Forrest. 398-430. New York: The Free Press.

Swignoski, M. E. 1996. Challenging privilege through Africentric social work practice. *Social work.* 41(2):153-161.

Taber, R. H. 1970. A systems approach to the delivery of mental health services in black ghettoes. *American journal of orthopsychiatry.* 40(4):702-709.

The family therapy networker. 1996. 20(3): May/June.

Thomas, V. G., N. G. Milburn, D. R. Brown and L. E. Gary. 1988. Social support and depressive symptoms among blacks. *Journal of black psychology.* 14:35-45.

Todd, T. 1991. Lecture given at New York City Health and Hospital Corporation Master Therapist Series. New York, NY, October 10.

Trimble, D. W. and J. Kliman. 1992. Network intervention. In *The family therapies: principal approaches,* ed. M. Elkaim. Paris: Les Editions du Sevil.

Tsui, P. and G. L. Schultz. 1985. Failure of rapport: why psychotherapeutic engagement fails in the treatment of Asian clients. *American journal of orthopsychiatry.* 55(4):561-569.

Tung, M. 1991. Insight-oriented psychotherapy and the Chinese patient. *American journal of orthopsychiatry.* 61(2):186-194.

van der Velden, E. H., L. L. Ruhf, and K. Kaminsky. 1991. Network therapy: a case study. In *Family therapy approaches with adolescent substance abusers,* eds. T. C. Todd and M. D. Selekman. 209-226. Needham Heights, MA: Allyn and Bacon.

Vasquez, J. 1994. Bilingualism and the Latino ascendancy. Unpublished paper.

Venables, R. W. 1992. American Indian influences on the America of the founding fathers. In *Exiled in the land of the free: democracy, Indian nations, and the U. S. constitution,* eds. J. C. Mohawk and O. R. Lyons. 73-124. Santa Fe: Clear Light Publishers.

Wachtel, E. F. and P. L. Wachtel. 1986. *Family dynamics in individual psychotherapy: a guide to clinical strategies.* New York: Guilford.

Wade, J. C. 1993. Institutional racism: an analysis of the mental health system. *American journal of orthopsychiatry.* 63(4):536-544.

Waldegrave, C. 1990. Just therapy. *Dulwich centre newsletter* (1). Dulwich Centre Publications.

Walfish, S., E. N. Goplerud and A. Broskowski. 1986. Survival strategies in community mental health: a study of management consensus. *American journal of orthopsychiatry.* 56(4):630-633.

Walters, M. 1990. The co-dependent Cinderella who loves too much. *The family therapy networker,* July/Aug.

Weatherford, J. 1988. *Indian givers: how the Indians of the Americas transformed the world.* New York: Crown Publishers, Inc.

Weick, A., C. Rapp, W. P. Sullivan, and W. Kisthardt. 1989. A strengths perspective for social work practice. *Social work.* 34(4):350-354.

Weiss, H. B. 1989. State family support and education programs: lessons from the pioneers. *American journal of orthopsychiatry*. 59(1):32-48.

Weissbourd, B. and S. L. Kagan. 1989. Family support programs: catalysts for change. *American journal of orthopsychiatry*. 59(1):20-31.

West, C. 1991. In *Breaking bread: insurgent black intellectual life*, eds. B. Hook and C. West. Boston: South End Press.

White, M. 1991. Deconstruction and theory. *Dulwich centre newsletter*. No. 3:3-11.

White, M. and D. Epston. 1990. *Narrative means to therapeutic ends*. New York: W. W. Norton and Company.

Wylie, M. S. 1996. It's a community affair. *The family therapy networker*. March/April: 58-65.

About the Contributors, Chapter Two

E. H. Auerswald, M.D. For the past thirty-five years, a predominant family therapist who headed neighborhood-based integrated biopsychosocial health care delivery systems in New York City and Maui, Hawaii. Dr. Auerswald has written over twenty definitive papers on ecosystemic , community-based models of care and the kind of thinking which fosters these models. He is co-founder of the Aion Foundation in San Francisco, where he now works to establish a "global community of differences".

Miriam Azaunce, Ed.D. Now a Senior Psychologist at Kings County Hospital Center in Brooklyn, working in Crisis Intervention Services in Out-Patient Psychiatry. She also is an adjunct professor at the College of New Rochelle and at New York University, and has a private practice in psychotherapy. Her primary field of academic interest is the psychological consequences of separation through migration of West Indian families.

Dionisio Cruz, C.S.W. Now a Senior Social Worker at St. Vincent's Hospital in New York City, and the Air Bridge Case Management Coordinator, working on AIDS treatment issues between New York City and Puerto Rico.

Brenda David, C.S.W.-R. Employed as a Family Counselor at Child and Family Services of Buffalo and Erie County, Buffalo, New York.

Cecilia Gaston, M.A. A public health administrator directing a residence for AIDS patients in the Bronx, New York.

Virginia Goldner, Ph.D. a prominent family therapist , writer, and workshop leader on feminist, psychoanalytic, and systems theory. She teaches at Ackerman Institute in New York City, maintains a private psychotherapy practice,and travels widely, focusing on work with violent men and their partners, and how to address ethical and political issues effectively in clinical practice.

Ena Johnson, C.S.W.-R. Now employed as a family therapist at the Therapeutic Preschool of Children's Hospital, Buffalo, New York. She co-leads a Men's Domestic Violence Group.

Mel King . Former Director of the Community Fellows Program at Massachusetts Institute of Technology, adjunct professor in the Department of Urban Studies and Planning at M. I. T., and a member of the Rainbow Coalition and Million Man March Political Mobilization Committee.

Eliana Korin, Dipl.Psic. A family therapist and community-oriented clinical psychologist working with immigrants and poor clients in the Bronx,New York for many years. She teaches at the Residency Program in Social Medicine/Department of Family Medicine, Montefiore Medical Center, where she supervises physicians and other professionals in developing health initiatives with the community. She has developed a participatory health education program with Latina patients at a medical clinic, applying Paolo Freire's ideas.

Bolaji Oladapo, R.N., M.P.H., C.A.S. clinical instructor of psychiatric nursing at Medgar Evers College; supervisor in a nursing home; and nurse's aides evaluator.

Barry White, Seneca, Turtle Clan. Registration Coordinator and Diversity Trainer with the Center for the Development of Human Services at Buffalo State College, Buffalo, New York. He is also the Director of Undergraduate Studies and lecturer in Native American Studies for theAmerican Studies Department of State University of New York at Buffalo.

Agnes Williams, C.S.W. Family Counselor for the Seneca Nation Mental Health Clinic, and board member of the national/international Indigenous Women's Network. She is engaged in interviews with elder Native women to learn and preserve their traditions.

About the Author

Jane Piazza is a social worker, family therapist, and family therapy trainer currently doing clinical work in a mental health setting, and family systems consultation and program design on a contractual basis. For the past twenty-nine years, she has provided therapy to poor families in a variety of settings in the public sector. For the past fifteen years, she has provided training in university, agency, and community settings in family systems and community-based frameworks. In directing family therapy training in the public sector, her primary focus has been the incorporation of natural extended family, spiritual, and cultural leadership into direct clinical work. She has helped clinicians to connect better to natural community strengths, and , thus, to be better supported themselves as clinicians.